INVENTING AMERICAN TRADITION

★ ★ ★

INVENTING AMERICAN TRADITION

★ ★ ★

FROM THE *MAYFLOWER* TO CINCO DE MAYO

JACK DAVID ELLER

REAKTION BOOKS

Published by Reaktion Books Ltd
Unit 32, Waterside
44–48 Wharf Road
London N1 7UX, UK
www.reaktionbooks.co.uk

First published 2018
Copyright © Jack David Eller 2018

Printed and bound in Great Britain
by TJ International, Padstow, Cornwall

A catalogue record for this book is available from the British Library

ISBN 978 1 78914 035 4

Contents

★ ★ ★

American Lifestyle Traditions

★

American Traditional Characters

★

Preface

★ ★ ★

Once upon a time there were no American traditions. But, then, once upon a time there was no America. There was surely a continent west of the Atlantic Ocean, but no one called it America, and there were surely people inhabiting that continent, but none of them called themselves American. America—the country or the identity—was invented fairly recently. The people who migrated from Europe, and then eventually from every other part of the world, to what would become America or the United States brought traditions with them; those traditions were European, African, Asian, and so on—traditions *in America* rather than "American" traditions. At the moment of American independence, there were few, if any, traditions that were originally and uniquely American.

It may sound counterintuitive to speak of "invented traditions." In our day of "fake news" and "post-truth" arguments and assertions, though, it is not preposterous to consider how humans fashion and inhabit their own realities—even more so than in previous eras, when knowledge was less certain and the pathways of knowledge were unreliable at best. Granted, the "traditional" idea of tradition implies (often, if not usually, spurious) continuity with the ancient past. The United States, however, has no ancient past; it is a society and country self-consciously created in the late eighteenth century but by no means completed in that era. It took many decades for the U.S. to accumulate—and to reflect on and fret about—the experiences out of which "tradition" was constructed.

And America is hardly unique in this regard. Even "traditional societies," which are sometimes imagined to be primordial and static, even ahistorical, have actually been dynamic and changing. This is certainly true of the native nations of North America, who had their own traditions, many not as traditional as we often assume. For instance, the Iroquois Confederacy of the northeast of the U.S. was not formed until the 1500s, shortly before Dutch and English settlers began arriving in numbers in their territory; after a period of intertribal war, a man of peace appeared, known to history as Dekanawida or Tekana:wita, The Great Peacemaker, traveling with a companion named Hahyonhwatha or Ayenwatha (made famous in Henry Wadsworth Longfellow's epic poem *The Song of Hiawatha*). The very name "Iroquois" is an invention and imposition, applied to them by the French; they called themselves *Haudenosaunee* or *Ongwanonsionni,* which means something like "the people of the longhouse." The western Plains culture is another example of a tradition that could not have existed far into the past; the classic horse-riding culture of groups like the Cheyenne and Lakota was an innovation, since horses were not indigenous to the Western Hemisphere. Only after horses were brought to and released on the continent could Native Americans begin riding them, so this tradition is an adaptation to a foreign introduction. Worse still is the fact that historical, linguistic, and archaeological evidence indicates that some of these groups, such as the Cheyenne, were not even indigenous to the West but migrated there because of population pressures brought on by European settlement.

Around the world, the story is the same. Traditions that appear or claim to hearken back to "time immemorial" prove to be creations, often in the quite recent past. The very societies themselves that purport to be traditional turn out to be products of contemporary forces. Anthropologists Meyer Fortes and E. E. Evans-Pritchard, for instance, commented in 1940 that some of the supposed "traditional tribes" of Africa in actuality "appear to be an amalgam of different people, each aware of its unique origin and history," often forged by European colonialism on the continent.[1] The same can be said of the Betawi, who are often touted as the indigenous people of the Jakarta region of Java, Indonesia; instead, the Betawi (a name derived from the Dutch colonial city of Batavia) are most likely the descendants of displaced societies and enslaved individuals who were lumped together in the colonial census and gradually melted in "a new, shared culture and identity and their own dialect, *Omong Betawi*" until they recognized themselves—and were recognized by the newly independent Indonesian state—as an authentic ethnic group and a model for all of Indonesia.2 Closer to home for Americans, the "Melungeons" have been dubbed a "traditional" group of the Appalachian region, despite the fact that the very name probably comes from a corruption of the French word *mélange* or mixture (in this case, a mixture of races in a highly race-sensitive time and place) and that no one avowed the identity or culture of "Melungeon" until recently. Thanks to a play from the 1960s titled *Walk Toward the Sunset* and the formation of the Melungeon Heritage Association, as well as books and articles about them, people who had never identified as Melungeon suddenly "became Melungeon"; according to Melissa Schrift, in more than a few cases "individuals do not recall being Melungeon before they chose to do so as adults,"3 inventing and joining a "traditional society."

The Melungeons are but one example of the fertile productivity of tradition-invention in the United States, a country and society that is itself, as mentioned above, thoroughly a recent achievement. And in a very real sense, the business of inventing American tradition could not commence until America itself was born, making many of those traditions of much later vintage—some no more than a few decades old and hardly any of them more than a century-and-a-half old. This book tells the story of a few of the signature traditions of American society. It does not attempt to be exhaustive; that would be impossible for a book of portable size, if not for an entire series or encyclopedia. I have made a selection of some of the most familiar, important, and revealing traditions in America. I have only included traditions that originated in America, which, for instance, excludes Christmas; assuredly, Americans do Christmas, and in a distinctly American way, but Christmas is not a fundamentally American tradition. I have also not included some domains of tradition, such as sports or music, which could easily fill—and have filled—volumes on their own. Finally, I have not included religion, although America has been the site of the invention of some prominent religions, from Mormonism and Seventh-Day Adventism to Scientology. I offer instead a sampling to make a point.

Further, this book does not strive to excavate the "true history" of the traditions, partly because their history is often shrouded in uncertainty and controversy and partly because there often is no "true history." That is, we are not in search of "the first Thanksgiving" or "the real national anthem," because the first or real one is not the main point (and, in the case of national anthems, there is no "real" one). As often as not, the myth and legend is as important—and revealing—as the "facts." The question is how a tradition gets started, transmitted, altered, and adopted. Many people contribute to a tradition, for many (often extremely partisan) reasons, and there is almost always a struggle over tradition. The outcome of the process—what we will call the "traditioning" process— is by no means assured. Nor should we ever consider the traditioning process finished.

The examples chosen for this book are organized into four categories. The first is political traditions, which have to do specifically and officially with the American government (or what social scientists call the American "state"). They include symbols or representations of the state such as its national song, its national flag, its national oath and motto, and its national personification (as "Uncle Sam"). The second section features holidays, which are a fertile area of tradition in all societies. Many holidays were invented in the United States, and many of them refer singularly to the United States (such as Thanksgiving or military holidays such as Veterans Day or Memorial Day);4 however, others do not refer exclusively to America—such as Mother's Day and Father's Day, and some, ironically, do not refer to America at all—such as St Patrick's Day or Cinco de Mayo. Some people may question whether these latter celebrations are American holidays, but if they were invented in or are principally celebrated in America, how could we exclude them?

The third category is everyday traditions of dress, food, and even gesture. Americans have contributed a remarkable number of such traditions to the world (for better or for worse), such as blue jeans, hamburgers, and the word and gesture "OK." It is truly fascinating and significant that most of the world knows, if not practices, these American-originated traditions, although once those other societies adopt and modify them, we might just as well call them traditions of those other societies (as in the Brazilian tradition of blue jeans or the Chinese tradition of the hamburger). Again, as we said already, the origin of a tradition is not as crucial as its transmission and integration into a society. Indeed, both blue jeans and hamburgers have a certain non-American and pre-American source too.

The fourth and final category consists of distinctive, even internationally representative, American characters, such as Superman, Paul Bunyan, and Mickey Mouse. Some of these legendary characters come from American folklore, but many of them are much more recent—and intentional—fabrications, what some scholars have dubbed "fakelore." But, as we will see, the line between folklore and fakelore is a thin and permeable one. The book ends with a glimpse into the future of American traditions, because traditions have not only a history but a future.

The chapters can be read in any order, and readers who do not want to engage in the scholarly analysis of tradition can skip the first chapter, but I would implore them not to, as the pervasive traditioning process will be much clearer if they attempt the first chapter before encountering the specific traditions. Accordingly, before the book begins the tale of particular American traditions, it spends some time discussing the nature, processes, and (perhaps most importantly) functions of tradition. What do we mean by "tradition"? How do traditions work—how do they begin, grow, adapt, often fail or disappear, and ultimately earn their way into American culture and consciousness? And, in a question that people seldom ask themselves, why do we have those traditions? In fact, why do we have any traditions at all? What purpose is served by tradition? Or, to put this question another way, whose interests are served by the creation, transmission, and acceptance of tradition?

Tradition, as we will acknowledge, is "about" the past in some way, but it is never only or even mainly about the past. As this notorious slogan in George Orwell's novel *1984* has it, he who controls the past controls the future, and he who controls the present controls the past. Thus, two critical and unavoidable factors are *authority* and *the future*. Who has authority to create, transmit, or adopt a tradition—and how does creating and transmitting a tradition *create* and *perpetuate* authority? And finally, how are tradition and authority today, in the name, if not in the image, of the past, related to the future? What new traditions, or new aspects of existing traditions, will be added to American culture, and how is the traditioning process really an exercise in shaping the future culture and identity of America?

The wonder is not that American tradition took so long to emerge and evolve but that American tradition exists at all. The United States was conceived, rather intentionally, as a country and society breaking the shackles of history, especially of European history, and thus as a society of the future. In the ironically appropriate source of the introduction to Marcel Proust's famous novel of memory, *In Search of Lost Time*, Richard Howard opined that Americans "have a kind of allergy to the past; it's our national disease, and the very assurance . . . that the past is *within the present* is likely to seem repellent, even offensive" to them.5 This suggests that the advent of, running into an obsession with, tradition in America has a deeper meaning. Each American tradition has its own story—a story of intention and accident, of institutionalization, competition, and opposition—but each is a scene in the bigger American story of *becoming* a "traditional" society. Born self-deliberately imagining itself breaking with tradition and looking only toward the future, by the centennial of the country's independence, many Americans perceived their nation and culture in peril. The half-century between 1870 and 1920 was especially and explicitly anxious for those Americans, and "tradition" was one bulwark against the specters of immigration and socialism, not to mention the traumatic near-self-destruction of the recently ended Civil War. It was perceived fairly overtly as a means to ensure or manufacture literally American self and society, which was endangered or altogether absent. We may then find that tradition-inventing is the prerogative not so much of an energetic and confident people but of a tired and stressed one, desperately striving to perpetuate an identity by actively creating it.

Introduction: Tradition is Not What It Used to Be

★ ★ ★

History is facts which become lies in the end; legends are lies which
become history in the end.—JEAN COCTEAU

*O*dissi is considered one of the classical forms of dance in India,
although it only became "classical" in 1958. Centuries ago, it
was a style of movement practiced by female temple dancers,
called *maharis*; in the 1700s, male dancers commandeered the genre,
and by the 1800s it was not considered entirely proper for decent
women, given its (fictitious?) association with temple prostitution.
However, it was only in the 1950s that these men—completely exclud-
ing actual *maharis*—codified the dance style, establishing its "rules and
aesthetics" and canonizing those newly minted norms as "classical"
odissi.[1] Amusingly, those fresh standards were granted such authority
that a controversy recently erupted over the apparel of dancers, some
clothing deemed to be intolerably nontraditional despite the fact that
the "costume worn by *odissi* dancers on stage today barely resembles
the one worn by *maharis*, and was specifically reconstructed during the
codification of *odissi* dance."[2]

Modern life is full of traditions and would-be traditions. And who
doesn't enjoy a good tradition? In fact, would life even be possible
without tradition? The fact that traditions are appealing and compel-
ling (sometimes verging on compulsory) habits and that they refer
to and, in a sense, revive the past does not mean, though, that they
are necessarily ancient or primordial. Some traditions are very old,
and some are quite new. Most Americans would consider the Super
Bowl an American tradition, but in the year 2017 only the 51st Super
Bowl was played, the first instance of this tradition having occurred

in 1967—although the term "super bowl" was not used at the time of the first contest between the National Football League and the upstart American Football League, and legend has it that Lamar Hunt, the owner of the Kansas City Chiefs, named the game after his daughter's Super Ball. The MTV Music Awards began in 1984 (there were no "music videos" much before that date), and the 89th Academy Awards were presented in 2017.

One might argue that these are not "real" traditions or that they are not "important" traditions. But of course, some traditions have deep meaning (to some people; to others they are meaningless or worse), and some are lighthearted fun. So let us consider some "real" and "important" traditions. Many Protestant Christians cherish their traditions, but naturally there are no Protestant traditions that go back more than five hundred years, since there was no such thing as Protestantism (at least in the familiar form of Martin Luther's revolution) before the 1500s. No Protestant tradition is more than five hundred years old, and some are much younger (for example, Methodism did not come along until the 1700s). Even worse is the fact that while Christians in general tout their traditions, there are no specifically Christian traditions that go back more than two thousand years, since there was no such thing as Christianity before two thousand years ago. There are, of course, pre-Christian roots to some Christian traditions, including what Christians have traditionally come to call "the Old Testament" (but which was the only testament in its time, and still is the only testament for the Jewish people). And there are also non-Christian roots to many Christian traditions, Christianity having absorbed various bits and pieces of Greek and Roman culture, as well as from Germanic, Nordic, and, more recently, African, Asian and Native American cultures during its history.

The same could clearly be said about Islam (the traditions of which date only from the 600s of the Common Era), Mormonism (the traditions of which date only from the 1800s), or Scientology (the traditions of which date only from the 1950s). And what is true for religion is true for all areas of human "traditional" behavior. Every tradition has an origin, and every tradition has evolved from the moment of its origin. In other words, tradition is not what it used to be.

In the American context, many traditions practiced in the United States, such as Christmas, certainly have a pre-American origin. Other traditions, such as Thanksgiving, were born on American soil (although not at the time or in the way that most Americans imagine, and the tradition of "giving thanks" long predates the u.s.); some American traditions appeared much more recently. And whenever it began and whatever its source of inspiration, every American tradition has a history, as it has morphed, adding or shedding elements or interpretations. Nor have American traditions "stayed at home": once a tradition is launched, it easily—often intentionally—flows across social boundaries, and maybe to the entire world. This is why we can find rock 'n' roll or hip-hop music, blue jeans, T-shirts, and hamburgers in virtually every society on earth. In the contemporary globalized world, tradition is not only not what it used to be; it is not *where* it used to be. Tradition, like all culture, is mobile, portable, plastic, and hybrid.

What is Tradition?

"Do you guys know any songs?" I asked the Aleuts (an indigenous people of Alaska).

"I know all of Hank Williams," the elder Aleut said.

"How about Indian songs?"

"Hank Williams is Indian."

"How about sacred songs?"

"Hank Williams is sacred."[3]

When Americans hear or use the word "tradition," they tend to have two things in mind. First, "tradition" and its variations such as "traditional" connote age: "traditional" is what has been done for a long time, maybe even "since the beginning." It is, in a word, a legacy and continuation of the past. Second, "tradition" tends to suggest what is good, what is authentic, what is "really us." This is particularly clear when we think about usages such as "traditional marriage," "traditional family," or "traditional values." For people who talk this way, "traditional" means *good* marriage, *real* family, or *the correct* values. But then, not everything that is "traditional" in America is equally good: slavery was a long-lasting tradition that we are all glad to be rid of. And there is no objective way to establish that one set of values is "more correct" than another. One kind of American is not better or more real than another; if America is anything, it is diverse.

So for most people, the essence of tradition is its connection—that is to say, its *continuity*—with the past, usually (selectively) remembered (or imagined) as a "noble past." Something really happened back then, and that something set the pattern for what we do, or should do, today. However, if we look at the derivation of the word "tradition," antiquity is not the key issue. From the Latin *tradere* for "to deliver/hand down/ transmit" (further, from *trans* for "across" and *dare* for "to give"), the kernel of the idea of tradition is the transmission process, not the age of the transmitted message. Thus, as Newell Booth expressed it over thirty years ago, tradition "is commonly understood as meaning 'the inherited wisdom' of the past, and 'traditionalist' as referring to one who preserves this heritage . . . but the emphasis is more on the process of transmission than on the content transmitted."[4]

The core quality of tradition, then, is not any specific detail (the "true" stuff or the "good" stuff) nor any specific age (the "old" stuff) but the process by which the related ideas, beliefs, behaviors, and artifacts are reproduced and perpetuated over time and between people. In a sense, anything that people transmit and share is "traditional" to some extent, making the word awfully vague and nearly synonymous with "culture" in general. In fact, for many listeners, "tradition" is hardly other than the "most authentic" or the "most important" elements of their culture—its language, its religion, its stories, its food, its clothing, and so on.

Accordingly, the scholars who have spent the most time thinking about tradition have been those most directly concerned with culture, language, stories, and religion, especially folklorists and theologians. For instance, in an influential analysis in 1984, folklorist Dan Ben-Amos argued that even the experts used the word in many different ways— seven, to be precise.[5] First, tradition could mean "lore," a corpus of knowledge, usually transmitted and practiced orally, including songs, tales, sayings, games, jokes, and the like. Second, tradition could refer to "the canon," that subset of cultural knowledge or lore that is most "official" or deemed most fundamental to a group: "narratives, songs, proverbs, and riddles that have withstood the test of time, and have become the main mental staple of a society, are conceived as the cultural canon,"[6] and it is those that are most essential to preserve and propagate. In this view, tradition is often the "high" culture, the sayings and doings of the elite, as opposed to "popular culture," which is more ephemeral and, quite frankly, sometimes lower in quality. (These are, of course, value judgments, and the line between high and low culture is a negotiable and permeable one.)

Third, folklorists have stressed that tradition is a "process"— namely, the process of transmission (again, usually seen as an oral process). But since a social process like transmission necessarily entails a social group, Ben-Amos's fourth sense of tradition redirects the focus from the contents of the tradition to the "bearers" of the tradition. As anthropologist and folklorist Richard Bauman phrased it,

> The folklore is the product through creation or re-creation of the whole group and its forebears, and an expression of their common character. It is spoken of in terms of traditions, with tradition conceived of as a superorganic temporal continuum; the folk are "tradition bearers," that is, they carry the folklore traditions on through time and space like so much baggage— particular people and generations come and go, but the group identity persists and the tradition lives on . . .[7]

This perspective not only emphasizes the "folk" in folklore but attunes us to the integrative and identity-fostering aspect of tradition.

After mentioning as his fifth definition that tradition can basically act as a surrogate and synonym for culture, Ben-Amos added two other observations. One (his sixth strand) sees tradition as an abstract set of rules for generating knowledge or behavior, like the grammar of a language; scholars have come to call this the *langue* dimension of language—that is, the underlying grammar or competence to say (and do) appropriate things, rather than actual things that people say (or do), which is known as *parole*, following the ideas of the linguist Ferdinand de Saussure. This view tends to highlight the stable, even timeless, nature of tradition. Ben-Amos's other observation (his seventh and final strand) takes exactly the opposite stance, envisioning tradition as "performance," what people actually say and do; this approach rein-troduces time, variability, and creativity. As the eminent linguist and folklorist Ruth Finnegan said, a tradition "has to be *used* by people for it to continue to exist."[8] And since different individuals and subgroups may have different knowledge, skills, interpretations, and motivations in regard to the same tradition, the performative quality of tradition opens up a whole new way of thinking about the subject.

Likewise, writing in the journal *Church History*, Richard Heitzenrater identified several distinct "common usages" for the word "tradition," including

1. "the repetitive practice of a certain activity or the regular recitation of an idea, a repetition through which something is being passed on from person to person, from generation to generation. The fact that we do or say something with routine recurrence down through the years within families, institutions, or countries, makes it a tradition."

2. "That which is being celebrated regularly, that which is being passed on, is also called a tradition. These traditions often point to an auspicious beginning for a group or a significant defining idea or event or a special development in the life of an individual or a group."

3. "We also speak about tradition in a more encompassing fash-ion to refer to the body of people who share a particular set of traditions relating to their origin, background, experience, perspective, and story. In this sense (as with the last sense), 'tradition' takes on a proprietary sense—'our tradition,' 'their tradition.' The totality of shared ideas, structures, and concom-itant events (that is, the traditions) that characterize a group or institution are also at times called a 'heritage'."

4. Additionally, calling something a tradition implies "that the story or bit of information has the aura of factuality through repetition, though it is not necessarily verifiable—'tradition has it that . . .' Such an acknowledgement makes explicit in this meaning of tradition what might be implicit in the last two uses of the term—a possible lack of historical or factual

verifiability as to origins of the tradition. These traditions are no less important to groups, however, and are as frequently and faithfully passed on."

5. Finally, in keeping with the performative and inventive dimension, tradition can be thought of as a verb, as an active process—*to tradition* or to participate in *traditioning*—that not only transmits but modifies and even generates tradition in the first place. We will have much more to say about this later in the chapter.[9]

Culture and Revitalization

As transmitted content, transmission processes, and a community among whom the content is transmitted, tradition partakes in the nature of "culture" generally; it might be more accurate to say that tradition is a subset of culture. Now, part of the convention of the social sciences has been to treat culture as an enduring, sometimes static, phenomenon—that which a society has been doing for an undetermined but presumably long time. However, at least since the middle of the twentieth century, anthropologists and sociologists have been acutely aware of the dynamic and creative quality of culture.

One of the most important and useful discussions of cultural change and innovation came from the anthropologist Anthony Wallace, who compared "many instances of attempted and sometimes successful innovation of whole cultural systems, or at least substantial portions of such systems."[10] He discovered that cultures commonly (and increasingly commonly in the modern world) experience many kinds of change processes, including "evolution, drift, diffusion, historical change, acculturation" and so forth,[11] all of which are relevant to the study of tradition. But his main interest was the *revitalization movement*, defined as "a deliberate, organized, conscious effort by members of a society to construct a more satisfying culture."[12] In other words, what is particularly significant about revitalization movements is that they are intentional, orchestrated, and sustained attempts to change culture in a particular way.

Social scientists have observed a wide and colorful array of revitalization movements over the past century or two. Wallace himself

The Ghost Dance by the Oglala Lakota at Pine Ridge Agency. Drawn by
Frederic Remington from sketches taken on the spot.

investigated the Handsome Lake movement among the Seneca at the
turn of the nineteenth century (named after its founder, a man called
Handsome Lake); other famous cases include the Taiping "Rebellion"
in China, the Ghost Dance among Plains Indians in the U.S., and, of
course, the many, often dramatic, "cargo cults" on Pacific Islands.[13] But
Wallace's real contribution was his summary of the standard course that
such movements take.

In his model, culture starts off in a relatively stable and satisfactory
condition that he called the "steady state"; in this pre-movement state,
individuals understand their world and possess the mental and cultural tools to navigate it successfully. The steady state is not necessarily
totally static, but change is slow and incremental rather than sudden
and disruptive. Then something comes along to disturb the steady state;
this could include environmental change or natural disaster but more
likely involves social processes such as contact with a radically different
society, invasion and conquest, war (especially defeat in a war), internal
division and conflict, severe economic trouble, and other such dislocat-
ing events. At first perhaps only a few individuals feel the change, but
the effects become more pronounced in this stage of "increased individual stress." As tensions build, the society enters a period of "cultural
distortion," resulting in more or less widespread failure of people's
cultural knowledge and practices. The distortion manifests in negative

behaviors such as "alcoholism, extreme passivity and indolence, the development of highly ambivalent dependency relationships, intra-group violence, disregard of kinship and sexual mores, irresponsibility in public officials, states of depression and self-reproach, and probably a variety of psychosomatic and neurotic disorders."[14] In short, individual and collective coping mechanisms break down.

For many societies, and for many individuals in such societies, this may be the end. More than a few societies have become extinct as a consequence of the corrosive experiences just mentioned, and many individuals either give up or cling tenaciously to failed habits. But in numerous cases, a period of revitalization ensues. Revitalization tends to start with a "reformulation," a new idea or a new interpretation of old ideas; frequently, this reformulation comes from a single person who operates as the "prophet" of a new vision of life. But the founder and prophet seldom claims (or maybe seldom believes) that he or she is really the originator of a new culture; instead, he or she often portrays the reformulation as a message from the spirits (God or gods, ancestors, or other spirits), giving the new vision a distinctly religious character. This is only natural, since religion adds a superhuman sheen—and authority—to the message. Also, the founder or prophet himself often exhibits charismatic or more-than-human qualities, sometimes surviving a near-death experience, receiving visions, and performing miraculous acts.

Not all of these would-be founders or prophets are listened to—not all even discuss their experiences—but when other people hear and attend to the proffered reformulation, the stage of "communication" begins. The visionary teaches the revelations to others, first family and friends, and then a widening circle of followers or "converts." Historical movements that ultimately achieved enormous, sometimes global, success started out this way: Jesus gathered his small circle of disciples and then preached to larger crowds, and Muhammad convinced his wife and kin before he assembled a growing group of believers.

These early days of a movement often depend on the personality of the founder or prophet and his charisma; the movement would collapse without direct contact with the originator and without repeated demonstrations of his special powers. But as the movement expands, it may no longer be possible to have direct access to the founder, and of course, despite what the founder or the movement may say, he eventually dies. So begins the stage of "adaptation," in which the movement adjusts to its social environment and to its very successes. One obvious and inevitable adaptation will be a succession scheme: who will be the next leader? In Christianity, Paul emerged as the leading (but not uncontested) figure in the so-called "Jesus movement," while the first successors of Muhammad were his kinsmen—establishing the tradition of the caliph which many Muslims still dream of today—until control of the congregation was seized by a military dynasty (the Ummayyads) and then subsequently a long line of dynasties, often claiming to be the caliph, leading all the way to today's "Islamic State."

Because the movement is growing, it can longer depend on personal relationships and direct contact; it must formalize and institutionalize. Some common forms of institutionalization include a chain of command and a set of officers, as well as group norms and even written rules. There may be more or less strict qualifications for membership, such as oaths and initiations. There will almost certainly be the invention and adoption of symbols, including uniforms, special gestures and words, and such. A mythology may coalesce, with tales of the founder's wonders, as well as reverence for the places where he or she lived and worked. All of these institutional forms help to build and maintain a common identity and an orthodoxy.

However, three further processes may challenge this simple identity and orthodoxy. As the movement grows, it integrates more kinds of people, who bring their prior ideas and practices with them. The movement will therefore absorb influences from other and older sources, deviating from the original form inherited from the master. Indeed, if the movement seeks to attract members, it may deliberately adopt outside practices (such as the Roman practice of worshipping on Sunday or the Germanic practice of decorating trees) or tone down its own rules and expectations (such as Paul's decision to eliminate the requirement of circumcision and dietary laws). Second and sometimes related to these developments, the movement may undergo schism or fission. Schism may merely be a power struggle for control of the movement, or it may represent real disagreement about doctrine, symbols, or tactics. Finally, a movement not uncommonly meets opposition and resistance, occasionally stiff and life-threatening resistance, in which case it may adopt a defensive or an offensive stance—arming itself, organizing itself into military-type units, and developing a martial attitude.

Wallace noted that most revitalization movements (perhaps thankfully) die out long before they reach this stage of maturity. Many other movements stall at a certain stage and remain small, peripheral, and largely ineffective subcultures. But some revitalization movements achieve dramatic success, working a transformation on culture, signaled "by the reduction of the personal deterioration symptoms of individuals, by extensive cultural changes, and by an enthusiastic embarkation on some organized program of group action."[15] This he called the "cultural transformation" stage. Such a successful movement tends to shift its character from a charismatic and radical force to a more "normal" and routine element of society, settled in its doctrine and conservative in its interests; this Wallace called the "routinization" phase. If, ultimately, the movement solves the cultural problem out of which it was born, and if it gains the approval or participation of most or all of society, then it reaches the status of the "new steady state," a new tradition if you will.

Traditioning, or the Invention of Tradition

Wallace's essay, while not mentioning tradition explicitly, nevertheless implies that elements of a culture that are deemed "traditional" often— no, necessarily—have an origin and a history. What is "traditional" today indisputably had a start, even if we do not and cannot know what that start was, and at its beginning it certainly was not yet "traditional." In fact, it may have been quite revolutionary—by some standards seditious—at the outset.

Eric Hobsbawm and Terence Ranger, in their epoch-making 1983 book, took up the question of the invention of tradition directly. In his introduction, which is the best-known part of the book, Hobsbawm defined an *invented tradition* as "a set of practices, normally governed by overtly or tacitly accepted rules and of a ritual or symbolic nature, which seek to inculcate certain values and norms of behaviour by repetition, which automatically implies continuity with the past. In fact, where possible, they normally attempt to establish continuity with a suitable historical past."[16] The contributors to the book thus presented examples of invented traditions such as the "Highland tradition" in Scotland, the rituals of the British monarchy, and various traditions in colonial settings such as India and Africa.

An example that Hobsbawm and the other authors in the collection do not discuss is Nazi Germany, which was a skilled inventor of traditions. One of the most obvious and egregious instances is the adoption and redefinition of the swastika, which was most definitely not of German origin. It was a very old South Asian symbol: folklorist W.G.V. Balchin, in the middle of the Second World War, published a short analysis arguing that the word "swastika" comes from Sanskrit, the ancient language of India, which is apparently where Nazis thought that their own race of "Aryans" originated. However, the shape has also been found in many other parts of the world, including ancient Europe and Native America, and "when used on small unimportant objects such as implements, household goods and the like was probably little more than a charm or amulet designed to bring long life, good fortune and good luck. But in some cultures it has always been held in veneration as possessing a special religious significance," particularly among Buddhists and ancient Egyptians.[17] Nazis also reinterpreted many local beliefs, objects, and places, such as the Atlantis myth or the Icelandic Edda tales, legends of former kingdoms such as Thule, and old stone formations and runes in Germany and Austria, to suit their political agenda; in extreme cases, they simply invented ceremonies and pageants and other "traditions" out of thin air, dubbing them as true and venerable German traditions.

Based on incontrovertible evidence like this, Hobsbawm insisted that, while traditions usually purport to be about "the past," this past does not have to be old or even factual.

> The historic past into which the new tradition is inserted need
> not be of length, stretching back into the assumed mists of time
> ... However, insofar as there is such reference to a historic past,
> the peculiarity of "invented" traditions is that the continuity

with it is largely factitious. In short, they are responses to novel situations which take the form of reference to old situations, or which establish their own past by quasi-obligatory repetition.[18]

Thus, it is not important that the asserted origin of the tradition is true—thankfully for tradition-inventors, since it is often untrue or at least cannot demonstrate its truth.

Hobsbawm perpetuated one strange (and false, I insist) claim about invented traditions, which is that they are invariant: "The past, real or invented, to which they refer imposes fixed (normally formalized) practices, such as repetition."[19] This he contrasted with "custom" which "does not preclude innovation and change up to a point, though evidently the requirement that it must appear compatible or even identical with precedent imposes substantial limitations on it."[20] But here Hobsbawm was uncritically accepting an *ideology* of tradition as a *reality* of tradition: surely, traditions like to allege their invariance—and they try to impose invariance—but that is hardly the fact of the situation. Invented traditions obviously *begin*, which is not invariant, and they adapt and change over time, as noted by Wallace, even if each adaptation once again alleges its invariance. Hobsbawm and the other writers in the volume also seemed to be restricting themselves to a particular kind of invented tradition—namely, the formal kind represented by political events and symbols or ceremonies of state. But these are hardly the only or most common sort of invented traditions.

As we indicated earlier, folklorists have been among the most active scholars to think about the question of tradition, if only because they long observed "traditional folklore" coming in and out of existence. So almost a decade before Hobsbawm, the eminent folklorist, linguist, and anthropologist Dell Hymes had already introduced the notion of tradition as a verb, as "to traditionalize" or "traditionalization." Hymes wrote that "every person, and group, makes some effort to 'traditionalize' aspects of its experience."[21] Moreover, traditionalizing is not limited to major official occasions nor to the minutiae of folklore, but rather "in every sphere of life, occupational, institutional, regional, personal, and familial, one can find expressions of traditionalization."[22] From this perspective, a tradition is the endpoint—let us emphasize, the *current* endpoint—in a historical process of tradition-alization: "something partakes of the nature of the traditional already when the effort to traditionalize has brought it into being."[23] If so, then this fundamentally changes our ordinary perception of traditions as simple and invariant repetitions of the past. As Hymes put it succinctly, "intact tradition is not so much a matter of preservation, as it is a matter of re-creation, by successive persons and generations, and in individual performances"; indeed, there are no non-traditionalized traditions, if by non-traditionalized "is meant the absence of creative interpretation and effort."[24]

Although Hymes gets much of the credit for the notion of making tradition a verb, the renowned sociologist Edward Shils actually beat him to the punch by four years, writing in an essay called simply "Tradition" about beliefs and practices that become "traditionalized."[25] Fully appreciating that change is not the antithesis of tradition, indeed that the "mechanisms of persistence are not utterly distinct from the mechanisms of change"[26]—that is to say, both persistence and change depend on human transmission and performance—Shils admitted that "modification is the inevitable fate of traditional norms."[27] Several crucial observations followed. First, a tradition need not really be about the past, so long as it has a certain aura of "pastness," and the "pastness" ascribed to any element of alleged tradition "may derive either from its presumed connection with symbols of authority in the past . . . or from the mere fact of its frequent anonymous occurrence in the past."[28] But sometimes—and more often than we think—it is not the past but the present that makes a tradition "traditional"; its power and appeal resides in what Shils called its "sheer massive factuality"—that is, the fact that everyone else is doing it and that it seems like the thing to do. As folklorist Alan Gailey added some years later, "those who espouse a tradition do not necessarily do so because of its pastness; it may simply, and perhaps informally, be taken for granted as the only reasonable thing to do or to believe."[29] For instance, most American Christians have no real idea why they put a pine tree in their house for Christmas, but they know that other American Christians do it and often feel quite strongly that they should do it too. Sometimes such traditions, especially in the religious realm, may carry an aura of sacredness, but Shils assured us that the "immediate pressure of 'givenness' is probably as important as the sacredness of the past, perhaps more so in most societies" and for most modern people.[30]

The final point that Shils made is that, while traditions are some-times just "there" or feel like they are just "there," frequently, if not usually, they are actively pursued and searched for. Tradition "is in other words not just a matter of passive reception of the given. There is an active seeking relationship to traditional belief which motivates recom-mendation and reception at least in part and which also appears in a more independent form. Traditions are sometimes sought for."[31] Traditions can be "found," and those that are not found can be, as Hobsbawm and Ranger emphasized, invented.

Many scholars have picked up the mantle of Shils and Hymes. Henry Glassie, also in an essay dubbed "Tradition," wrote that "trad-ition is the creation of the future out of the past."[32] Tradition, like history, "is not the past; it is an artful assembly of materials from the past, designed for usefulness in the future"; furthermore, both tradition and history "exclude more than they include, and so remain open to endless revision. They are functionally congruent in their incorporation of the usable past."[33] More recently, Tom Mould, examining the nar-rative and prophetic practices of contemporary Choctaw people, offered a compact definition of traditionalization, as "a process that evokes the traditional past not merely as part of a general dialogue with the past, but as part of an attempt to provide authority for one's own narrative performance and interpretation by supporting or contributing to a community's sense of what is 'traditional'."[34] Traditionalization, as Shils also held, "must be understood to describe an active effort to imbue a performance with the aura of the traditional"[35]—that is, to give the appearance of great antiquity, sacredness, or givenness. Thus, Mould proposed the following features for traditionalization:

> it is 1) a conscious process undertaken by a performer that 2) refers to the past, 3) adopts an anti-modern stance, 4) asserts the continuity of a specific cultural element, and 5) makes refer-ence to and may even reconstruct "the traditional," rather than simply referring to "a tradition." In other words, as I define it,

traditionalization is the act of explicitly referencing some element of the past considered traditional within the community.[36]

Dorothy Noyes and Roger Abrahams actually identified a set of stages through which the "past" achieves the status of a tradition (or invented tradition). The first stage is "customary memory" or "the mindfulness of the body, the incorporation of past experience in forceful ways that both allow the body to reproduce it and call the conscious mind to a realm of feeling usually left unarticulated."[37] If a potential tradition is implanted in the mind and body, then the second stage is "practical traditionalization," which involves giving the tradition a name, talking about it, and showing pride in it. The third stage is "ideological traditionalization," defined rather technically as "a translation of community meta-commentaries into hegemonic terms,"[38] which means that the various opinions and forms of the potential tradition get settled and made "official," which implies and requires the efforts of leaders or elites. Finally, if all goes well, the aspiring tradition becomes a tradition, albeit an invented tradition, with its customary forms and its customary evocation of the past.

It is perhaps no surprise that one of the most fertile domains in culture for traditionalizing is religion, which, above all other domains, claims a continuous connection with the past, as well as a sacred, obligatory, and invariant nature. What may be a surprise is that religion scholars are particularly aware of the invention of tradition, which they tend to refer to as "traditioning" (see Heitzenrater above). Serious students of religion cannot help but concede that many "religious traditions" are not very old and that even the old ones have not been handed down unchanged *ab origine*. For instance, biblical scholars fully accept that the Bible was composed over many years out of many different sources; moreover, writings that were candidates for inclusion were left out, and the writings that were included and became canonical have suffered many divergent interpretations. So scholars like Gerhard von Rad in his 1957 study of Old Testament theology found it incumbent to discuss, in Bernhard Anderson's words, "the history of the transmission of traditions antedating the biblical texts in their final form."[39] Today, according to Anderson, "Traditio-historical theologians go even further than von Rad by emphasizing the process . . . of transmission of traditions—the 'traditioning process,' as it is sometimes called."[40] When applied to scriptures, this traditioning approach means that the community of believers was "not allowed to settle down in any fixed formulations of the heritage but was constantly summoned into a new understanding of its place in the unfolding drama of the Bible."[41] The horrifying or thrilling consequence (depending on your point of view) is that the Bible specifically or religion generally is not a closed and invariant thing but rather a living and changing thing, continuously undergoing reinvention. Indeed, Anderson cited the great Karl Barth, who also concurred that there are religious claims "which can be historically proved," while there are also other claims which have "been consciously fashioned, or invented, in a later synthetic view."[42]

Returning to biblical history, in 2003 Walter Brueggemann reaffirmed the traditioned character of Judeo-Christian scripture. It is people, he asserted, who must generate scripture, transmit scripture, interpret scripture, and make scripture relevant to their lives. This traditioning process, therefore,

> is endless and open-ended . . . First, there was a long process of traditioning prior to the fixing of the canon as text in normative form. Much of that process is hidden from us and beyond recovery . . . Second, the actual formation of the canon is a point in the traditioning process that gives us "scripture" for synagogue and for church . . . But third, it is important to recognize that the fixing of the canon did not terminate the traditioning process. All of the force of imaginative articulation and ideological passion and the hiddenness of divine inspiration have continued to operate in the ongoing interpretive task of synagogue and church until the present day.[43]

One of the ironies, or ideologies, of the traditioning process is that each version or interpretation asserts its absolute authority:

> each version of the retelling (of which there were surely many in the long-term process) intends, perforce, that its particular retelling should be the "final" and surely the correct one. In the

event, however, no account of traditioning turns out to be the "final" one, but each act of traditioning is eventually overcome and in fact displaced ("superseded") by a fresher version. The later, displacing form of the tradition no doubt is assumed to be the "final and correct" one, but is in turn sure to be overcome and, in part, displaced by subsequent versions of the memory.[44]

This endless process, this "interplay of historical reportage and canonical formation," this *work of tradition*," was recognized by Brueggemann as a kind of "imaginative remembering."[45]

To prove that theologians and religious scholars are fully aware of the traditioning phenomenon, let us cite one final source, a 2006 volume titled *Futuring Our Past: Explorations in the Theology of Tradition*. The book leads off with a chapter by co-editor Orlando Espín called "Traditioning," in which he first acknowledged that, while some of the Catholic Church's doctrines and rituals are old and unchanged, "some other doctrines and ethical expectations cannot claim such unquestioned, constant reception throughout Christian history."[46] Espín clearly understood that Christianity or the Catholic Church depends on processes of transmission; however, "anytime that Christianity is transmitted (expressed, taught, preached, ecclesially organized, and so on), and anytime that Christianity is lived by human communities, culture acts as the unavoidable means and prism."[47] In the process, people in different cultural or historical settings can and inevitably will traditionalize Christianity differently, such that "*there cannot be one single way of being Christian or of experiencing and interpreting the Christian religion*. The different ways will reflect the conflicts, the social places, the classes, the cultures, the genders, and everything else that is common part and parcel of human societies."[48] In sum, then,

> it seems reasonable to suggest that *whatever is traditioned (the tradition or contents of Christianity) is shaped, selected, presented, and received according to the social position, gender, culture, and so forth, of those who ordinarily transmit Christianity as well as of those who ordinarily listen to the gospel and accept it across generations and across cultural boundaries*.[49]

The Catholic Church in particular is well aware of this issue and has developed a sophisticated understanding of and policy toward what it calls "inculturation"—the injection of religion into culture as well as the injection of culture into religion.

Christianity, of course, is no more prone to traditioning than any other religion. Indeed, entire new religions have been traditioned into being in the last century or two, several of them in the United States (Church of Jesus Christ of Latter-day Saints, Christian Scientists, Jehovah's Witnesses, and so on), with many more in other parts of the world, from ayahuasca cults in Brazil to the Unification Church in Korea (also known pejoratively as the "Moonies" after founder Sun Myung Moon and subsequently transferred to the U.S.). Indeed, so many new religions appeared in Japan after the Second World War that Neill McFarland referred to the period as "the rush hour of the gods."[50]

And although religion is especially ripe for traditioning, no domain of culture is exempt, including food, clothing, music, dance, and every other collective behavior. The "traditional" cuisine of Italy—pasta with tomato sauce—would have been impossible prior to the sixteenth century, as the tomato was not indigenous to Europe and was unknown until explorers found it in the Americas; even pasta is a variation of Chinese noodles, made from local wheat instead of exotic rice. Likewise, what Koreans consider to be traditional "royal court cuisine" was actually established and codified in the twentieth century, largely through the efforts of one woman, Hwang Hye-Seong, who founded the Institute of Korean Royal Cuisine and won a national award for preserving and modernizing it.

We have already seen how the "classical" dance form of *odissi* was fabricated only in the mid-twentieth century. Other venerable dance "traditions" have just a slightly longer pedigree, such as Argentine tango. Like the United States, Argentina is a product of European colonialism, but the first tango music did not appear until the mid-1800s. As a dance, tango is a hybrid of the many different cultures and ethnicities that inhabited the country—Spanish and African, German, Italian, and Polish among others. Furthermore, when it first emerged, it was seen as scandalous, performed on the streets by the lower class and featuring a modern dance-hold in which a man and a woman put their arms around

Tango dancers,
Buenos Aires, 2009.

each other, which was considered shocking at the time. Additionally, lacking a standardized form, it was a basically improvisational dance, quite the opposite of traditional. The tango only became the "national" dance of Argentina in the early 1900s after it became known in Paris, became respectable, and circulated back to its country of birth.

Even what is frequently taken for "traditional culture" is often a late historical innovation. According to John Clammer, the "traditional" social organization of Fiji was actually designed by colonial officials such as Native Lands Commissioner G. V. Maxwell, who was so frustrated by the absence of a clear-cut local system of landownership and kinship that he imposed one on the Fijians—one that was "immediately enshrined as the 'official' doctrine of native social structure"[51] and has been accepted by outsiders and natives alike as authentic and traditional. Often dubbed the oldest and most traditional peoples in the world, the Australian Aboriginals had traditions for modifying their traditions; individuals might dream new material (songs, dances, symbols, entire ritual complexes) that could be added to "traditional knowledge," and tribes could exchange cultural material, such that a particular song, dance, etc. might be part of "traditional culture" one year and not the next. Memory being wonderfully porous, erroneous information might also slip into tradition: Deborah Bird Rose mentioned how one Yarralin man from the Victoria River Downs area of Australia recounted the adventures of Captain Cook in their territory, notwithstanding that Cook never set foot anywhere near the place.[52] As one final example, in 2001 China unveiled a new national garment on the occasion of an international economic summit in Shanghai. Called the *tangzhuang*, a name invoking the proud Tang dynasty (618–907 CE), the silk jacket was described as—and was intended to be—"ambiguously traditional" and to convey "both traditional Chinese flavor and modern ideals"; as Jianhua Zhao put it, it was "something new that appeared to be old" and something international that appeared to be local.[53]

The Processes of Traditioning

Traditions are made, not born—or rather, their shaping is ongoing after they are historically born. The next question, then, is how they are made. If traditioning or traditionalizing is a historical process that requires time and effort, how precisely does that process operate?

It is customary and attractive to think of traditioning as fundamentally a function of remembering. That cannot be the whole story, though, since traditions are often, if not ideally, things that we never personally experienced and therefore could not personally remember; also, as Henry Glassie insisted, there is always more available in the past and in memory than is actually embedded in tradition—as well as more than a few items in tradition that did not actually occur in the past or at least in the same moment in the past. So traditioning is not only a product of remembering, but of *forgetting*. We forget a lot of the details of the past; more significantly, we forget that there were other versions and interpretations of and in the past which, as Brueggemann stated, were just as confident of their accuracy as we are of ours. This reminds us, of course, that much of the point of traditioning is *interpreting*, so

that even what we remember—and perhaps remember correctly—
is and must be interpreted in the light of the present. And finally,
sometimes traditioning is a literal and intentional act of *inventing*, of
manufacturing bits and pieces and calling them traditional.

We can, however, be still more specific about traditioning processes,
the most common and powerful of which include the following:

Absorption, or *syncretism.* As some item of culture circulates
through a society or gets transmitted and reproduced over
time, it invariably picks up and integrates other elements of
culture along the way. The tradition-complex of Christmas is
a perfect example. Over the years and miles, the original (and
originally not terribly important) notion of Christmas (Easter
was the celebration par excellence in early Christianity) absorbed
numerous bits of culture such as the tree and the yule log (and
the very idea of "yule"), and Santa Claus and reindeer, etc. ad
infinitum. Every contemporary tradition is, in reality, a blending
of many different sources and traditions. Naturally, in the course
of syncretism there is often a crucial re-tasking of the elements
of other or former cultures: in their contact with native peoples,
Christian missionaries typically redefined local spirits as either
Christian demons or Christian saints and adopted aspects of
local ritual and language while reassigning Christian meanings
to them. In the American context, a British song called "To
Anacreon in Heaven" was reassigned as the tune of the national
anthem (see Chapter One).

Addition. As a tradition evolves, members of a society frequently
create new elements to enhance and extend it. To continue our
Christmas example, in 1822 Clement Clarke Moore composed
the rhyme "'Twas the Night Before Christmas," also known as
"A Visit from St Nicholas." Many Americans would not consider traditional Christmas well and truly done without a
rendition or two of the poem. In the 1940s Mel Tormé and Bob
Wells added "The Christmas Song" (better known to most folks
as "Chestnuts Roasting on an Open Fire"), and in between, an

adman working for Montgomery Ward added Rudolph the Red-nosed Reindeer (see Chapter Fifteen). Each generation can, and seems compelled to, fashion its own adornments to a tradition, such that the tradition grows over time.

Elaboration. In every tradition there are aspects that are not fully exploited and that can be developed in more detail. One such instance is the Christian doctrine of "the Rapture." It does indeed say in the New Testament that those Christians who are alive at the time of Christ's return will "be caught up" in the air (1 Thessalonians 4:17), while other passages make more arcane references to coming up to heaven at the sound of a trumpet (Revelation 4:1–2) or at the call of a loud voice (Revelation 11:3–12). The fact that these verses are more than a little obscure allows for a variety of interpretations and embellishments. The credit often goes to John Nelson Darby in 1827 for formulating and spreading the popular vision of the Rapture, which has been further elaborated since by the likes of Hal Lindsey (in his 1970 *The Late Great Planet Earth*), not to mention the *Left Behind* novels of Tim LaHaye and Jerry Jenkins—which, incidentally, have been further elaborated in a children's series and a military series penned by various other authors. Leaving this example behind, we can also see how Rudolph the red-nosed reindeer, after having been appended to the Christmas tradition, has been further elaborated in songs and animated television programs—given a family, a girlfriend, and an elf-dentist buddy.

Subtraction or *deletion.* Just as elements can be added to a tradition, so they can be removed from it too. Sometimes there is an intentional rejection of certain bits of the tradition, because they are deemed false or inappropriate in the present context. Such actions may take the form of "purification," an attempt to get back to the authentic version or source of the tradition— to cleanse the tradition of its accretions and elaborations—and at the extreme we might call such a project "fundamentalism."

Sometimes there is a more or less intentional thrust toward "simplification," to make the tradition more easily remembered or practiced. Aspects of the tradition that were formerly elaborated may undergo a process of de-elaboration, as some of these refinements or developments are jettisoned or forgotten. One variety of simplification mentioned by Shils relates to the "poor intellectual quality" of "the custodians" of the tradition,[54] who forget, misunderstand, or garble the tradition; the cause may be their own inadequate training in the tradition. Monica Ringer describes an interesting instance of this process in the Zoroastrian religion, which first appeared in ancient Persia. By the nineteenth century, the most vibrant community of Zoroastrians, known as Parsis, was based in India. When those Parsis went in search of ancient Persia and their religious roots, what they found was a disadvantaged and depressed minority in contemporary Iran, where "many religious texts had been lost and . . . the few texts that community preserved were poorly understood by the priests."[55] Ironically at first glance, but totally in keeping with our new understanding of traditioning, the Parsis took a certain pride in their long-lost ancestors but also set out to improve not only the living conditions but the religious knowledge and practice of their Iranian confreres, including "the reinstatement of 'lost' practices and the purification of Zoroastrianism from historical accretions of Islamic or Arab origin."[56]

Schism or *fission*. Finally, as indicated previously, one familiar way in which traditions evolve is through division and multiplication, which we might call, on the evolutionary metaphor, a kind of "speciation." That is, for doctrinal or practical or political reasons, a tradition may split into two or more contrasting—and often competing—versions. Whether we are then talking about one tradition or two is moot for the time being: when Protestantism split from Catholicism, we might argue that the outcome was two competing versions of the Christian tradition or two distinct traditions of Christianity. And naturally, since a branch of a tradition can itself branch further, the result may be a tree of related traditions, constituting a set of traditions with some "family resemblance" but often with all of the stresses and hostilities common to families.

Traditioning for (and against) the Nation and State

Having explored the "how" of traditioning, we must still ask two other questions: who and why? Who—what individual, group, or institution—is behind the traditioning, promoting it and profiting from it? And why: what are the motivations and interests driving tradition-making—and tradition-resisting?

Traditioning is never the work of a single individual, although one person may be key to any particular traditioning project. An example is Pierre de Coubertin, who, beginning in 1892, spearheaded the modern revival of the "tradition" of the Olympic games, which had not been held since 393 CE; ultimately, while a few of the "traditions" of the ancient Olympics were brought back to life, many new traditions have since been added (such as opening and closing ceremonies, modern sports, medals, and mascots) and others have been deleted (such as competing in the nude). An example of a crucial traditioning group or institution in America is the Grand Army of the Republic, which, as we will see in coming chapters, was instrumental to many patriotic traditions such as the flag, the national anthem, and the Pledge of Allegiance.

Every tradition, including the ones discussed in this book, has one and usually more than one such decisive actor or originator or promoter: someone, after all, had to compose the lyrics to the American national anthem, write the first Pledge of Allegiance, design the first pair of Levi's blue jeans, or draw the first cartoon mouse. Likewise, religious traditions have their founding prophet or teacher, such as Jesus, Muhammad, or Gautama (the Buddha). Many, if not all, religions have their energetic champions too, who helped spread and articulate the faith, such as Christianity's St Paul, the "apostle" of Jesus who never actually met Jesus (since Jesus was dead by the time Paul began preaching) and who never actually read the Gospel accounts of Jesus (since those documents were not written yet). We might call all of these

"Lest We Forget,"
the First World
War Memorial
in Marlborough,
Massachusetts.

figures the "tradition entrepreneurs," who make it their business to
formulate and foment the tradition.

As the cross-cultural and historical examples in this chapter have
shown, traditioning is, of course, by no means a new or uniquely Western
phenomenon; there is little doubt that humans have been inventing and
rethinking their traditions since the species emerged. However, there is a
strong consensus, and plenty of justification for saying, that traditioning
is particularly characteristic of the modern era. In fact, it is extremely
interesting to note that much traditioning occurred in the late nineteenth
and early twentieth centuries (which were also the key era of research for
Hobsbawm and Ranger). A surprising number of American traditions
arose and entered the culture in the late 1800s and early 1900s, just as
the modern Olympic tradition did. Those were also the crucial years

for the founding of modern states such as Germany, Italy, Japan, and Yugoslavia, among others. Since the modern state (what most people call "country" or "government") is a relatively late invention itself, it needed to instill itself in the hearts and minds of its citizens (that is, to breed "patriotism" and "nationalism"), to reshape the identities of individuals who may not previously have had a strong sense of or attachment to the state—if the state even existed.

States have been the most determined traditioners and tradition entrepreneurs of the past century or two. Because modern states are such large, abstract, and bureaucratic entities, in which members cannot possibly actually know everyone else and in which they may really have fairly little in common with each other, conceiving oneself as a citizen of such a society requires some imagination. Indeed, Benedict Anderson famously referred to modern states as "imaginary communities" integrated by forces such as shared media, shared economy, and shared political projects (such as war).[57] Part of this imagination is a (frequently imaginary) shared past—which naturally shapes a shared present of habits and holidays—which is provided by national "traditions."

These state traditions represent the collective memory of the society. Maurice Halbwachs was perhaps the first to comment on the significance and omnipresence of collective memory, traces of the past that are "continually reproduced" and re-enacted in the present and therefore become part of each individual's memory despite the fact that she or he was not there.[58] States go to very great lengths to create and imprint these collective memories in such forms as monuments and memorials, songs and stories, parades, and slogans and sayings (sometimes literally exhorting memory, as in "Remember the Alamo" or "Lest We Forget"), not to mention history books, speeches, movies, and everyday conversation.

So traditions are vitally important for creating and maintaining the modern state. But must the traditions be "traditional"? Most observers agree that the virtue of a tradition is not antiquity, certainly not veracity, but *authenticity*. Richard Bauman regarded the very phenomenon of traditionalization as "an act of authentication, akin to the art or antique dealer's authentication of an object by tracing its provenience."[59] And for the modern state, as for the art or antique market, authenticity confers authority, in at least three ways:

1. The putative age of the tradition. Older traditions (like older works of art) have a certain inherent *gravitas*, based on what Mircea Eliade called "the prestige of the past." Sheer age itself means longevity, which tends to translate into quality. Furthermore, the distant past has a certain mythical dimension: things were better, brighter, closer to the "source" back then. Very old (or allegedly very old) traditions partake in the "perfection of the beginning." And this, of course, provides a sense of continuity: as in the case of every myth, the myth of the deep-past origins of a tradition "assures man that what he is about to do *has already been done*."[60]

2. The "status of the acknowledged originator."[61] Related to and dependent on the first point, the founder/prophet—if known (and sometimes being unknown can convey an aura of timelessness and naturalness that is also very powerful)—often adds authority not only for being in the past but for being "on the spot" and for being more creative or more brilliant, verging on, if not literally, "sacred." If the Pilgrims were actually there at the first Thanksgiving, or if Francis Scott Key was actually there at the Battle of Fort McHenry, then they had a special insight; if the "Founding Fathers" were not only present at the signing of the Constitution but wrote it themselves, then they were smarter than we are. Whatever the details, the originator is typically seen as having the *right* to establish a tradition that binds us today.

3. The invariance of the tradition. As Heitzenrater asserted, a tradition's "continuing authenticity depends upon care in its transmission ('faithful' passing on and receiving)."[62] In other words, it is important that the tradition be—or *seem*—true and unchanging. But since time makes changes, it is necessary to indulge in "imaginative remembering," which also entails some *strategic forgetting*. Therefore, the "truth" of a tradition—that is, its historical accuracy, the claim that it happened exactly as we remember it and as we practice it today—is less important than the "sense of authenticity" that we build and sustain around it. Invariance—indeed, factuality in the first place (that

something, *anything*, happened in the past)—is an ideology and an imagination that we construct and defend around the tradition; it is part of the traditioning process—more than it is a reality of the tradition. Heitzenrater called this "the cloak of historical authenticity and continuity,"[63] and it is a little trick that we effectively and happily play on ourselves.

States have been happy enough to invent and promulgate traditions out of thin air or out of the raw material of art, culture, and history (for instance, "The Star-Spangled Banner" was a poem before it was a song and before it was an anthem). But states are also eager to exploit, manipulate, and co-opt preexisting traditions for their own use. Among many such instances, contemporary China has actively reworked *minjian*, or "folk culture," as in Yan'an (Shaanxi province), which is significant to the current regime as the early headquarters of the Chinese Communist Party. One tradition in that area is cutting elaborate and deeply symbolic paper designs. Chairman Mao Zedong inspired Chinese intellectuals and urbanites to study folk traditions such as paper-cutting with an eye toward crafting "a socialist art form that would absorb local cultural resources, yet reject elements considered as superstitious and feudal."[64] Researchers under the auspices of the Communist Party collected samples of folk art, selecting some motifs while ignoring or criticizing others; in the process, they "refashioned paper-cuts into a modern socialist art form by discounting their imagery and narrative themes connecting to a traditional past, thus highlighting the CCP's role in breaking away from the past and charting a new course for the country."[65] This overtly political work culminated in the Ansai Hall of Culture, with its classes to teach the locals (the "proper" version of) their own tradition. In Tibet, China has seized certain traditions (such as naming local lamas or religious leaders), banned others, and turned yet others into public televised spectacles.

As this case illustrates, the state is not above injecting itself into tradition, using tradition to legitimate itself and inculcate its power and its view of the world in its population. In extreme but not rare cases, tradition and folklore were employed to conjure the state and the nation (the people, who share a culture and putative birthright) into existence and into alignment in the first place. Across Europe and elsewhere, researchers and collectors scoured the countryside for folklore (songs, tales, dances, etc.), which allegedly proved the reality of an authentic nation; based on the romantic nationalism of thinkers such as Johann Herder (1744–1803), it was believed that each nation, people, or folk had its own distinct *Volksgeist*, its "spirit" and "genius," expressed in its arts and culture.

In short, traditioning has commonly been by and for the state (in the name or under the guise of the nation), but Nicholas Thomas reminded us to ask not only what traditions are invented *for* but what they are invented *against*.[66] One thing that they are invented against is *difference*, and traditioning can be an effective weapon for erasing difference—especially identities and nationalities that possess their own traditions. This means that the process of establishing and extending the hegemony of the state involves not only traditioning but *detraditioning*, the disqualification, if not suppression or eradication, of competing and potentially disintegrating traditions. In Turkey's struggle with the Kurds, the Turkish state has outlawed Kurdish songs, symbols, and language. In the United States, various means were tapped to detraditionalize the native peoples, from war and genocide to breaking up tribal territories and social organization, to boarding schools that prohibited traditional language, religion, clothing, food, and even hairstyles. In places such as Yugoslavia during its conflict of the 1990s, locations and storehouses of tradition—including mosques, museums, libraries, and the historic Mostar bridge—were intentionally targeted for destruction.

Yet despite their power, states have not monopolized the field of traditioning; indeed, in the modern world, traditions are sometimes created and wielded *against* the state, for instance in the name of ethnic groups and indigenous peoples. Richard Handler and Jocelyn Linnekin offered two examples in the cases of Quebec and native Hawaii. In both situations, and in many others like them, "tradition" became a valuable resource and weapon in staking a claim to the authenticity and thus to the political identity and rights of the Quebecois and Hawaiian nation in opposition to Canada and the United States, respectively. As they expressed it, "Nationalist ideology requires the existence of a culture—'we are a nation because we have a culture'—but most people are hard put to specify the traits and traditions that constitute that culture. It then becomes the business of specialists to discover and even to invent national culture, traditions, and heritage."[67] The surprising but inevitable realization is that what they called the "cult of tradition" is not only crucial to national identity and national sovereignty but in many, if not most, cases is *prior to* national identity and sovereignty. That is to say, there is a fundamental relationship between tradition, the past, and a social group (such as an ethnic group, indigenous society, or modern state), but often, if not ordinarily, both the past and the group are largely a product of the tradition, of traditioning, rather than the other way around.

Nor are states the only entities or forces against which groups, institutions, and nations exercise their traditioning. In Central and Eastern Europe, neo-pagan movements, such as Asatru, Wotanism, Ukrainian "Sylenkoism," and many many more, often resist contemporary states, to be sure, as well as past states such as the Soviet Union and its communist satellites, but also twenty-first-century globalization and ancient imperial conquest and domination, by appealing to what they consider their true and authentic traditions. Many of these movements-cum-religions reject Christianity as a foreign imposition, looking back further to pre-Christian and pre-Roman beliefs and practices. Members of these groups are often avid readers of history and ethnography, seeking information on their lost or denied cultures and identities. In such places, "tradition" or "folklore" is a central notion or trope in the quest for the authentic nation, resulting in what scholars have dubbed "ethno-paganism," the intersection of ethnicity or nationalism, and tradition, folklore, and religion. Neo- or ethno-paganism accordingly often pursues—and finds—the "sacred nation," the "true" culture and identity suppressed, as some partisans say in Hungary, by "a 'falsified' mainstream history" that excludes them while empowering and legitimating false and foreign influences such as Christianity or the (often multinational) state.[68] Some fairly fantastic counterclaims may ensue, such as the notion "of a direct continuity between the Sumerian and Hungarian people"[69] or even the assertion that the ancient Huns came from the distant star Sirius,[70] but as we have stressed, factuality has little to do with tradition; for Hungarian neo-pagans, the goal is "to sacralize the Hungarian nation. It makes Hungary stand out from other nations in origin and mission, and its fate influences the whole of human civilization."[71] It is no wonder then that neo-paganism, like many another tradition-oriented movement, tends not only to sanctify the group but in so doing to adopt exclusive and intolerant identities based on what they regard as not invented, but revived or restored traditions—and to translate those identities and traditions into political action.

If there is one thing that native Hawaiians, European neo-pagans, and many enthusiasts of "tradition" have in common, it is a sense of loss. One of the ironies of tradition is that often, in the words of Joni Mitchell's popular song "Big Yellow Taxi," you don't know what you've got till it's gone. Social scientists in many different fields have observed that traditioning requires, or at least thrives on, a certain distance from one's own culture and self; in the words of Thomas Sowell, too much cultural continuity can be a veritable hindrance in the traditioning process, and "those who have lost a culture have often been its most strident apostles . . . Genuine continuity of cultural identity is seldom as strident or as dramatic as artificial revivals."[72] This underscores the contrast between being traditional and being tradition-minded and emphasizes the point that those who are the most tradition-minded are frequently those who are already alienated to some extent from tradition.

Perhaps no one is more alienated, literally distanced, from their culture and tradition than refugees. According to Remo Guidieri and Francesco Pellizi, *exile* is a creative force, making difference painfully clear and driving an urgent sense of loss for the home culture—and often enough, an urgent search for it.[73] In groundbreaking fieldwork among Hutu refugees living in camps after the 1972 ethnic conflict in Burundi, Liisa Malkki found that the "most unusual and prominent social fact about the camp was that its inhabitants were continually engaged in an impassioned construction and reconstruction of their history as 'a people'."[74] In such an environment, people reconstructed a life out of memories and imaginings, because their old taken-for-granted life really was threatened, if not destroyed. In particular, she described the "mythico-history" in which they indulged when they told stories about the recent and ancient past. In these tales, they explored recurrent themes of their ancient origins and a "golden past" before the Tutsi came—or before the evil of the Tutsi arrived and their own consequent subordination—or of the purported physical and psychological differences between "them" and "us," and of course of the apocalypse that was the 1972 war and its atrocities. Narratives like these were commonly not factual nor was factuality their function; they were polemics, pleas, and hopes.

Many people today and in recent years have felt the same sense of loss even in their own homes and homelands. Refugees are lost in place, but neo-pagans, indigenous peoples, and many more groups and nations are (or at least feel) lost in time. Traditioning is, in the final analysis, a mighty engine for both nation-building and nation-restoring. As the American traditions in the following chapters illustrate, American traditioning has been a strenuous combination of building a nation that has not yet become and restoring a nation that is already un-becoming.

AMERICAN
POLITICAL
TRADITIONS

ONE

Of Thee I Sing:
National Anthem

★ ★ ★

Question: What national song is named in the U.S. Constitution?
The answer, of course, is none. At the time when the Constitu-
tionwas ratified in 1787 (not a date that Americans customarily
observe with any excitement) and the United States of America formally came into existence, it had no national anthem. In fact,
according to Marc Ferris, who recently published a comprehensive
history of the American national anthem, the very idea of a "national
anthem" was still new, the mother country of England only having
adopted its own song, "God Save the King," in the mid-eighteenth
century; furthermore, the English song was "born of war, as most
lasting national anthems are"[1]—including America's "The Star-
Spangled Banner," which is explicitly about a specific, although largely
forgotten, battle and war, as well as the French anthem *La Marseillaise*
that preceded it, arising in the midst of the traumatic French Revolution
of 1789.

Although it is now normal for a country to have an anthem, it was
not countries that first promulgated the musical form. Originally an
"anthem" was a style of church music, the word derived from the
Greek *antiphona*, or "anti-/opposite-sound," a kind of call-and-
response singing. The lyrics of an anthem are typically celebratory;
the Merriam-Webster dictionary characterizes it as "a song or hymn
of praise or gladness." The words and the tunes are usually rousing
and more—*they are motivating*: as the Greek source suggests, an anthem
asks us not only to feel, not only to identify, but to *respond*; an anthem

is a call to action. This is especially clear in the anthems or theme songs of universities and their sports teams, which are commonly referred to as "fight songs." Some examples are the University of Wisconsin's "On, Wisconsin," Notre Dame's "Notre Dame Fight Song" (or in some sources "Victory March"), Louisiana State University's "Fight for LSU," and Pennsylvania State University's "Fight On, Penn State." These songs, with their bellicose lyrics and their martial beats, aim to inspire loyalty and stimulate exertion.

Other entities also have their anthems or official songs, including the branches of the U.S. military (for example, the Army's "The Army Goes Rolling Along," the Marines' "The Marine's Hymn," and the Navy's "Anchors Aweigh") and the various states of the United States. As a sovereign country, the United States toyed with different songs before settling on "The Star-Spangled Banner" (sometimes rendered without the hyphen, as "The Star Spangled Banner"), which, to many ears, was an unlikely choice given its subject-matter and its musical difficulty.

During the American Revolution, the most popular marching and fighting song was actually "Yankee Doodle," an appropriation of a derogatory term of the British for their American inferiors (Ferris reminds us that "Yankee" was a condescending name for American colonials and that "a 'doodle' is a fool.")[2] Shortly after independence, a new song entered American culture. Philip Phile is generally credited with composing the tune for the inauguration of the first president, George Washington, in 1789, titled "The President's March"; lyrics were added by Joseph Hopkinson in 1798.[3] The song became known as "Hail, Columbia," Columbia being a common term for the United States in its early years. The first verse and chorus go:

Hail Columbia, happy land!
Hail, ye heroes, heaven-born band,
Who fought and bled in freedom's cause,
Who fought and bled in freedom's cause,
And when the storm of war was gone
Enjoyed the peace your valor won.
Let independence be our boast,
Ever mindful what it cost;

Ever grateful for the prize,
Let its altar reach the skies.

Firm, united let us be,
Rallying round our liberty,
As a band of brothers joined,
Peace and safety we shall find.[4]

In the race to choose a national anthem, "Hail, Columbia" was, in the words of Ferris, "the coequal of 'The Star-Spangled Banner' through the late 1800s" (just as the image of Columbia was a rival to Uncle Sam for the same period).[5] In fact, it was not until a century and a half after its independence that America would finally have an official anthem, its competitors sinking into obscurity.

Oh Say Can You See: America Meets England in War and Verse

The life of "The Star-Spangled Banner" began in 1814, during a barely remembered clash in a barely remembered war. In 1812 the United States found itself defending its hard-won and tender independence against England, and by 1814 the war was not going well. On August 24, a British army sacked Washington, DC, and burned the Capitol and the White House (which was not known as the White House at the time: its first names were the President's Palace or the Presidential Mansion, and its official designation was "Executive Mansion" until Theodore Roosevelt began using the phrase "White House" on his presidential stationery in 1901). The British moved on to threaten Baltimore, Maryland, the next month, and for about 25 hours a minor poet and lawyer from Georgetown watched the shelling of Fort McHenry, which defended the harbor of the city.

Francis Scott Key was a prominent citizen of the Baltimore/Washington vicinity. George Svejda, who has offered his own history of "The Star-Spangled Banner," described him as "an active social worker, helping to organize the Lancaster Society of Georgetown for the free education of Georgetown's poor children," as well as "a charter member of the American Colonization Society."[6] The latter was an organization committed to sending Africans in America back to Africa, and Key— ironically, as the author of the words "land of the free"—was himself a slave owner. He was also at first an opponent of the War of 1812,

> on moral and political grounds. At one point he had even taken pleasure in his country's military failures, writing to a friend in 1813 that he would rather see the American flag lowered in disgrace than have it stand for persecution and dishonor, as he believed was the case in the United States' attempted invasion of British Canada.[7]

Nevertheless, Key was called upon to try to win the release of one Dr William Beanes, who had been detained by the British, so Key was negotiating with the enemy and staying on British ships at the time of the assault on Fort McHenry. Becoming aware of the impending attack, he was not allowed to leave until it was over; otherwise, an American would not have been on board a hostile ship at that moment. The bombardment of the stronghold lasted from 6 a.m. on September 13 until 7 a.m. the following day, at which time the British attackers withdrew from the nearly impregnable fort. Key and other onlookers waited for the dawn and the clearing of the smoke to learn whether the fort had survived the shelling, which it had.

There are two somewhat conflicting accounts of how Key's resulting poem came to be written, both offered decades after the event. One was given by John Stuart Skinner in 1849, who accompanied Key on his diplomatic mission 35 years prior. Skinner claimed that the verses were composed the night after the pair returned to Baltimore. A decade later in 1859, Key's brother-in-law Roger Brooke Taney (who by that time was the Chief Justice of the U.S. Supreme Court and, two years earlier, authored the infamous *Dred Scott* decision that African slaves were not citizens and that Congress could not ban slavery or force owners to free their slaves) filed a different report, asserting that Key had begun to draft the poem on board the ship, writing "brief notes, that would aid him in recalling the lines, on the back of a letter. For some lines he relied on his memory, finishing them before reaching shore. He wrote the final version, however, at his hotel on the night he reached Baltimore."[8] Svejda regarded both stories as "the products of old-age memories,"[9] which extended to how the poem came to be published.

In Taney's account, Key took his verses to a Judge Joseph H. Nicholson the next day, who sent it to a printer; however, Svejda considered this unlikely, as Nicholson was himself on military duty at Fort McHenry at the time. Skinner, on the other hand, claimed that it was he who delivered the poem to the *Baltimore Patriot and Advertiser* the day after it was written. In whatever way it fell into the hands of a publisher, many years later, in 1874, Samuel Sands maintained that he was the one who set it in type, the poem appearing on September 30, 1814 (Oscar Sonneck said the name of the newspaper was the *Baltimore American* and the date September 21[10]) by the title of "Defence of Fort McHenry" without Key's name attached but with a short introductory comment about the scene that the poem depicted. The text of the poem read

O say, can you see, by the dawn's early light,
What so proudly we hailed at the twilight's last gleaming,
Whose broad stripes and bright stars, through the perilous fight,
O'er the ramparts we watched, were so gallantly streaming?
And the rockets' red glare, the bombs bursting in air,
Gave proof through the night that our flag was still there;
O say, does that star-spangled banner yet wave
O'er the land of the free and the home of the brave?

On the shore, dimly seen thro' the mist of the deep,
Where the foe's haughty host in dread silence reposes,
What is that which the breeze, o'er the towering steep,
As it fitfully blows, half conceals, half discloses?
Now it catches the gleam of the morning's first beam,
In full glory reflected, now shines on the stream
'Tis the star-spangled banner. Oh! long may it wave
O'er the land of the free and the home of the brave!

And where is that band who so vauntingly swore
That the havoc of war and the battle's confusion

A home and a country should leave us no more?
Their blood has washed out their foul footstep's pollution.
No refuge could save the hireling and slave
From the terror of flight, or the gloom of the grave,
And the star-spangled banner in triumph doth wave
O'er the land of the free and the home of the brave.

Oh! thus be it ever, when freemen shall stand
Between their loved homes and the war's desolation,
Blest with vict'ry and peace, may the Heav'n-rescued land
Praise the Pow'r that hath made and preserved us a nation!
Then conquer we must, when our cause it is just,
And this be our motto: "In God is our trust."
And the star-spangled banner in triumph shall wave
O'er the land of the free and the home of the brave.

Finally, there was a notation that the words were to be sung to the tune
of "Anacreon in Heaven."

A Poem Becomes a Song

Two things are clear. Francis Scott Key never called his poem "The Star-Spangled Banner"—or anything else, for that matter, the title "Defence of Fort McHenry" having been assigned by a newspaper editor—and Key did not write the melody in which it was to be sung. Indeed, "Anacreon in Heaven," also called "To Anacreon in Heaven" and "The Anacreontic Song," has a long, disputed, and checkered story of its own.

The Anacreontic Society was a social club of gentlemen and professionals in eighteenth-century London; in addition to general conviviality and drinking, its special interest was music. The organization was named after the ancient Greek poet Anacreon, commonly associated with "wine, women, and song." In the late 1700s its members felt that the club needed its own anthem (some call it a "drinking song" or bacchanalian; Ferris dubs it "a bawdy, boozy ballad"[11]), so probably sometime in the 1770s the song was composed (Sonneck argued that the Society was dissolved in the early 1790s[12]), either by

Samuel Arnold or more likely by John Stafford Smith. The first of its six verses apparently went as follows:

> To Anacreon in Heaven, where he sat in full glee,
> A few sons of harmony sent in a petition
> That he their inspirer and patron would be;
> When this answer arrived from the Jolly Old Grecian
> "Voice, fiddle, and flute,
> "No longer be mute,
> "I'll lend you my name and inspire you to boot,
> "And, besides, I'll instruct you, like me, to intwine
> "The Myrtle of Venus with Bacchus' Vine."

From England it diffused to the taverns of America, where it became a popular melody. In fact, "The Star-Spangled Banner" was hardly the first American song set to the tune: Svejda stated that 85 different sets of words employed the melody between 1790 and 1820,[13] including Robert Treat Paine's "Adams and Liberty" (1798):

> Ye sons of Columbia, who bravely have fought,
> For those rights, which unstained from your Sires had descended,
> May you long taste the blessings your valor has brought,
> And your sons reap the soil which their fathers defended.
> 'Mid the reign of mild Peace,
> May your nation increase,
> With the glory of Rome, and the wisdom of Greece;
> And ne'er shall the sons of Columbia be slaves,
> While the earth bears a plant, or the sea rolls its waves.

Key indisputably knew the melody; in fact, he used it for a poem in 1805 called "When the Warrior Returns from the Battle Afar" in honor of Stephen Decatur, and he almost certainly had it in mind when he wrote his verses on Fort McHenry, since Sonneck concluded that the "form and meter of 'To Anacreon in Heaven,' 'Adams and Liberty,' and 'The Star-Spangled Banner' are practically the same, as the juxtaposition of the first stanza will prove, if such proof be necessary."[14]

So Key's poem had acquired its tune, but it still had not acquired its name. All sources agree that the verses were originally published as a "broadside"—that is, a large paper sheet printed on one side, like a poster or advertisement. It was quickly circulated and reprinted in various East Coast newspapers, but it became a song when Thomas Carr, a music store owner in Baltimore, transferred it to sheet-music format no later than November 18, and as early as October 19, with the title "The Star-Spangled Banner." Svejda reported that the song was publicly performed on the October date by a Mr Hardinge after a play called *Count Benyowsky*.[15]

The song spread rapidly from that point, appearing in various printed collections of American music. But its very popularity subjected it to diverse treatments, some rougher than others. One adaptation was the addition of verses: a new verse was tacked on in an 1816 songbook, referencing the Battle of New Orleans. In 1824 George Spowers addressed one of the more serious and persistent complaints about Key's composition, namely the ugly and anti-British third verse, with a verse of his own that was decidedly friendlier:

> But hushed be that strain! They our Foes are no longer;
> Lo Britain the right hand of Friendship extends,
> And Albion's fair Isle we behold with affection
> The land of our Fathers—the land of our Friends!
> Long, long may we flourish,
> Columbia and Britain,
> In amity still may your children be found,
> And the Star-Spangled Banner and Red Cross together
> Wave free and triumphant the wide world around!

Few people sing or even know this verse, but then few sing or even know the verses of "The Star-Spangled Banner" beyond the first (or realize that that entire first verse is a question!). More successful but still largely unknown today was the stanza suggested by Oliver Wendell Holmes in 1861 after another bombardment, this time the Southern attack on Fort Sumter, ushering in the Civil War:

DEFENCE OF FORT M'HENRY.

The annexed song was composed under the following circumstances—A gentleman had left Baltimore, in a flag of truce for the purpose of getting released from the British fleet, a friend of his who had been captured at Marlborough.—He went as far as the mouth of the Patuxent, and was not permitted to return lest the intended attack on Baltimore should be disclosed. He was therefore brought up the Bay to the mouth of the Patapsco, where the flag vessel was kept under the guns of a frigate, and he was compelled to witness the bombardment of Fort M'Henry, which the Admiral had boasted that he would carry in a few hours, and that the city must fall. He watched the flag at the Fort through the whole day with an anxiety that can be better felt than described, until the night prevented him from seeing it. In the night he watched the Bomb Shells, and at early dawn his eye was again greeted by the proudly waving flag of his country.

Tune—ANACREON IN HEAVEN.

O ! say can you see by the dawn's early light,
    What so proudly we hailed at the twilight's last gleaming,
Whose broad stripes and bright stars through the perilous fight,
    O'er the ramparts we watch'd, were so gallantly streaming?
And the Rockets' red glare, the Bombs bursting in air,
Gave proof through the night that our Flag was still there;
    O ! say does that star-spangled Banner yet wave,
    O'er the Land of the free, and the home of the brave?

On the shore dimly seen through the mists of the deep,
    Where the foe's haughty host in dread silence reposes,
What is that which the breeze, o'er the towering steep,
    As it fitfully blows, half conceals, half discloses?
Now it catches the gleam of the morning's first beam,
In full glory reflected now shines in the stream,
    'Tis the star spangled banner, O ! long may it wave
    O'er the land of the free and the home of the brave.

And where is that band who so vauntingly swore
    That the havoc of war and the battle's confusion,
A home and a country, shall leave us no more?
    Their blood has washed out their foul footsteps pollution.
No refuge could save the hireling and slave,
From the terror of flight or the gloom of the grave,
    And the star-spangled banner in triumph doth wave,
    O'er the Land of the Free, and the Home of the Brave.

O ! thus be it ever when freemen shall stand,
    Between their lov'd home, and the war's desolation,
Blest with vict'ry and peace, may the Heav'n rescued land,
    Praise the Power that hath made and preserv'd us a nation!
Then conquer we must, when our cause it is just,
And this be our motto—" In God is our Trust ;"
    And the star-spangled Banner in triumph shall wave,
    O'er the Land of the Free, and the Home of the Brave.

Broadside printing of "Defence of Fort McHenry."

When our land is illumined with liberty's smile,
If a foe from within strikes a blow at her glory,
Down, down with the traitor that tries to defile
The flag of the stars, and the page of her story!
By the millions unchained,
Who their birthright have gained,
We will keep her bright blazon forever unstained;
And the star-spangled banner in triumph shall wave,
While the land of the free is the home of the brave.

An 1814 copy of "The Star-Spangled Banner," the first printed edition
to combine the words and sheet music.

The song, or at least the melody that it borrowed, was also put to
various partisan uses. Political campaigns, for example, drafted their own
lyrics for the tune—eight campaign songs alone for William Henry
Harrison's Whig campaign of 1840, and then at least one, "Our Brave
Rough and Ready," for the 1848 race, not to mention a victory song, "On
Mexico's Plain," celebrating the U.S. defeat of its southern neighbor.[16]
Other causes too exploited the popularity and familiarity of "The Star-
Spangled Banner," such as abolition (anti-slavery), including one parody
that allegedly ended with the lines "O say, does that blood-striped banner
still wave / O'er the land of the fetter, and the hut of the slave?"[17] Another
usurper of the tune was the temperance (anti-alcohol) movement, as in
this 1843 takeoff:

> Oh! Who has not seen by the dawn's early light,
> Some poor bloated drunkard to his home weakly reeling,
> With blear eyes and red nose most revolting to sight;
> Yet still in his breast not a throb of shame feeling!
> And the plight he was in
> Steep'd in filth to his chin,

While the pitiable wretch would stagger along
To the shame of his friends, 'mid the jeers of the throng.[18]

Clearly, then, there was no great reverence just yet for the future national anthem.

The Competition to Become the Anthem

Meanwhile, the respectful and even official uses of "The Star-Spangled Banner" were growing. By 1842 it was regarded as a national patriotic song, especially by the u.s. Navy and the Marine Band. It was played, along with other patriotic songs, at Fourth of July celebrations, and it was performed at the inauguration of Abraham Lincoln (who, coincidentally, was sworn in by Chief Justice Taney). But it still had no special status: it was one song among others, including "Yankee Doodle" and, of course, the de facto anthem "Hail, Columbia." But no national anthem was officially defined, although Americans began to feel the need to have an official anthem. Accordingly, contests were held throughout the 1800s to find a suitable "national hymn," but none was selected, and many were true abominations.

Remarkably, Ferris asserts that there was another competition over the anthem too—not for which song would hold the honors, but for which country would hold the song. At the outbreak of the Civil War, some rebels in the Confederacy wanted to adopt the song as their own; when they failed to wrest it from the Union, Northerners occasionally showed irreverence themselves by penning parodies to spite their Southern kin, as in "The Flag of Fort Sumter" which intoned, "O say have you heard how the flag of our sires, is insulted by traitors in boastful alliance / When the Union's dear cause over Sumter's red fires, in front of Rebellion it waved in defiance."[19]

Why wasn't "The Star-Spangled Banner" simply embraced as the theme song of the United States? There are a number of answers. Some critics found it impossible to sing, with a very demanding melody and confusing lyrics (as evidenced by the struggle that contemporary singers still have in remembering the words correctly). Others thought that its topic was too obscure and too specific, a minor battle in a minor war. Some objected to its anti-British sentiment, while some regarded it as too British, perhaps a joke or a jab by Key at his host's and enemy's expense. For instance, Richard Grant White, who studied patriotic music, opined that

> as a patriotic song for the people at large, as the National Hymn, ["The Star-Spangled Banner"] was found to be almost useless ... The words, too, are altogether unfitted for a national hymn. They are almost entirely descriptive, and of a particular event ... The lines are also too long, and the rhyme too involved for a truly popular patriotic song. The rhythm, too, is complicated, and often harsh and vague.[20]

Stephen Salisbury, in his 1872 essay, conceded that the instrumental version of the song "will be a constant and untiring gratification to the ear and the heart of an American"—which is ironic, since the music was not of American origin—but "the words in use will not be accepted as a permanent national song."[21] Some felt that it was too combative, such as the New Jersey Federation of Women's Clubs as late as 1927 or the educators at the Teachers College of Columbia University in 1930. Then there were its rivals, not only "Hail, Columbia" and "Yankee Doodle" (the latter of which was never taken seriously as an anthem) but "America" (otherwise known as "My Country 'Tis of Thee," with lyrics by Samuel Francis Smith in 1832 but a melody mimicking the British anthem "God Save the King," which fascinatingly also provided the mold for the national anthem of Denmark, adopted in the 1790s), "The Battle Hymn of the Republic" (the preference of President Theodore Roosevelt), and "America the Beautiful" (which came together in 1910 from Katharine Lee Bates's 1895 poem "Pike's Peak," or "America," and Samuel A. Ward's 1882 hymn "Materna," or "O Mother Dear, Jerusalem," but that is another story).

So, late in the nineteenth century "The Star-Spangled Banner" was a familiar and beloved (by many) patriotic song in the panoply of American songs. What really tipped the balance in its favor was its gradual integration into military usage. In July 1889, by General Order No. 374, Secretary of the Navy Benjamin F. Tracy specified it as the music for morning Colors (the raising of the flag in the morning), with "Hail, Columbia" prescribed for evening Colors (the lowering of the flag at day's end). By 1893 Key's song earned its spot at both moments of the day (Article 157, U.S. Naval Regulations), and the Navy mentioned it as the "national air."[22] John Philip Sousa's Marine Band helped popularize "The Star-Spangled Banner," particularly during the band's tours around the country; however, Sousa himself alternated between performing it and "Hail, Columbia" at official events and still believed that the latter was the rightful "national air" of the United States.[23] Meanwhile, the U.S. Army also took note of "The Star-Spangled Banner," ordering in the U.S. Army Regulations of 1895 for it to be performed as the flag was lowered in the evening. Eventually increased respect was added: soldiers were drilled to stand at attention, facing the flag and saluting "uncovered" (that is, with their hats off) while the song played.

In 1917, after the U.S. entered the First World War, "Military engagements on the battlefields of Europe elevated the importance and visibility of the flag, 'The Star-Spangled Banner,' and other historic national songs . . . 'The Star-Spangled Banner' also made repeated appearances at community singing events during the war years."[24] Consequently, Army regulations (Changes No. 50, Paragraph 264) named "The Star-Spangled Banner" as the national anthem of the United States. But the Army did not have the authority to make such a designation; in fact, "The Star-Spangled Banner" was not yet officially the national anthem, nor was any other song. Nevertheless, the push was on to select a national anthem, and "The Star-Spangled Banner" had its champions—unsurprisingly, especially among patriotic organizations in Maryland and the vicinity as the dramatization of a local event and the product of the native son. As early as 1903, the Maryland state president of the U.S. Daughters of the War of 1812, Mrs Robert Barry, petitioned the Army to choose "The Star-Spangled Banner" as the anthem. But again, neither the Army nor the War Department (which we call the Department of Defense today) had such authority.

So partisans of the song turned their efforts to Congress, proposing bills almost every year from 1912 until their ultimate success. The first in the series was introduced by Congressman George Edmund Foss of

Illinois in 1912, which, like many bills after it, died in committee. In 1918 the president of the Maryland State Society, United States Daughters of 1812, Mrs Reuben Ross Holloway, found an ally in Congressman J. Charles Linthicum—Representative from Maryland and native of Baltimore—to nurse a bill through Congress. Two other patriotic organizations, the Veterans of Foreign Wars and the American Legion, also joined the initiative for the anthem. Still, only on Linthicum's sixth try, on April 15, 1929, did a national anthem bill pass, although it took another full year before House Resolution 14 was adopted by the House on April 21, 1930. The Senate took almost another year to approve it (March 3, 1931), but President Herbert Hoover signed the bill into law that very day. The entire Act read as follows: "Be it enacted by the Senate and House of Representatives of the United States of America, in Congress assembled, that the composition consisting of the words and music known as 'The Star Spangled Banner' is designated the national anthem of the United States of America."

Observers could not help but notice that this was a victory for a certain constituency, namely the sons and daughters of Baltimore and of Maryland. Indeed, shortly thereafter the *Baltimore Evening Sun* earnestly wrote

> It must be pleasing to all Marylanders to have a Maryland song thus honored, and yet the occasion is not yet quite one for unreserved joy. Unofficially, "The Star-Spangled Banner" has long been recognized as the national anthem, so nothing much is added to its dignity by this act of Congress. On the other hand, now that it has official standing, we formally prophesy that not six months will pass before some one comes forward with a proposal to inflict pains and penalties upon those who do not accord the song what the proposer regards as a proper measure of respect.[25]

And interestingly, while the "tradition" of "The Star-Spangled Banner" was now settled, a number of the details had not been—and still have not been—settled. For instance, there is a law stipulating how listeners should behave during the performance of the national

Tommie Smith and John Carlos raise the "black power salute" during the national anthem at the 1968 Olympics.

anthem—standing, facing the flag, right hand over heart, according to Title 36, Section 301 of the U.S. Code—but there are no standards for the performance itself. Ferris actually mentions that there was a mild difference between how the opening notes were sung in the nineteenth and early twentieth centuries: previously, faithful to the original "To Anacreon in Heaven," the words "O say" were sounded as two notes of the same pitch, but eventually they were divided into the familiar three notes of descending pitch ("O-O say").[26]

Furthermore, there is no regulation about where and when the anthem can or must be played, outside of military venues. However, it has become customary to begin sporting events with a rendition of "The Star-Spangled Banner," which may date back to before it was the official anthem, as early as 1903 at a New York Highlanders (Yankees today) baseball game; clear evidence indicates that it was performed during the 1918 World Series in Chicago, although it was not yet the actual national anthem.[27] Since then it has been played and sung thousands of times in hundreds of ways, some more controversial than others. In 1944 the great composer Igor Stravinsky debuted his personal arrangement of the song, but popular reaction—as well as a Massachusetts state law that bans "embellishment of the national anthem"—prevented him from ever repeating the performance.[28] Another attempt to standardize the anthem, promoted by Representative Joel T. Broyhill, a Republican from Virginia, failed in 1955, partly because he advanced a version sometimes known as the "education version" that lacked one of the verses and failed to acknowledge Key; the public outcry against such perceived tampering killed the measure.[29]

And musicians of diverse styles—from José Feliciano's blues/folk rendition during the 1968 World Series to Jimi Hendrix's psychedelic version at Woodstock in 1969, to the warbling interpretations of Mariah Carey and Whitney Houston—have made the "traditional" song their own, to mixed responses from the American public. Probably the most reviled (mis)treatment of the song was Roseanne Barr's butchery of it before a San Diego Padres game on July 25, 1990, in which she included a crotch-grab and a spit for good measure. A new controversy erupted in 2016 when San Francisco Forty-Niners quarterback Colin Kaepernick refused to stand for the performance of "The Star-Spangled Banner" before football games, as a political statement about racial violence in the U.S.; nor was his protest the first of its kind: two African American track and field stars, Tommie Smith and John Carlos, raised their fists in a "black power salute" during the podium rendition of the anthem at the 1968 Olympics. And efforts to replace "The Star-Spangled Banner" with a different song have not disappeared.

Americans continue to reinvent and even resist their "traditional" national anthem. And whatever happened to "Hail, Columbia"? It is used today as the theme song of the vice president, played when he enters a room, just as "Hail to the Chief" is played for the president.

TWO

You're a Grand Old Rag: American Flag

★ ★ ★

Then flag—the Stars and Stripes, Old Glory—is perhaps America's oldest, proudest, and most omnipresent tradition. It is the fullest representation of the United States of America, recognizable around the world. It has also been the inspiration or focus of other prominent traditions, such as the national anthem (see Chapter One), the Pledge of Allegiance (see Chapter Four), and Memorial Day and Flag Day (see Chapter Seven). Many other days, indeed every other day, you can see homes, schools, offices, trucks, and even people decked out in the national colors.

The U.S. hardly invented the concept of a flag; every modern country has one, and vexillologists (scholars who study flags, from the Latin *vexillum* for flag) maintain that cloth banners were used by ancient Egyptians and Chinese, mainly as military identifiers and signals and especially on ships. Particular armies or regiments might fly their own "colors," and flags and other emblems were part of heraldry and symbols of clans and royal houses. By the Middle Ages flags came to be associated with emerging nation-states, and the English carried a red cross of St George into the Crusades. In 1606 the English red cross was superimposed on the Scottish flag (that is, the red cross of St George superimposed on Scotland's white saltire and blue background of St Andrew) to produce the first "Union Jack"—a red, white, and blue banner that also flew over the British colony of Massachusetts Bay in 1634.

America's love affair with its flag is unique, though. American flag expert Marc Leepson wrote, "Nowhere on earth do citizens fly their national flags, as Americans do, everywhere they live and everywhere they go, from our front porches to our pickup trucks . . . Nor does any nation turn to its flag as an emotional, political, and patriotic symbol in good times and bad the way Americans do."[1] Some observers have judged that there is an American "cult of the flag," and Italian historian Arnaldo Testi goes so far as to call the flag "the totem of the nation" and to accuse Americans of "flag fetishism."[2]

Finally, the American flag is uncommon among traditions in that it is officially intended to change: "It is a flag that changes over time as the national territory changes and increases"—a new star added for each new state—and the change and growth are foreseen and regulated by law. "The flag is a variable icon geared to automatic expansion, the appropriate emblem of an empire in the making," according to Testi.[3] This means that there has not been a single stable American flag but multiple American flags over time—and often many versions of the flag at any one time.

Lest the reader feel that the title of this chapter conveys intentional disrespect, it is worth noting that "You're a Grand Old Rag" was the original title and lyric of George M. Cohan's classic song, "You're a Grand Old Flag." Based on a quote from a veteran, Cohan used the line in his song, but popular reaction compelled him to replace it. This is but one example of how some elements of tradition are rejected and best forgotten.

The Dawn's Early Light of American Flags

According to Marc Leepson, "This unalloyed and unique feeling that Americans have for their flag is even more remarkable given the fact that the American flag's origins are murky and that Americans labor under several widespread misunderstandings about our national emblem"; even more surprisingly, says Leepson, for the first century of the country's history, "it was not customary for private individuals to fly the American flag. Until 1861, the flag was flown almost exclusively at federal facilities and by the American military, primarily on U.S. Navy ships."[4]

Obviously, there was no "American" flag for the first century-and-a-half of colonialism (early 1600s to late 1700s), since there was no

"America," only British settlements on the North American coastline. These British communities hoisted banners that were mostly variations on the Union Jack, although there were many exceptions, such as the so-called Bedford (Massachusetts) flag (from 1705), a crimson banner with an arm raising a sword through a cloud in silver, black, and gold. Interestingly, most similar to the eventual American flag was the ensign of the British East India Company, which featured red and white horizontal stripes and a white canton (in vexillology, the space in the upper left corner) with the St George's Cross. There is no evidence that the American flag has a direct connection to that standard, however.

The evolution of American flags is naturally related to the growing antipathy and rebelliousness towards England in the mid-1700s, and many of the early banners were explicit symbols of defiance, such as the well-known coiled snake flag and its slogan "Don't Tread on Me," attributed to Benjamin Franklin. Reportedly Commodore Esek Hopkins flew a yellow version of the "Don't Tread on Me" flag over the first Continental Navy fleet. Other designs existed as well, including flags with images of the pine tree or with words such as "Liberty."

At the time of the Declaration of Independence (1776), there was still not a single official American national or battle flag, and the Founding Fathers did not get around to considering one for almost a year. This means, of course, that American Revolutionary War soldiers fought under a number of different pennants, including

- the Bennington flag, with thirteen horizontal stripes (seven white and six red) and a canton with eleven stars in a semicircle, two more stars above, and the number "76" below;
- the Stark flag, "a green silk banner with a blue canton in which thirteen white or gold five-pointed stars are painted";[5]
- the Cowpens flag, with thirteen stars and thirteen stripes in red, white, and blue, twelve of the stars encircling a central star (which may have been made after the Battle of Cowpens, South Carolina);
- the Brandywine flag, a red banner with a canton of red and white stripes and its own mini-canton of thirteen red stars on a white background.

Grand Union Flag, also known as "Continental Colors," is considered
to be the first flag of America.

By 1775 there was also a flag in use known as the Continental Colors, which flew alongside Esek Hopkins's yellow snake flag, and by late 1776 the Continental Congress, America's revolutionary government, "considered the Continental Colors as the de facto official flag of the American naval forces"—but not the standard flag of the country.[6] One significant drawback of the Continental Colors was that it still included the Union Jack (in the canton), which suggested loyalty to England and could be confused with the British flag in battle. George Washington was reportedly against its use.

The Continental Congress finally took up the issue of a national flag in mid-1777, issuing a brief resolution on June 14 subsequently known as the Flag Resolution: "Resolved, That the flag of the United States be thirteen stripes, alternate red and white; that the union by thirteen stars in a blue field, representing a new constellation." Note several important facts about the proposed flag. First, there are no specifics about its size or shape or the proportions of its components. Nor is there guidance on the shape or arrangement of the stars. Nor were the stars overtly associated with the thirteen colonies; rather there is a cryptic reference to a "constellation." In his 1853 book *The History of the National Flag*, Schuyler Hamilton contended that the

Congress had an actual celestial constellation, Lyra, in mind, which was allegedly "a time-honored emblem of the union"[7]—although one completely unknown to today's Americans. Nor was any explicit meaning assigned to the choice of colors; although various individuals have offered interpretations for the red, white, and blue—in 1782 Secretary of the Continental Congress Charles Thomson mused that white stood for "purity and innocence," red for "hardness and valor," and blue for "vigilance, perseverance, and justice"—Leepson concludes that the colors "do not have—nor have they ever had—any official imprimatur. What historians believe is the explanation of the derivation of red, white, and blue in the Stars and Stripes is the simple fact that those colors were used in the first American flag, the Continental Colors"[8]— and before it, the hated Union Jack.

It will also be noted that no one was given formal credit for the design, although the most likely candidate is Francis Hopkinson, a congressional member from New Jersey and prolific designer of seals and symbols, including the Great Seal of the United States, the Treasury Board seal, and the Board of Admiralty Seal, all noble symbols but ones that excite less (if any) passion in most Americans.[9] And last but not least, Kevin Keim and Peter Keim hold that "very little evidence suggests use of the flag was common during the war, particularly on land."[10] As already mentioned, military regiments tended to fight under their local colors, not the common flag, notwithstanding romantic images such as Emanuel Gottlieb Leutze's renowned 1850 painting *Washington Crossing the Delaware*, with its prominent but ahistorical Stars and Stripes waving over his boat. "If Washington did carry an ensign" on that fateful crossing, "it was likely a simple blue field with stars— without stripes—as depicted in Charles Wilson Peale's original *George Washington at the Battle of Princeton*, painted in 1779" and therefore much more reliable.[11]

Betsy Ross: Mother of the Flag?

One of the most beloved sub-traditions within the American flag tradition is the story of Betsy Ross, who, as every schoolchild learns, sewed the first flag. According to the story, George Washington visited the

Philadelphia tailor shop of Betsy Griscom Ross in 1776 as part of a congressional flag committee. One problem with the tale is that there is no record in any document—congressional minutes, personal diaries and letters, or the like—of any such committee, and Washington, as a commanding general but not a member of Congress, would not likely have been a member of any such party. Another problem is the date: previously we discovered that the Flag Resolution was adopted in 1777, a year after the supposed commission of Ross to sew the flag. "Virtually every historian who has studied the issue," Leepson summarizes, "believes that Betsy Ross did not sew the first American flag."[12]

This particular bit of mythmaking owes its origin to Ross's grandson, William Canby, who in 1870 read an essay to the Historical Society of Pennsylvania by the title of "The History of the Flag of the United States." Canby began by surveying the available research and documentation, admitting that "the search was fruitless . . . as to the finding of any matter throwing light on the origin of the design, and the making of the flag."[13] Since "no such history there exists," he moved on to the dubious, if not dangerous, claim that the "next and the last resort then of the historian (the printed and the written record being silent) is tradition"; surely, long after the fact and in the absence of facts, traditions and tales are less than trustworthy, but Canby insisted that a story told by the interested parties themselves, "uncontradicted by the written record, stands unimpeachable, quite as reliable and often more so, than the books." Subsequently he provided the now-canonical legend (in his own words, "Let us now return to our Legend") of Betsy Ross and the first flag.

So, the source of the Betsy Ross tradition is—tradition. And an appealing tradition it was. Ross served as the missing woman, the Founding Mother, in a patriarchal history of nation-building. There is even a semi-mystical quality to the story: Leepson quotes historian Morris Vogel as saying, "It is the immaculate conception: George Washington comes to visit and the flag literally issues forth from Betsy's lap."[14] But such a lovely myth still needed assistance, which it got from Ross's descendants, who made and marketed "Betsy Ross flags," as well as from an 1873 article in *Harper's New Monthly Magazine* that essentially repeated Canby's version uncritically. And already the legend was

A mythical image of Betsy Ross sewing the first flag, from Edward Percy Moran's painting *The Birth of Old Glory*.

growing: the article's author, H.K.W. Wilcox, added the claim that Ross became the "manufacturer of flags for the government"—a boast that not even Canby had made.[15] Another pillar of the legend was a book by Canby's nephew Lloyd Balderson, *The Evolution of the American Flag*, based on material from Canby and Canby's brother, George. Further aid came from the Betsy Ross Memorial Association, a movement to preserve the Betsy Ross House (which may actually be at the wrong address), and Charles Weisberger's evocative but historically inaccurate 1893 painting *Birth of Our Nation's Flag*, reprinted "in school textbooks for years, deceiving generations of unsuspecting students."[16]

The Flag Grows—and Goes to War—with America

History apparently cannot resolve the question of the person—possibly a woman—who stitched the first flag, and it is unlikely that facts would dislodge an entrenched and beloved legend like Betsy Ross. We do know two things, though. First, "in the post-Revolutionary War era, the flag, as a symbol of the nation, played a minor role. Other images of the nascent nation were used much more widely," including "sculptures, paintings, and engravings of George Washington" and "images such as the eagle and the female figures of Liberty and Columbia".[17] Second, there was no settled and standardized American flag at that time, since the instructions in the original resolution were so vague. Many variants existed, especially in regard to the shape and layout of the stars. Americans today expect the five-pointed star, but stars on past flags featured five, six, seven, and sometimes eight points; worse is the fact that "individual stars might point in any direction, often in a variety of directions on the same flag."[18] Worst of all is the fact that flag makers were free to arrange the stars in almost any pattern: circles were common, sometimes with one or more stars in the middle or in the corners, while rows of stars might be even or staggered, horizontal or vertical, featuring any number of stars per row or even in a square.

Then there was the question of the relation of stars to states in the Union. Vermont joined the U.S. in 1791 as the fourteenth state and Kentucky in 1792 as the fifteenth, but no particular thought was given to modifying the flag until 1793. For some Americans, thirteen stars and stripes was *the* flag once and for all, while for others the flag was a living chronicle of a growing nation. Accordingly, the flag was adjusted to fifteen stars and fifteen stripes for the now fifteen states. It was such a fifteen-star flag that flew over Fort McHenry in Baltimore during the War of 1812 and that inspired Francis Scott Key's poem, which would be set to music and eventually become the national anthem, affectionately known as "The Star-Spangled Banner".

The number of stars and stripes did not directly follow the number of states, as several more states were admitted to the Union (Tennessee, 1796; Ohio, 1803; Louisiana, 1812; and Indiana, 1816) before the flag was altered again in 1818. The idea of adding a new stripe for each state was rejected, as the stripes would become too thin, so the Flag Act of 1818 reset the number of stripes to thirteen and ordered that a new star be added for each new state—twenty at the time. By 1845 there were 27 stars on the flag, and by 1847 there were 29. This was the flag that the U.S. Army carried into Mexico during the successful war against its southern neighbor, leading poet Walt Whitman to dream of "more stars . . . a cluster of new stars" formed from conquered territories.[19] Whitman also

presaged the adulation of the flag that would follow the Civil War in his
1855 poem "Song of the Banner at Daybreak," culminating in the lines

> O you up there! O pennant! where you undulate like a snake
> hissing so curious,
>> Out of reach, an idea only, yet furiously fought for, risking bloody
> death, loved by me,
>> So loved—O you banner leading the day with stars brought from
> the night!
>> Valueless, object of eyes, over all and demanding all—(absolute
> owner of all)—O banner and pennant!
>> I too leave the rest—great as it is, it is nothing—houses,
> machines are nothing—I see them not,
>> I see but you, O warlike pennant! O banner so broad, with stripes,
> I sing you only,
>> Flapping up there in the wind.

No event in American history had more impact on citizens' attitudes
toward the flag than the Civil War. Understandably, with a rebel country
and a rebel flag occupying a large chunk of American territory, popular
enthusiasm for the Stars and Stripes reached a level previously utterly
unknown. Kit Hinrichs and Delphine Hirasuna asserted that once
secessionists attacked Fort Sumter, "Outraged Northerners reacted by
raising the Star-Spangled Banner in every town and village."[20] In fact,
the flag became for the first time a popular symbol rather than merely
a governmental or military emblem. Historian Whitney Smith dubbed
the Civil War "a fight for the flag," adding

> Every school flew a flag and prior to that there was only one
> known instance—in 1817—of a school flying an American flag.
> Union soldiers carried miniature flags called Bible Flags, small
> enough to fit in the Bible they would take with them to the
> battlefield. The start of the Civil War was the beginning of the
> sense we have today of the American flag as an everyday object
> and of something that belongs to everyone.[21]

The flag also increasingly appeared in poems and songs (like Whitman's verse above), such as George Root's 1862 "The Battle Cry of Freedom," alternatively titled "We'll Rally Round the Flag, Boys," not to mention Gustave Scott's "Defend the Stars and Stripes," J. D. Dickson's "The American Flag," John Savage's "The Starry Flag," and James T. Field and O. B. Brown's "The Stars and Stripes," which included the memorable and bellicose words

Let the Traitors brag;
Gallant lad, fire away!
And fight for the flag.
Their flag is but a rag
Ours is the true one
Up with the Stars and Stripes!
Down with the new one!

It was also during the Civil War that the flag got the moniker "Old Glory," attributed in 1862 to William Driver, who reportedly raised his flag in Tennessee and christened it Old Glory—although the name did not really stick until James Whitcomb Riley immortalized it in his 1898 poem "The Name of Old Glory," which has the flag itself make this statement:

By the driven snow-white and the living blood-red
Of my bars, and their heaven of stars overhead
By the symbol conjoined of them all, skyward cast,
As I float from the steeple, or flap at the mast,
Or droop o'er the sod where the long grasses nod,
My name is as old as the glory of God.
. . . So I came by the name of Old Glory.

The victory of the Union in the Civil War did not end the cult of the flag; if anything, successful reunification enhanced it. Indeed, just nine years later the United States celebrated its centennial (1876), which gave another boost to the patriotic popularity of the banner. Another iconic representation of the flag was born that year: Archibald Willard's painting *The Spirit of '76*, unveiled at the Centennial Exhibition and depicting two Continental Army drummers and a fife player marching under the Betsy Ross thirteen-star flag, an event we now know never actually happened.

More effective still were the flag reverence and "flag protection" movements of the late 1880s, driven particularly by Civil War veterans' organizations such as the Grand Army of the Republic (GAR). Formed in 1866, the GAR developed sufficient clout to achieve the requirement that flags be flown at all schools (and was, as we will see in Chapter Seven, instrumental in establishing Flag Day), aided by patriotic magazines such as *The Youth's Companion*, which was key to the creation and promotion of the Pledge of Allegiance ("to the flag, and to the Republic for which it stands").

The popular embrace of the flag led to rousing tributes, most inspirationally John Philip Sousa's 1896 concert march, "Stars and Stripes Forever," a staple of patriotic occasions such as the Fourth of July. A decade later, George M. Cohan introduced his "You're a Grand Old Flag" (originally, as noted, "Rag") for the stage musical "George Washington, Jr.," with the triumphant lyric

> You're a grand old flag,
> You're a high-flying flag,
> And forever in peace may you wave.
> You're the emblem of the land I love,
> The home of the free and the brave.

But this flag fervor led to some excesses and questionable uses, too. "Images of the flag found their way into an astonishing number of advertisements for scores of different types of products. The long, long list includes baking powder, bicycles, beer, cigarettes, corned beef, toilet paper, tobacco products, window shades, and whiskey barrels."[22] Politicians also opportunistically appropriated the flag for their campaign signs, slogans, and buttons. In reaction, regulations and laws for the proper use of the flag began to appear. In 1890 the U.S. House of Representatives passed the country's first flag desecration bill, and in 1912 President William Howard Taft finally promulgated some standards for the flag itself, establishing (in Executive Order 1556) the exact ratio of height (technically, "hoist") to length as 1-to-1.9 and the 48 stars to be arrayed in six horizontal rows of eight.

Predictably, another war—the First World War, involving the United States in 1917–18—stirred another burst of flag zeal. Arnaldo Testi reminds us that, "In their federal anti-sedition legislation, patterned on similar laws already existing in some states," President Woodrow Wilson and the Congress "made insulting national symbols a criminal offense . . . And they put the national colors at the service of the federal Committee of Public Information, which, headed by progressive jour- nalist George Creel, promised to 'advertise America' and 'the gospel of Americanism'" with the flag as one of its chief brand logos.[23] But as any logo does, the flag required final standardization. On June 14, 1923, on the anniversary of the 1777 Flag Resolution (which had spawned the holiday of Flag Day), the National Flag Code was published at the National Flag Conference. Promoted by the American Legion, the Flag Code stipulated how and when the flag should be displayed, its proper handling, and the approved performance of the Pledge of Allegiance, including the right hand over the heart. In 1934 the official shades of red and blue were formalized—"as O. G. Red and O. G. Blue, where 'O. G.' stands for Old Glory."[24]

Stars and Stripes Forever?

The Second World War gave still more impetus to the flag, with flags on recruiting posters, a refinement of flag etiquette in the popularized Flag Code, more references to the flag in music and movies, and of course one of the most famous images of the American flag ever seen—the photo- graph of the flag-raising at Iwo Jima in 1945. The flag reached its final (so far) configuration in 1960, when the fiftieth star was added, and it reached it furthest (so far) destination when it was planted on the moon by American astronauts on July 20, 1969.

The American flag is alive and well in the twenty-first century, but it is not without its controversies and even opponents. During the Vietnam War in the 1960s and 1970s, disrespect if not outright abuse of the flag became a political issue, with the flag worn in offensive ways and publicly burned. As mentioned, various states and the federal government had enacted laws against flag desecration (implying the *sacred* status of the object), such as the 1968 Federal Flag Desecration Law aimed at anti-war activists.

But the Supreme Court repeatedly (for instance, in 1969, 1972, and 1974) ruled against such laws in New York, Massachusetts, and Washington State, on the basis that insulting, offensively wearing (the 1972 case involved a Massachusetts man who stitched a flag on the seat of his pants), defacing, or even destroying the flag was a form of con-stitutionally protected speech. In 1989 the Court reiterated, in *Texas v. Johnson*, that flag-burning was First Amendment-guaranteed symbolic speech. Undaunted, President George H. W. Bush signed the Flag Protection Act of 1989, which sparked a flurry of flag burnings in pro-test and another Supreme Court case, *United States v. Eichman*, which again asserted the unconstitutionality of prohibiting such free-speech acts. Nevertheless, at war again in 2005, Congress passed a resolution empowering itself to ban "the physical desecration of the flag of the United States," and all fifty states have declared their approval of a future flag protection amendment to the Constitution. The Stars and Stripes, the Star-Spangled Banner, Old Glory, may be a grand old flag, but its meaning differs for different Americans, and it pits some of America's most prized principles against each other.

THREE

The New American Man: Uncle Sam

★ ★ ★

In his 1782 *Letters from an American Farmer*, Hector St John de Crèvecoeur asked the pivotal question about the nascent United States of America: "What then is an American, this new man?" Truly, Americans—or Europeans in America—had long felt that there was something special about their land and their people, that they were starting history over again, that they were inventing a better world and a more perfect union. And while de Crèvecoeur believed that the new American was "leaving behind him all his ancient prejudices and manners," he had to receive "new ones from the new mode of life he has embraced, the new government he obeys, and the new rank he holds."[1]

One habit that even the new Americans could not shake was the need to represent themselves to themselves. Most humans cannot really relate to an abstraction like "the United States," and no one can live by abstraction alone. Thus a society, even—or perhaps especially—a newly minted one, needs symbols, material manifestations, and ultimately personifications that they can identify with. That is, of all representations, an anthropomorphic representation is best. And the best-known and most-used personal representation of America is certainly Uncle Sam.

The United States hardly invented the idea of representing their country with or as a fictional character. At least since the early 1700s Britain had depicted itself with or as the character of John Bull, usually credited to writer John Arbuthnot in his 1712 *The History of John Bull*, which contrasted Britain's John Bull to France's Lewis Baboon (a caricature of Louis XIV). When John Bull was eventually drawn, particularly in the pages of the British magazine *Punch* in the 1800s, he became a rotund fellow in a vest, waistcoat, and top hat, occasionally portrayed with an actual bull's head.

Well acquainted with John Bull and the tradition of depicting a country as a cartoon character, it was inevitable that America would develop its own mascot. Interestingly but not surprisingly, Uncle Sam was not the first choice; in fact, colonial and early post-independence Americans had never heard of such a figure. The first personification of America was as a woman, namely Columbia (note the competitor to "The Star-Spangled Banner," "Hail, Columbia," which was discussed in the first chapter), whose moniker (although clearly not gender) was based on Christopher Columbus (the term "America," after all, was based on the name of another sixteenth-century explorer, Amerigo Vespucci). Columbia was used to refer to America as early as the 1730s or 1740s and is generally attributed to Samuel Johnson. As the war for independence approached, the African American poet Phillis Wheatley even composed a poem titled "His Excellency, General Washington" in 1775, invoking Columbia four times:

> Celestial choir, enthron'd in realms of light,
> Columbia's scenes of glorious toils I write.
> While freedom's cause her anxious breast alarms,
> She flashes dreadful in refulgent arms.
> See mother earth her offspring's fate bemoan,
> And nations gaze at scenes before unknown!
> See the bright beams of heaven's revolving light
> Involved in sorrows and the veil of night! . . .

> One century scarce perform'd its destined round,
> When Gallic powers Columbia's fury found;
> And so may you, whoever dares disgrace
> The land of freedom's heaven-defended race!
> Fix'd are the eyes of nations on the scales,
> For in their hopes Columbia's arm prevails.
> Anon Britannia droops the pensive head,
> While round increase the rising hills of dead.

William Charles, 'Columbia Teaching John Bull his New Lesson', featuring on the left the U.S. as Columbia gesturing towards John Bull as the UK; Napoleon stands in the center.

> Ah! Cruel blindness to Columbia's state!
> Lament thy thirst of boundless power too late . . .²

According to Ruth Miller, and as is apparent, "Described as 'a virtuous lady garbed in classical robes,' Columbia was used to represent 'values and standards of the colonies and later the United States'."³

Another popular and prior contender for national personification was Brother Jonathan, whose glory days were from the 1780s until the Civil War. Some accounts attribute the source of the character to one Jonathan Trumbull, a governor of Connecticut during the late-colonial and revolutionary period and a confidante of Washington; Washington allegedly once said before making an important decision, "We must consult Brother Jonathan," and the phrase "We must consult Brother Jonathan" still appears on the diplomas of Trumbull College, a school of Yale University in New Haven, Connecticut. As a New England everyman,

> Brother Jonathan was a projection of what many wanted to
> think was American. As such, Jonathan belonged to the kind
> of small community where neighbors, greeting one another

Brother Jonathan welcoming other countries to the U.S. Centennial , c. 1876.

in the morning on their way to work in their fields or small shops, acknowledged their kinship with the honorific "Brother" attached to one another's name. The title suited a cohesive circle of people who shared the same life style, ideals, and limitations.[4]

Brother Jonathan's finest moment was probably his appearance in James Kirke Paulding's political novel *The Diverting History of John Bull and Brother Jonathan*, in which he and his father "Squire Bull" shared many adventures. In fact, the first chapter is titled "Squire Bull quarrelled with his youngest Son, Brother Jonathan, and forced him out in the woods; and how the Squire, when Jonathan had cleared away the woods, grew to be very fond of him, and undertook to pick his pockets, but got handsomely rib-roasted for his pains."[5]

Along Comes Uncle Sam

"Arising in obscure ways, often originating in derision or abuse or satire, sometimes repudiated by those to whom they are applied, at other times adopted in spite of the ridicule, the origin of nicknames is singularly elusive, and there are few words or phrases of which it is more difficult to trace the history," wrote Albert Matthews in his study of the origins of Uncle Sam over a century ago.[6] Matthews went on to evaluate three versions of the invention of Uncle Sam. In the first account, Thomas Chandler Haliburton created the character "Sam Slick of Slickville" in Nova Scotia, Canada, around the time of the War of 1812, but Matthews dismissed this claim since Haliburton was supposedly too young (only eighteen years old in 1812) and did not use the name "Sam Slick" until 1835. The origin story that Matthews preferred holds "that the sobriquet was merely a jocular extension of the letters U.S." during the War of 1812.[7] He offered as an argument in favor of this answer that Americans of the era were enamored of acronyms, abbreviations, and wordplay (see Chapter Nine on the history of "OK"), and he concluded that while "U.S." was a relatively recent invention itself,

> the initials U.S. were well known in 1812 and 1813, yet no doubt the war made them still more common. "The letters U.S.," explained the *Troy Post* of September 7, 1813, "on the government waggons, &c are supposed to have given rise to it." On October 1, 1813, a writer spoke of "Uncle Sam, the now popular explication of the U.S."[8]

The explanation that Matthews rejected was the one that most scholars seem to accept today and that has been most ably defended by Alton Ketchum, probably the leading historian of Uncle Sam. In his 1990 article "The Search for Uncle Sam" and his much earlier 1959 book *Uncle Sam: The Man and the Legend*, he gave the honor of being the original Uncle Sam to Samuel Wilson of Troy, New York.

Samuel Wilson was born on September 13, 1766, in Massachusetts and relocated with his brother Ebenezer to Troy in 1789, where they opened a meatpacking business. When the War of 1812 erupted, the brothers' company, E. & S. Wilson, won a contract to supply the army in New York and New Jersey, and the barrels of meat that they shipped were marked with two sets of initials, "E.A." for Elbert Anderson (an army contractor) and "U.S." for United States. Ketchum asserted that "everybody around Troy knew Uncle Sam" Wilson,[9] so it was not unlikely that some of the locals, especially his workers, might have

understood "U.S." on the barrels to refer to their Uncle Sam. So the
story goes, as reported in the *New York Gazette* on May 12, 1830:

> This work fell to the lot of a facetious fellow in the employ
> of Messrs. Wilson, who, on being asked by some of his fel-
> low-workmen the meaning of the mark (for the letters U.S. for
> United States were almost entirely new to them) said that he did
> not know unless it meant Elbert Anderson and Uncle Sam—
> alluding exclusively then, to the said "Uncle Sam" Wilson. The
> joke took among the workmen, passed currently and, "Uncle
> Sam" himself being present, was occasionally rallied by them
> on the increasing extent of his possessions.[10]

This "facetious fellow" was identified as the chief butcher, Jonas Gleason,
by Wilson's great-nephew Lucius Wilson more than a century later in
his account of the origin of Uncle Sam. Gleason's jest was that it was
Uncle Sam Wilson "who is feeding the army."[11] Ketchum continued,

> This, he tells us, was considered a huge joke and it quickly
> spread. In the army the soldiers, some of whom had worked
> for him, called the beef and pork Uncle Sam's as attested by
> the initials on the barrels, and said that Uncle Sam was caring
> for them. And thus the joke spread throughout the land, much
> as "G.I." did during the Second World War to denote govern-
> ment supplies.[12]

Interestingly, Lucius described his great-uncle thus: "In form and
carriage he greatly resembled Abraham Lincoln. He was tall, well
preserved and the type of the well-to-do old gentleman of this day.
Had high cheekbones, was clean-shaven and wore his grey hair rather
long."[13]

Whatever the starting point of the Uncle Sam idea, it obviously
traveled quickly. The earliest documented use of the term (outside
Wilson's meatpacking establishment) was in a broadside reliably dated
to the spring of 1813: along with caricatures of John Bull, Bonapart
[*sic*], and Tom Patriot are two mentions, "If Uncle Sam needs, I'll be

glad to assist him" (spoken by Bonapart [*sic*]) and "But if Uncle Sam lives, they will all be Burgoyn'd" (Burgoyne being a British general who was soundly defeated in a revolutionary battle).[14] By September 7 of the same year, the *Troy Post* ran an article including the sentence, "'Loss upon loss, and no ill luck stirring but what lights upon UNCLE SAM's shoulders,' exclaim the Government Editors, in every part of the country."[15] Significantly, the figure of Uncle Sam appeared and grew popular during a time of war, but Matthews asserted that "it was avoided by those who favored the war, and was employed only by those who opposed the war. Hence the term was at first apparently used somewhat derisively."[16]

Matthews raised a number of objections to the provenance of Uncle Sam as referring to Samuel Wilson, many of which were resolved by evidence that Ketchum unearthed after Matthews's time. The strongest argument against the Wilson story is that people in 1812 would not have known what "U.S." stood for; but even so, contemporaries of the War of 1812 might still have been inclined to make an in-house joke about it. So whether or not Samuel Wilson is the real Uncle Sam, he has largely come to be accepted as such. Indeed, Samuel Wilson's obituary in 1854 from the *Albany Evening Journal* repeated the credit:

> "UNCLE SAM"—The death of Samuel Wilson, an aged, worthy, and formerly enterprising citizen of Troy, will remind those who were familiar with the incidents of the War of 1812, of the origin of the popular sobriquet for the "United States." Mr. Wilson was an extensive packer, had the contract for supplying the northern army with beef and pork. He was everywhere known as "Uncle Sam," and the "U.S." branded on the heads of barrels for the army were at first taken to be the initials of "Uncle Sam" Wilson, but finally lost their local significance and became throughout the army the familiar term for "United States."[17]

The Art of Uncle Sam

Whatever his source, the fame of Uncle Sam spread quickly. By 1816 he was the hero of his own book, *The Adventures of Uncle Sam, in Search*

After His Lost Honor, published under the name of Frederick Augustus Fidfaddy. Matthews found the first foreign usage of the term in a book by W. Faux sometime around 1820, in which Mr Faux quotes a Mr Perry to the effect that "Almost all Americans are boys in everything but vice and folly! In their eyes Uncle Sam is a right slick, mighty fine, smart, big man."[18] And Paulding, the author of *The Diverting History of John Bull and Brother Jonathan*, also wrote a "skit" called "The History of Uncle Sam and his Boys: A Tale for Politicians" in 1831, which includes the following:

> Once upon a time there lived, and still lives, in a country lying far to the west, a famous squire, rich in lands and paper money. Report made him out to be the son of John Bull, who everyone knows has children in all parts of the world . . . John Bull had christened this son of his by the name of Jonathan; but by and by, when he became a man grown, being a good hearty fellow, about half horse half alligator, his friends and neighbors gave him the nickname of Uncle Sam.[19]

Note not only the reference to John Bull (Britain, America's "father") but to Brother Jonathan, who continued to share the stage with Uncle Sam—and in this case, to be equated with Uncle Sam. For the appearance of Uncle Sam did not immediately erase Brother Jonathan; rather, the two actually occurred together, Brother Jonathan increasingly representing the American people while Uncle Sam *represented the American government*.

This last point is amply made in the first visual image of Uncle Sam, traced by Ketchum to 1832 and a drawing (with no identified artist) captioned "Uncle Sam in Danger," intended as a political attack on President Andrew Jackson, pictured standing over an ailing Uncle Sam. Sam is seated, beardless and draped in an American flag. As Ketchum noted, this inaugurated something of a sub-tradition of depicting poor Uncle Sam as a weakling or hapless victim:

> The cartoonists' favorite pose for him seems to be as in desperate straits—bilked, puzzled, disgusted, riled, at his wits' end. Seldom is he shown happy and at peace with himself and the

world, which again may be only a reflection of the times we live in. There seems to be almost a rule about this. Uncle is usually on the short end.[20]

In short, Uncle Sam was no superpower just yet.

Two important facts must be emphasized here. First, Uncle Sam was at this point in history shown no great respect: not only was he often passive and frail, but he was usurped for various political purposes, for or against particular candidates or causes. Second, he had no standard visual characteristics yet. "He has not yet been cast in a single mold; each artist depicts his own version."[21] Sometimes he was old, sometimes young; sometimes bearded, sometimes clean-shaven; and sometimes clad in flag-like attire, sometimes in ordinary clothes.

Remarkably, it was not Americans but the British who established the bearded tradition, and even then it was Brother Jonathan (who survived longer across the Atlantic than in the States) who first wore the beard. This was actually prior to the Civil War, but once the war began, Abraham Lincoln became the model for the American government, with

Uncle Sam, 1898, on the occasion of the Spanish–American War.

his tall lanky frame and his iconic beard. As with John Bull himself, the British magazine *Punch*, renowned for its political cartoons, was the site of much of this visualizing. John Leech gave Brother Jonathan a beard in an 1856 drawing called "The Spoilt Child," in which John Bull looked disparagingly at his wayward son. During the Civil War, "the artists of

u.s. as Columbia: "Wake Up, America."

Punch and *London Fun* drew Lincoln as a sinister and saturnine character
. . . But even as they did so, they were helping to fix the bearded image of
the United States."[22] So America owes one of the most lasting features
of one of its most lasting figures to non-Americans.

Uncle Sam evolved in the U.S. in the hands (quite literally) of political cartoonists such as Thomas Nast and Joseph Keppler. Nast, born
in Germany, was a highly influential journalist who brought great
attention to the corruption of the New York Tammany Hall political
machine in the late 1800s. It was he who largely settled the image of
Uncle Sam as sporting a white beard, red-and-white-striped trousers,
and a top hat. The Uncle Sam who flowed out of the Austrian immigrant Keppler's pen was, by contrast, "potbellied and looks rather like
a German music hall comedian of that era."[23] But even at this late
date Jonathan and Columbia sometimes appeared, and Uncle Sam still
shifted his appearance; Fred Oppler, for instance, drew him in a police
uniform.

If there is one version of Uncle Sam with which Americans are
most familiar, it is the powerful First World War recruiting poster, in
which a considerably more serious and realistic Sam pointed directly
out of the picture while declaring "I Want You for U.S. Army." Drawn
by James Montgomery Flagg in 1917, even this version is not, however,
entirely original: it bears a striking resemblance to a British war poster
of General Kitchener pointing and proclaiming "Your Country Needs
You." And in the early twentieth century, the female image of America,
Columbia, had not totally faded from memory: Flagg also produced a
drawing of a woman in repose, decked in red-white-and-blue regalia,
with the emphatic caption, "Wake Up, America!"

Is Uncle Sam America?

Thus by the second decade of the twentieth century, Uncle Sam has
assumed his modern form—or perhaps we should still say *forms*. Since
there is no official version of Uncle Sam (and even if there were), artists
remain (and would remain) free to portray him in diverse ways. Arthur
Schlesinger went so far as to insist, "Every generation of American life
re-creates Uncle Sam in its own image."[24] Worse still is the fact that not

all Americans have approved of Uncle Sam at all. In 1959 historian Allan Nevins called the old man "an infantile folk image" and "a mischievous oversimplification" and advocated that it was "time that the most complicated nation on earth disowned this crude stereotype."[25]

In fact, Ruth Miller makes a still more salient critique of Uncle Sam as the representation of America:

> In a country where the white-skinned majority is rapidly dwindling and minority ethnic groups are receiving greater opportunities for achievement in society, the nineteenth century upper-class white male figure of Uncle Sam is suspiciously arrogant and foreign-looking. Yet a realistic solution to such a problem is evasive. Should there be an Uncle Sam for each race in the u.s, or perhaps an "Aunt Sam," which actually has been depicted on a few rare occasions?[26]

Yet what single image or personification *could* capture all of this diversity? And if we remember that Uncle Sam has historically tended to represent the American *government* rather than the American *people*, then perhaps an old white man in ridiculously patriotic clothes is just the right image.

At any rate, while there is no official Uncle Sam, Samuel Wilson did get formal recognition as the source of all later Uncle Sams in a September 15, 1961, congressional resolution, to wit: "Resolved by the Senate and the House of Representatives that the Congress salutes Uncle Sam Wilson of Troy, New York, as the progenitor of America's National symbol of Uncle Sam." So whether or not the Samuel Wilson story is true, it is now official. Mr Wilson also enjoys two physical memorials to his role in American traditioning, one at his birthplace in present-day Arlington, Massachusetts (the Uncle Sam Memorial Statue), and the other at Riverfront Park in Troy, New York. In 1989, a joint resolution (predictably, introduced by a Congressman, Samuel Stratton, from New York) designated September 13 as "Uncle Sam Day," but that is a tradition that has not quite succeeded in traditioning. Oddly, as Ketchum noted, the one place where Uncle Sam is noticeably absent is his adopted home city, Washington, DC:

there are almost no mentions of Uncle Sam in the official publications that come from the Government Printing Office. Whether this is because bureaucrats do not identify themselves with Uncle Sam, or because they are afraid that he is too popular with all persons and parties to be safely political, is not clear. But in Washington itself, where Uncle Sam may be presumed to walk abroad at noonday and nightfall, and to exercise at all times the fullness of his authority, visual and verbal notice of his presence is perhaps rarest.[27]

In conclusion, then, the best evidence suggests that Uncle Sam was born from a joke and given life through cartoons (and not always flattering ones at that). But one thing we can be sure of is that

Uncle Sam is not the same as he was when first created nor is his namesake the same, but the two are inseparably intertwined. The changes made to Uncle Sam's image have almost reflected the features and actions taken by people within the administration of the United States. Some of these have been positive for Uncle Sam while others are not so complimentary. Yet it is only natural and befitting that the nation's most prominent human symbol should be a flexible, adaptable figure, able to adjust his physical and temperamental condition to reflect and comment on the state of the nation.[28]

FOUR

The Republic for Which It Stands: Pledge of Allegiance and Motto

★ ★ ★

Tradition itself is a kind of fidelity to the past and to the identity supposedly founded on that past. But modern nation-states tend to demand a special kind of fidelity or loyalty that we call patriotism (from *patrios*, Greek for "of one's fathers," literally devotion to the fatherland or country) or sometimes allegiance. "Allegiance" derives from the feudal term *liege* for a nobleman or lord to whom a vassal or serf owed obedience and service; allegiance thus refers to the fidelity that subjects or citizens are—or are asked to believe that they are—duty-bound to pay to their sovereign or government.

Allegiance has historically often been associated with oaths, spoken promises, or commitments to act or even feel in a certain way. For instance, the U.S. Constitution specifies an oath of office for the president, and witnesses in court are customarily administered an oath that binds them to tell the truth. Average Americans, though, were not expected to perform any oaths of allegiance for the first century of the country, nor especially were children required to make such pledges. Indeed, Richard Ellis, a scholar of the Pledge of Allegiance, held that "democracies generally do not require their children to pledge allegiance to the nation on a daily or even regular basis,"[1] and American children did not begin to do so until the late 1800s. And at that time, America still lacked an official motto.

The Prehistory of the Pledge of Allegiance

The Pledge of Allegiance cannot be understood apart from the "flag movement" of the 1880s, which cannot be understood apart from the Civil War. Ellis instructed us that, just as American (that is, Union) flags became more omnipresent during the war, so "loyalty tests" also spread. Persons suspected of disloyalty were often arrested, eligible for pardon if they submitted to an "oath of allegiance" swearing to "support, protect and defend the Constitution and Government of the United States against all enemies, domestic and foreign, and that I will bear true faith, allegiance and loyalty to the same."[2] Such oral and signed performances were thought to be rehabilitative and reconstructive, to shape and win hearts and minds and to make real Americans out of those whose devotion was questionable.

The practice of oath-taking and pledging did not extend beyond captured Confederate soldiers and their suspected Northern sympathizers during the war, but the "cult of the flag" that emerged two decades later began to stir a desire in many Americans to have more citizens—maybe all citizens—demonstrate their respect for the flag and the country in word and gesture. By the 1880s, various spontaneous patriotic activities were being observed around the country, many of them set in schools, where the "school flag movement" focused its energy. One such ceremony was conducted in 1888 in New York City, spearheaded by George T. Balch, a West Point graduate and veteran of the Civil War. He encouraged schoolchildren to demonstrate their patriotism with what he called "The American Patriotic Salute" to the flag:

> Balch's salute began with students touching their foreheads and then their hearts and saying: "We give our Heads! And our Hearts! To God! And our Country!" The students then extended their right arms, palms down, and said, "One Country! One Language! One Flag!"[3]

Balch's was the first recorded pledge to the flag, and the next year he wrote a book titled *Methods of Teaching Patriotism in the Public Schools*. Providentially, Charles Homer of the Grand Army of the Republic, the veterans group so instrumental in placing flags in and over schools, attended one of the New York events and encouraged the organization to promote "flag presentation ceremonies" in schools around the country.

Equally instrumental in the school flag movement and particularly in the "flag presentation ceremonies" phenomenon was the weekly magazine *The Youth's Companion*, founded in Boston in 1827. In October 1888 the magazine started running advertisements selling flags, although it did not endorse flag-raising and -lowering rituals as the best means for instilling patriotism. Even so, in 1890 it sponsored an essay contest for students on the topic "The Patriotic Influence of the American Flag When Raised over the Public School," offering the winner in each state a large flag for their school.[4]

That same year, James B. Upham, head of the magazine's "premium department," concocted an idea for what was to be a "Public School Celebration" on the occasion of the 400th anniversary of Columbus Day (1892). He took his plan, renamed the National School Celebration, to the National Education Association (NEA), which appointed a committee to guide the process, with Francis Bellamy as its chairman. Bellamy was a Baptist minister and pastor at Bethany Baptist Church in Boston. He was also a prominent Christian socialist (and cousin to Edward Bellamy, author of the 1888 utopian-socialist novel *Looking Backward*), renowned for speeches with such names as "Jesus the Socialist" and "The Socialism of the Bible." He shared with the Society of Christian Socialists (renamed from the Nationalist Club in 1889) the desire "to show that the aim of Socialism is embraced in the aim of Christianity" and "to awaken members of Christian Churches to the fact that the teachings of Jesus Christ lead directly to some specific form or forms of Socialism" rather than to the runaway individualism, materialism, and capitalism that characterized his (and our) era.[5] In 1891 Upham hired Bellamy as an assistant editor for *The Youth's Companion*.

Becoming the Pledge of Allegiance

What would eventually be known as the Pledge of Allegiance originated as a minor element of a multipart ceremony of Columbus Day 1892. By summer of that year, Congress had recognized "Discovery Day" as

Children pledging allegiance to the flag with the "Bellamy Salute," 1915.

October 21—not the more familiar October 12—complete with "suitable exercises in the schools and other places of assembly." Upham, Bellamy, and *The Youth's Companion* designed the specific exercises and published them in a September issue of the magazine, under the heading "The Official Program of National Public School Celebration of Columbus Day." Included in the day's activities were a presidential proclamation, a flag-raising by veterans, a song, a speech, a poem, and a salute to the flag. Section 3 of the program, "Salute to the Flag," contained these guidelines:

> At a signal from the principal the pupils, in ordered rank, hands to the side, face the flag. Another signal is given; every pupil gives the flag the military salute—right hand lifted, palm downward, to a line with the forehead and close to it. Standing thus, all repeat together slowly: "I pledge allegiance to my flag, and to the republic for which it stands: one nation, indivisible, with liberty and justice for all." At the words, "to my flag," the right hand is extended gracefully, palm outward, toward the

flag, and remains in this gesture till the end of the affirmation; whereupon all hands immediately drop to the side. Then, still standing, as the instruments strike a chord, all will sing America—"My Country 'Tis of Thee."

Buried in the program then was the first incarnation of the Pledge of Allegiance, composed by Bellamy, complete with Balch's arm salute but conspicuously missing two prominent names—the United States and God. But it is important to remember that, according to Ellis, the Pledge "was written for a single, admittedly grand occasion. When Francis Bellamy penned the Pledge he did not know he was writing anything more lasting than the advertising copy he would later make his vocation."[6]

Bellamy's simple inspirational oath probably would have remained in obscurity if not for the efforts of patriotic organizations and state governments. And those organizations and governments would not have taken the steps they did without two other historical pressures—immigration and war. Ellis added that we "cannot understand the timing of the schoolhouse flag movement and the creation of the Pledge of Allegiance without understanding the intense anxiety about immigrants that began to grip many native-born Americans in the 1880s."[7] It has been estimated that more than 2.7 million immigrants landed on America's shores in the 1870s, followed by over 5.2 million in the 1880s (and another 14.5 million between 1900 and 1919). Bellamy shared the alarm of many at the threat to American values and identity by this onslaught, asserting in a presentation in 1892 to the NEA that "Americanism brings a duty . . . it must be made a force strong enough to touch the immigrant population which is *pouring over* this country,"[8] and the public schools were a key site for the inculcation of identification with and loyalty to the United States.

As it always does, war played a critical role in the development and institutionalization of this particular tradition, and the states were leading players. New York passed the first flag salute law, requiring students to recite an allegiance pledge at the start of one school day in 1898—the very day after the outbreak of the Spanish–American War.[9] The state went so far as to promulgate its own *Manual of Patriotism* containing more than four hundred patriotic poems, salutes, and songs for schools. Interestingly, Bellamy's pledge had no special status yet, coexisting with many other candidates for students' heads and hearts. The New York manual actually suggested five different flag salutes, the first four of which were

"Flag of Freedom! True to thee, All our Thoughts, Words, Deeds shall be, Pledging steadfast Loyalty"

"The toil of our Hands, The Thoughts of our Heads, The love of our Hearts, We pledge to our Flag!"

"By the memories of the Past, By the Present, flying fast, By the Future, long to last, Let the dear Flag wave!"

"I pledge myself to stand by the flag that stands for Loyalty, Liberty, and Law!"[10]

Bellamy's was the fifth and last version on the list. And then there was Balch's old pledge to the country, language, and flag, which was endorsed by the Woman's Relief Corps and by the Grand Army of the Republic (at least for elementary students; the GAR supported Bellamy's words for high school students).

Soon other states enacted mandatory flag salute laws in schools— Rhode Island in 1901, Arizona in 1903, and Kansas in 1907. Still, Bellamy's Columbus Day salute was *a* pledge of allegiance but not *the* Pledge of Allegiance until after the First World War. Indeed, few Americans remember that the country was yet in search of a national creed as late as 1918, when another contest was dreamed up by New York State's Commissioner of Education, Henry Sterling Chapin. The winner was William Tyler Page, whose "The American's Creed" was entered into the *Congressional Record* on April 13, 1918. It went as follows:

I believe in the United States of America as a Government of the people by the people, for the people, whose just powers are derived from the consent of the governed; a democracy in a Republic; a sovereign Nation of many sovereign States; a perfect Union, one and inseparable; established upon those principles of freedom, equality, justice, and humanity for which American patriots sacrificed their lives and fortunes.

I therefore believe it is my duty to my Country to love it; to support its Constitution; to obey its laws; to respect its flag, and to defend it against all enemies.

Who today knows or recites those words?

At any rate, by 1918 there were new enemies afoot—radicals, subversives, and especially communists. To advance the fight for the American way, the National Americanism Commission believed that it was time for a single standard flag code, and it held a flag conference in Washington, DC, in 1923. Among the decisions made by this nongovernmental body was to recognize Bellamy's salute as the national "Pledge to the Flag," with one small change of language. It was felt that "my flag" was too generic, so the conference recommended "the flag of the United States" instead. In a second meeting in 1924, the delegates appended "of

President Eisenhower with Reverend George MacPherson Docherty (left), c. 1954.

America" to the Pledge and specified that words should be accompanied by two gestures by civilians—right hand over the heart, then right arm raised palm up at the words "to the flag"; persons in uniform would offer the military right-hand salute. Interestingly, Bellamy allegedly disliked this tinkering with his work, thinking that the added syllables disrupted the flow of the pledge. But all of this activity was unofficial until June 22, 1942 (in the midst of yet another war), when Congress passed the U.S. Flag Code, including Bellamy's Pledge of Allegiance—with the removal of the stiff-arm salute, which too closely resembled the Nazi gesture.

The Pledge of Allegiance had still not arrived at its final form, as two familiar words were absent. In 1954 Congress inserted "under God" into the Pledge, between "one nation" and "indivisible." "Under God" was not a particularly common political slogan until the late 1940s; Lincoln had uttered it in his immortal Gettysburg Address—"that this nation, under God, shall have a new birth of freedom and that government of the people, by the people, and for the people shall not perish from the earth"—but Ellis found that no president used it in the ensuing fifty years.[11] President Harry Truman was heard to invoke it, as the Cold War against communism turned into a hot war in Korea. President Dwight Eisenhower, taking office in 1953, used it even more frequently.

But once again it was nongovernmental organizations and interests that promoted the religious reference as law and tradition. At the center of the campaign to insert "under God" in the Pledge was a Catholic organization, the Knights of Columbus. Significantly also founded in the 1880s, this group had been adding the religious phrase at its meetings, but now it began to urge Congress to embrace the practice. The reasoning was rather clear: in an existential battle with godless communism, as Reverend George MacPherson Docherty opined in a sermon in 1954 at the New York Avenue Presbyterian Church in Washington, DC, "By adding 'under God' to the Pledge the nation would affirm the distinctive and defining characteristic of the American way of life: belief in God."[12]

Congress introduced eighteen "under God" resolutions in 1953 and 1954—ten of them from Catholic members[13]—and Public Law 83-1683 of May 28, 1954, amended the Pledge to include the words, with this justification:

At this moment of our history the principles underlying our American Government and the American way of life are under attack by a system whose philosophy is at direct odds with our own. Our American Government is founded on the concept of the individuality and the dignity of the human being. Underlying this concept is the belief that the human person is important because he was created by God and endowed by Him with certain inalienable rights which no civil authority may usurp. The inclusion of God in our pledge therefore would further acknowledge the dependence of our people and our Government upon the moral directions of the Creator. At the same time it would serve to deny the atheistic and materialistic concepts of communism with its attendant subservience of the individual.

Eisenhower signed the bill, symbolically, on Flag Day, June 14, 1954, and released a statement from the White House, proudly claiming, "From this day forward, millions of our schoolchildren will daily proclaim in every city and town, every village and rural school house, the dedication of our nation and our people to the Almighty."[14] Hence the Pledge of Allegiance as it is known today was finally settled:

I pledge allegiance to the flag of the United States of America, and to the Republic for which it stands, one Nation under God, indivisible, with liberty and justice for all.

Surprisingly, congressmen and -women did not recite the Pledge on the floor of the House of Representatives until 1988, and the Senate only started reciting the Pledge in 1999.[15]

America Gets a Motto

Look at the back of a U.S. dollar bill and you will see a variety of inscriptions, including two Latin phrases, *Annuit coeptis* ("He approves [the/ our] beginning/undertakings") and *Novus ordo seclorum* ("a new order of the ages"), surrounding an odd pyramid with an eye peering out. In

Detail of the back of a $1 bill, with the motto "In God We Trust."

the center of the bill is an English phrase, "In God We Trust," which has been America's motto for sixty years.

Webster's defines a motto (from the Latin *muttire*, to mutter) as a phrase or short sentence that expresses a guiding principle of a person, group, or institution and/or indicates the character or use of the object on which it is etched. It is customary for countries to have a motto that sums up their philosophy, such as France's *Liberté, Égalité, Fraternité*, or Nazi Germany's *Ein Volk, Ein Reich, Ein Führer* ("One People, One Country/Empire, One Leader"), but other entities may adopt a motto too, such as the Boy Scouts ("Be Prepared"), Harvard University (*Veritas* [Truth]), or West Virginia ("Mountaineers are Always Free"). As many Americans know, the de facto motto of the United States for most of its history was *E pluribus unum*, a phrase—"Out of Many, One"—that perfectly captures the aspiration of the country, whether the "many" refers to its constituent states or to its multiple ethnic and racial groups. The familiar phrase was never officially enacted as the national motto, although it was proposed by a committee consisting of Franklin, Jefferson, and Adams in 1776 and was included in the design of the Great Seal of the United States from 1782, which began to appear on coins in 1795. (Amusingly, a coin issued by the Continental Congress in 1776 bore the motto or phrase, "Mind Your Business," allegedly designed by Benjamin Franklin.[16])

Interestingly, a possible source of the present-day motto is another American tradition, Francis Scott Key's poem that eventually became the national anthem. In the final verse, which few Americans know or ever sing, the poem features the line, "And this be our motto, 'In God is our trust'." But, of course, this was one man's suggestion, not federal policy, and when Congress ordered that mottoes and other symbols be engraved on U.S. coins on January 18, 1837, the only details it specified were the word "Liberty" and the image of an eagle. It was in the midst of the Civil War, in 1863, that the Director of the Mint, James Pollock, offered a number of possible new mottoes for coins, including "Our God and Our Country," "God and Our Country," "God Our Trust," and "Our Trust is in God." The Secretary of the Treasury, Salmon P. Chase, decided that the one-cent coin should bear the words "Our God and Our Country" and, with the imprint of a shield, "In God We Trust," which was approved by Congress in 1864.

First appearing only on the penny—and not yet bearing the imprimatur of the official national motto—"In God We Trust" was added to other coins in 1866, and the Coinage Act of 1873 empowered the Treasury to "cause the motto IN GOD WE TRUST to be inscribed on such coins as shall admit of such motto." As the Treasury reports, the words were omitted from the five-cent coin in 1883, not to return until 1938. "Since 1938, all United States coins bear the inscription."[17] Meanwhile, in 1905 President Theodore Roosevelt commissioned a new design for coins, which dropped "In God We Trust" and restored *E pluribus unum*. Roosevelt actually expressed disapproval of the religious motto on money, calling it a gesture of "irreverence, which comes dangerously close to sacrilege."[18] But his view did not prevail, and in 1908 Congress mandated "In God We Trust" on all coins on which it had previously been engraved; the penny and nickle were exempt, until they were brought into line in 1909 and 1916, respectively.

At this point, a century of the phrase (since Key's invocation of it) and a half-century of its use on money still did not constitute an official national motto. That occurred, just as with "under God" in the Pledge of Allegiance, in the Cold War climate of the 1950s. In a report to the House of Representatives dated March 28, 1956, a joint resolution noted that, "At present the United States has no national motto," and that "In God We Trust" was forthwith established as such. The report cited the history of American coinage and Key's poem and asserted that it "will be of great spiritual and psychological value to our country to have a clearly designated national motto of inspirational quality," one that is "superior and more acceptable" than *E pluribus unum*. Eisenhower signed the bill into law on July 30, 1956. The historical website of the House of Representatives records the statement of Florida congressman Charles Bennett, who proclaimed that "Nothing can be more certain than that our country was founded in a spiritual atmosphere and with a firm trust in God," of which the motto on money, buildings, and elsewhere would "serve as a constant reminder."[19]

Clashing Traditions: "Under God" versus the First Amendment

While traditions often engender controversy and resistance, probably no American traditions have sparked more opposition than the Pledge and the motto, and not just from atheists. Indeed, as Ellis aptly reminded us, "The most important and enduring sources of resistance to the flag salute and the Pledge of Allegiance were religiously based,"[20] coming not only from anti-religion types but from religious minorities with objections to the wording of pledges and mottoes and sometimes to the act of saluting or pledging to a flag. A very early illustration was the 1918 case of a Mennonite girl in Ohio who refused to salute and pledge allegiance to the flag on religious grounds; she was sent home from school, and a judge rejected her family's religious appeal. In 1926 the American Civil Liberties Union entered into a Denver, Colorado, case of Jehovite (not Jehovah's Witnesses) children who were excluded from school for their objection to saluting the flag as a form of "idol worship."[21]

The problem was exacerbated when the Pledge attained the force of law. In state after state, schools had the legal right to expel students who broke the law by abstaining from the Pledge, long before "under God" was appended to the text. A key moment was the case of Lilian Gobitis, an eleven-year-old Jehovah's Witness who was expelled from her school in Minersville, Pennsylvania, for religious opposition to the Pledge. A judge in 1938 ruled in her favor, but the school declined to accept her and appealed the decision all the way to the Supreme Court, which decided in 1940 (*Minersville School District v. Gobitis*) that mandatory flag salutes in school were constitutional and thus that the expulsion was legal. The matter was hardly settled, as more children around the country were subsequently banned from school for object-ing to the Pledge and flag salute. The Supreme Court heard another case on behalf of a different Jehovah's Witness family and on Flag Day 1943 (*West Virginia State Board of Education v. Barnette*) reversed the previous ruling, declaring that children could not be forced to recite the Pledge. In a stirring opinion, Justice Robert H. Jackson wrote,

> There is no mysticism in the American concept of the state or of the nature or origin of its authority. We set up government by consent of the governed, and the Bill of Rights denies those in power any legal opportunity to coerce that consent. Authority here is to be controlled by public opinion, not public opinion by authority.
>
> If there is any fixed star in our constitutional constellation, it is that no official, high or petty, can prescribe what shall be orthodox in politics, nationalism, religion, or other matters of opinion or force citizens to confess by word or act their faith therein.

Obviously, none of these complaints reacted to the reference to God in the Pledge, as the reference was not there yet. But in May 1954, as Congress proceeded in that direction, the Unitarian Ministers Association "adopted a resolution opposing the addition of the words 'under God' to the Pledge of Allegiance. In their view it was as much 'an invasion of religious liberty' as was the practice of issuing coins with the words 'In God We Trust' on them."[22] The constitutionality of the new motto was directly challenged in 1970, when Stefan Aronow argued that it violated the First Amendment, stipulating that the government "shall make no law respecting an establishment of reli-gion." But Aronow's claim was dismissed by the Ninth Circuit Court of Appeals (*Aronow v. United States*) on the spurious premise that the motto "is of patriotic or ceremonial character and bears no true resemblance to a governmental sponsorship of a religious exercise." The Supreme Court declined to hear the case. In 1979 the Fifth

Circuit Court also rejected atheist Madalyn Murray O'Hair's challenge to the motto (*Madalyn Murray O'Hair v. Michael Blumenthal*) with the determination that it is essentially secular, not religious—merely what has been dubbed "ceremonial deism." Even so, in the 1978 *Lipp v. Morris* case, a federal court asserted that students had the right to remain seated and silent during the Pledge—putting the burden of nonconformity on the individual child.

The most recent and successful challenge to the Pledge was made by atheist Michael Newdow on behalf of his school-age daughter. In June 2002 the Ninth Circuit Court (*Michael A. Newdow v. U.S. Congress et al.*) ruled in Newdow's favor, correctly recognizing that the 1954 Pledge

> takes a position with respect to the purely religious question of the existence and identity of God. A profession that we are a nation "under God" is identical, for Establishment Clause purposes, to a profession that we are a nation "under Jesus," a nation "under Vishnu," a nation "under Zeus," or a nation "under no god," because none of these professions can be neutral with respect to religion.[23]

Justice Alfred Goodwin added that, historically, the insertion of "under God"—and by extension, the adoption of the motto—had the "sole purpose . . . to advance religion, in order to differentiate the United States from nations under communist rule," which is precisely what the record shows. The Supreme Court reviewed the lower court's ruling and, rather than deciding the merits of the argument, dismissed Newdow as lacking the legal standing to raise the objection in the first place. Justice Sandra Day O'Connor reiterated that "under God" was not a religious claim, just ceremonial deism.

Nevertheless, on the fiftieth anniversary of the proclamation of the motto in 2006, President George W. Bush urged Americans to "reflect on these words that guide millions of Americans, recognize the blessings of the Creator, and offer our thanks for His great gift of liberty"[24]—a religious profession if there ever was one. Shortly thereafter, the House of Representatives introduced the "Pledge Protection Act of 2007," denying any court the jurisdiction "to hear or decide any question pertaining to the interpretation of, or the validity under the Constitution of, the Pledge of Allegiance." The bill was never enacted, but it is an interesting instance of government using its power to defend a tradition that indisputably means different things to different Americans.

AMERICAN
HOLIDAY
TRADITIONS

FIVE

We Gather Together: Thanksgiving

★ ★ ★

For many people, Thanksgiving is the quintessential and original American holiday. The observance of Thanksgiving includes the things that Americans hold most dear—faith, family, and food. Oh, and football. Thanksgiving also has the oldest putative provenance, harking back to one of the earliest events on (what would become) American soil. Yet, whatever happened on that fateful day in 1621, two things are perfectly clear: the givers of thanks did not imagine that they were creating an annual national holiday (in fact, the very idea would have been scandalous to them), and no annual national holiday resulted from it for over a century, and even then the observance, dating, and practices were spotty and inconsistent.

Nor is thanksgiving unique to America. Canada has a Thanksgiving Day, not only celebrated on a different day (the second Monday in October) but commemorating a different—and earlier—event, the successful transit of Martin Frobisher through the treacherous northern waters of Canada in 1578. Still earlier days of thanks were proclaimed in Spanish America, perhaps even in Florida (as long ago as 1565), which would become American territory, and other thankful days were celebrated in Virginia (1607, 1610, and 1619) and Maine (1607). Giving thanks for bountiful harvests and hunts was also a tradition among many Native American peoples, as it is and long has been among farming societies around the world. Finally, Thanksgiving was not the only or first attempted holiday to be spun off from the adventures of the "Pilgrims" of Plymouth.

Of course, thankful days were already common in Christianity centuries before Europeans reached the Western Hemisphere. The Catholic Church put many days of feasting and fasting on the ritual calendar, and special occasions and accomplishments would often earn an additional one-time day of thanksgiving. So, when English Christians arrived in North America, they brought with them most of the raw materials for a thanksgiving tradition. According to Diana Appelbaum, in one of the most thorough studies of the invention of American Thanksgiving, these raw materials included four specific elements: the "Harvest Home," or end-of-the-farming-season festival; Christmas; religious days of thanksgiving and prayer; and proclamations of thanksgiving by the civil authorities.[1] In a word, then, "Certain as it is that the Plymouth colonists held a gay and grateful feast in the early autumn of 1621, it is unclear that the celebration can be labeled a 'thanksgiving.' America's Thanksgiving Day, as we know it, did not originate in one place and year."[2] Instead, as James Baker put it in his more recent examination of Thanksgiving, the holiday is not a faithful re-enactment and continuation of events four centuries ago but rather an invented tradition "bound up with our sense of the mythic past"[3]—a vision of who we think (or wish) we were, who we think we are, and who we think we will be.

That Day in 1621

In 1620 a group of plucky freedom-seekers—or religious fanatics, depending on your perspective—left Europe for the "New World." Although they were mostly English, they did not initially embark from England, since as "separatists," they had already forsaken their mother country in search of more favorable conditions in the Netherlands. Whatever one thinks of their religious motivations, it is worth noting that their voyage—indeed, any such long, dangerous, and expensive voyage—was not about religion alone: in 1620 a chartered English company known as the Plymouth Company hatched a plan to send a colony to America for profitable business reasons. The financial backers of the company were called "the Adventurers," and those who were contracted to travel and establish the colony were dubbed "the Planters." Further, the passengers on board the *Mayflower* were not all radical Protestant partisans: 57 were members of the emigrant church, but almost as many (48) were referred to as "strangers," many, if not most, of whom

> were simply young Londoners who hoped to prosper and in particular to become landowners in America . . . Some eighteen of them were "indentured servants," young people, that is, who agree to work for low wages, or no wages at all, for seven years in return for their keep and for freedom to start a new life in America after their years of servitude were over.[4]

The ill-considered party left Holland in July and finally sailed away from Plymouth in September, guaranteeing a landing in late autumn or early winter—a very bad time of the year to set up a new colony. The winter was hard, costing the "Pilgrims" half of their population and most of their stores. Those 53 who survived into the spring and summer and then to the harvest season of 1621 were understandably thankful to be alive, and they reportedly held a feast in the fall of 1621, although the details—including the date—are vague. The best and earliest record is a description credited to Edward Winslow in the 1622 *Mourt's Relation*, which read

> Our harvest being gotten in, our governor sent four men on fowling, that so we might after a special manner rejoice together, after we had gathered the fruits of our labors; they four in one day killed as much fowl, as with a little help beside, served the Company almost a week, at which time amongst other Recreations, we exercised our Arms, many of the Indians coming amongst us, and amongst the rest their greatest king Massasoit, with some ninety men, whom for three days we entertained and feasted, and they went out and killed five Deer, which they brought to the Plantation and bestowed on our Governor, and upon the Captain and others. And although it be not always so plentiful, as it was at this time with us, yet by the goodness of God, we are so far from want, that we often wish you partakers of our plenty.[5]

Jennie A. Brownscombe, *The First Thanksgiving at Plymouth*, 1914, oil on canvas.

While this description reminds us somewhat of the iconic Thanksgiving, it is missing a number of key ingredients, which must have been missing on that occasion. Chief among them is the food. Appelbaum insisted that "the feast bore little resemblance to the modern Thanksgiving dinner," not even definitively including turkey; the "fowl" referred to by Winslow probably meant ducks, geese, and partridges, and maybe turkey.[6] There would have been no bread (as the flour had long been used up, and wheat was not indigenous to America; no apple cider (as apples were not indigenous to America); no butter, cheese, or other dairy products (as the Pilgrims failed to bring cows on their ship); no potatoes (as potatoes were not indigenous to North America); and pumpkins but not pumpkin pie (as the settlers had no flour or molasses). Seafood was probably abundant.

So the "first thanksgiving" sounds more like a standard harvest festival, and a rather meager and un-American one at that, rather than a national holiday or the start of an annual tradition. Indeed, Appelbaum concluded that, "Had the governor proclaimed a day of thanksgiving to Almighty God, Edward Winslow, one of the Pilgrim Fathers, would have written about the religious services the settlers held. Thus this feast was more harvest celebration than prayerful day of thanksgiving."[7] More significantly, the Plymouth colonists did not see themselves as doing anything particularly unique or noteworthy: "Whatever happened in 1621, the Puritans did not have special memories of it. They made no subsequent mention of that autumn and did not commemorate it in later years."[8] In fact, the Pilgrims, as fundamentalist Protestants, were opposed to revelry (they had already discontinued Christmas and other "popish," or Catholic, and pagan celebrations, such as Easter and saints' days), and they would have found setting an annual day of thanksgiving blasphemous and presumptuous: they "feared that such yearly celebrations when no particularly noteworthy beneficences had been received, would make the people overly confident of the Lord's generosity and insufficiently humble and chary of Providential wrath."[9] In short, they would have opposed the modern Thanksgiving holiday.

The Politics of Thanksgiving

"It was not a thanksgiving at all, judged by Puritan customs, which they kept in 1621; but as we look back upon it after nearly three centuries, it seems so wonderfully like the day we love that we claim it as a progenitor of our harvest feasts,"[10] wrote William DeLoss Love in his 1895 commentary on the evolving holiday. Instead, New England settlers, as all other Christians did, proclaimed periodic days of thanksgiving as deemed appropriate, including on June 30, 1623. Nonconformist Rhode Island refused to establish official days of thanksgiving until the late 1700s. And the seventeenth-century New England thanksgiving "tradition" was not much fun, either: it was dominated by church attendance and governed by "blue laws" that banned "any Game, Sport, Play, or Recreation" as punishable by fine.[11] Charles Dudley Warner was probably not the only contemporary to feel that "Thanksgiving itself was rather an awful festival—very much like Sunday, except for the enormous dinner."[12]

The other exception from a typical New England Sunday was that Thanksgiving was generally not held on a Sunday, which was the Sabbath. But no day of the week, or even date of the year, was fixed as *the* Thanksgiving Day. Wednesdays and Thursdays were the most likely candidates, especially since New England towns often had a preexisting tradition of "lecture day" on Thursdays, which availed itself for feasts as well as fasts. Still, "no colony west or south of New England celebrated a New England-style thanksgiving although every colony did, on occasion, observe the separate and ancient custom of appointing special days of thanks."[13] Thanksgiving was, as of the 1700s, very much a regional custom.

As the United States began to meld into a single nation, it began to have occasions to be nationally thankful. One was the defeat of the British army at the Battle of Saratoga in 1777, which called forth a national day of thanksgiving on December 18; this had little or nothing to do with the Plymouth feast, though. Soon, nevertheless, the Continental Congress began to issue annual thanksgiving proclamations, as on December 30, 1778; December 9, 1779; and December 7, 1780. The end of the Revolutionary War certainly merited days of gratitude, which were scheduled for December 11, 1783, and October 19, 1784. But givings-of-thanks were not universally accepted by early Americans, many of whom outside New England "were beginning to resist this attempt to impose a 'New England holiday' on the other states. After the Congress of 1784 adjourned, no nationwide thanksgivings were proclaimed until Washington assumed the presidency under the new constitution."[14]

As mentioned, George Washington declared two days of thanksgiving during his presidency (November 26, 1789, and February 19, 1795), both of which appear unrelated to the Plymouth event, as indicated by the language of his first presidential proclamation, which read in part

> Whereas it is the duty of all Nations to acknowledge the providence of almighty God, to obey his will, to be grateful for his benefits, and humbly to implore his protection and favor— and Whereas both Houses of Congress have by their joint Committee requested me "to recommend to the People of the United States a day of public thanksgiving and prayer to be observed by acknowledging with grateful hearts the many signal favors of Almighty God, especially by affording them an opportunity peaceably to establish a form of government for their safety and happiness."

Now therefore I do recommend and assign Thursday the 26th day of November next to be devoted by the People of these States to the service of that great and glorious Being, who is the beneficent Author of all the good that was, that is, or that will be—That we may then all unite in rendering unto him our sincere and humble thanks . . .[15]

Among Washington's immediate successors, John Adams and James Madison also issued thanksgiving proclamations—Adams for May 9, 1798, and April 25, 1799, and Madison for January 12, 1815, and April 13, 1815. None of these was cognizant of the alleged date or doings of the Pilgrim feast; in fact, both of Adams's declarations were actually for days of "solemn humiliation, fasting, and prayer" rather than days of giving thanks. And no presidential tradition was thereby inaugurated: Thomas Jefferson never proclaimed a thanksgiving day, and John Quincy Adams actually turned down a demand for one in 1825.

But traditions do not depend solely on acts of government, so as New Englanders migrated westward, they carried their regional harvest-feast holiday with them—especially because, as late as the 1830s, New Englanders still did not celebrate Christmas, and Thanksgiving was an acceptable seasonal substitute. Thus we see Thanksgiving radiating out from the northeast in local and state proclamations, such as in New York in 1817, Pennsylvania in 1817 and 1818, and eventually Ohio, Michigan, Illinois, and Iowa through the 1820s and 1830s. It even reached King Kamehameha's Hawaii in the late 1830s, although His Majesty was free to set the date as he pleased, so for 1856 it was celebrated on December 25. However, there was not yet national consensus on Thanksgiving, as non-New Englanders, including Long Islanders and Pennsylvania Dutch, resented and ignored it. In the mid- and late 1800s Southern states continued to resist it, Virginia governor Henry Wise disparagingly referring to "this theatrical national claptrap of Thanksgiving"[16] in the 1850s and Texas governor Oran Milo Roberts in the 1880s labeling it "a damned Yankee institution."[17]

Nor was Thanksgiving the only contending damned Yankee institution. In 1769 descendants of the Plymouth planters, organized as the Old Colony Club, inaugurated Forefathers' Day, to be observed on December 22, the calendar-adjusted date of their first landing at Plymouth. This, they insisted, and not Thanksgiving "was the original holiday honoring the Pilgrims—long before the Plymouth colonists had any association with Thanksgiving."[18]

Yet times of tribulation are good opportunities for giving thanks, and both sides of the Civil War issued thanksgiving proclamations, including the Confederate date of September 12, 1862, and the Union date of April 13, 1862. Lincoln's declaration, significantly, was exactly 47 years to the day since the last presidential thanksgiving of Madison. However, it was only in 1863 that Lincoln issued his famous proclamation for Thanksgiving Day as a national holiday, in the following words:

> The year that is drawing towards its close, has been filled with the blessings of fruitful fields and healthful skies. To these bounties, which are so constantly enjoyed that we are prone to forget the source from which they come, others have been added, which are of so extraordinary a nature, that they cannot fail to penetrate and soften even the heart which is habitually insensible to the ever watchful providence of Almighty God. In the midst of a civil war of unequaled magnitude and severity, which has sometimes seemed to foreign States to invite and to provoke their aggression, peace has been preserved with all nations, order has been maintained, the laws have been respected and obeyed, and harmony has prevailed everywhere except in the theatre of military conflict; while that theatre has been greatly contracted by the advancing armies and navies of the Union. Needful diversions of wealth and of strength from the fields of peaceful industry to the national defense, have not arrested the plough, the shuttle or the ship; the axe has enlarged the borders of our settlements, and the mines, as well of iron and coal as of the precious metals, have yielded even more abundantly than heretofore. Population has steadily increased, notwithstanding the waste that has been made in the camp, the siege and the battle-field; and the country, rejoicing in the consciousness of augmented strength and vigor, is permitted to expect continuance of years with large increase of

freedom. No human counsel hath devised nor hath any mortal hand worked out these great things. They are the gracious gifts of the Most High God, who, while dealing with us in anger for our sins, hath nevertheless remembered mercy. It has seemed to me fit and proper that they should be solemnly, reverently and gratefully acknowledged as with one heart and one voice by the whole American People. I do therefore invite my fellow citizens in every part of the United States, and also those who are at sea and those who are sojourning in foreign lands, to set apart and observe the last Thursday of November next, as a day of Thanksgiving and Praise to our beneficent Father who dwelleth in the Heavens. And I recommend to them that while offering up the ascriptions justly due to Him for such singular deliverances and blessings, they do also, with humble penitence for our national perverseness and disobedience, commend to His tender care all those who have become widows, orphans, mourners or sufferers in the lamentable civil strife in which we are unavoidably engaged, and fervently implore the interposition of the Almighty Hand to heal the wounds of the nation and to restore it as soon as may be consistent with the Divine purposes to the full enjoyment of peace, harmony, tranquility and Union.[19]

Note that there is no direct reference to "the First Thanksgiving" or the Plymouth settlers. Be that as it may, Lincoln's successor, Andrew Johnson, not only perpetuated Lincoln's precedent in 1865 but for the first time acknowledged it *as a tradition*, when he opened his proclamation with the words, "In conformity with a recent custom that may now be regarded as established on national consent and approval."[20] Note, again, Johnson's reference to *a recent custom*.

The (Art) Work of Thanksgiving

It took many years and the effort of many people to spread the custom of Thanksgiving across the American land and into the American mind. However, more important and interesting than the mere fact of

Thanksgiving is the *image* of Thanksgiving, which was the product of many more people, especially writers and artists.

The story of the look and feel of Thanksgiving obviously begins in New England, with its autumn snows and its cozy kitchens and big families. But even the most robust memories require a carrier, an entrepreneur, to give them shape and expression. Key to the image, as well as the politics, of Thanksgiving was Sarah Josepha Hale, who published a novel called *Northwood*, subtitled *Life North and South*, in 1827. Among other things, her purpose in writing the book was "to demonstrate the superiority of democratic, virtuous, rural New England by contrasting it with decadent, slaveholding southern society."[21] Among its chapters were "A Thanksgiving Sermon," "Thanksgiving Dinner," and "The Day After Thanksgiving." By her description, on the supper table "the roasted turkey took precedence on this occasion, being placed at the head of the table"; she proceeded to recount the other meats and treats at the meal, including the enormous chicken pie, the bread, the plum pudding and "pies of every name and description ever known in Yankee land; yet the pumpkin pie occupied the most distinguished niche."[22]

This was only the beginning of Mrs Hale's contribution to the invention of Thanksgiving. In 1835 she added a book of short stories called *Traits of American Life*, in which she once again lauded Thanksgiving. But it was in the pages of the *Lady's Magazine* of Boston, which in 1837 became *Godey's Lady's Book*, that she mounted a relentless campaign in favor of her regional holiday. As editor, she published a steady stream of items about the custom, and in 1847 she commenced her personal campaign to have it recognized nationally, writing, "The Governor of New Hampshire has appointed Thursday, November 25th, as the day of annual thanksgiving in that state. We hope every governor in the twenty-nine states will appoint the same day—25th of November—as the day of thanksgiving! Then the whole land would rejoice at once."[23] For two decades starting in 1850 she featured Thanksgiving editorials, advocating the need for a unifying national day in late autumn:

it would be better to have the day so fixed by the expression of public sentiment that no discord would be possible, but, from Maine to Mexico, from Plymouth Rock to Sunset Sea,

the hymn of thanksgiving should be simultaneously raised, as
the pledge of brotherhood in the enjoyment of God's blessings
during the year.[24]

She also waged a letter-writing crusade, including letters to Abraham
Lincoln, such as the one dated September 28, 1863, that may have
profoundly influenced the President to issue his decisive proclamation:

> Permit me, as Editress of the "Lady's Book," to request a few
> minutes of your precious time, while laying before you a sub-
> ject of deep interest to myself and—as I trust—even to the
> President of our Republic, of some importance. This subject
> is to have the day of our annual Thanksgiving made a National
> and fixed Union Festival . . .

> Now the purpose of this letter is to entreat President Lincoln
> to put forth his Proclamation, appointing the last Thursday in
> November (which falls this year on the 26th) as the National
> Thanksgiving for all those classes of people who are under
> the National Government particularly, and commending this
> Union Thanksgiving to each State Executive: thus, by the
> noble example and action of the President of the United States,
> the permanency and unity of our Great American Festival of
> Thanksgiving would be forever secured.
>
> An immediate proclamation would be necessary, so as to reach
> all the States in season for State appointments, also to anticipate
> the early appointments by Governors.[25]

Not content with a presidential decree, she persisted in pressing for a
congressional declaration of Thanksgiving in 1871. (In passing, it is curious to note that Hale is also recognized as the author of the "traditional"
rhyme "Mary Had a Little Lamb" in 1830.)

As influential as she was, she did not work alone. Cornelius
Mathews gave Americans another dose of Thanksgiving in his 1850
Chanticleer, followed by George Hill's 1854 *Dovecote*. Harriet Beecher
Stowe wrote about it in her 1869 *Oldtown Folks*, as did Julia Mathews

in her 1876 *Uncle Joe's Thanksgiving*. Three of the most significant literary treatments of Thanksgiving and its origin were Louisa May Alcott's 1881 "An Old Fashioned Thanksgiving," Jane Goodwin Austin's 1889 *Standish of Standish: The Story of the Pilgrims*, and Henry Wadsworth Longfellow's 1858 *The Courtship of Miles Standish*, the latter two of which helped form the romantic portrayal of the Pilgrims that would stick to this day.

Beyond poets and novelists, artists added to the vision of Thanksgiving. Two of its greatest champions were Winslow Homer the painter and Thomas Nast the cartoonist (the latter of whom also gave Uncle Sam his familiar look, as mentioned in Chapter Three; in fact, he even brought Thanksgiving and Uncle Sam together in an 1869 drawing). Homer painted *Thanksgiving Day in the Army: After Dinner the Wishbone* in 1864, and eventually Thanksgiving images were gracing postcards and other newfangled media of the day. And no discussion of the look of Thanksgiving would be complete without a mention of the homiest of American artists, Norman Rockwell, whose 1943 Second World War-era picture *Freedom from Want* pushed all of the buttons about Thanksgiving, turkey, and grandma.

Finally, James Baker stresses the role that schools played in securing Thanksgiving in the American psyche: "It was in the classroom that Thanksgiving had its greatest impact at the turn of the twentieth century."[26] Booklets were composed for children featuring stories, poems, songs, and other material about Thanksgiving, such as Schell's 1901 *The Celebrations* and Dickinson's 1916 *Children's Book of Thanksgiving Stories*. Thanksgiving decorations, displays, pageants, and costumes brought the tradition to life for successive generations. Sunday schools also appreciated the value in the holiday and featured it in their teaching tools. As Baker concludes, "Once the print media created a new, multifarious symbol system for the holiday, an 'authentic' Thanksgiving had to involve turkey dinners, Pilgrims and Indians, family reunions, and autumnal associations, whatever an individual's earlier conception of it might have been."[27] That is, having learned Thanksgiving, Americans endeavored to teach Thanksgiving.

One more point is worth emphasizing. As we have repeatedly observed, while proclamations of thanksgiving were customary in

Thanksgiving postcard, c. 1910.

Thanksgiving Day is here again,
And come this year to crown:
Oh pray receive my wholesome wishes,
For well prepared Thanksgiving Dishes.

the early United States, they usually made no particular reference to Pilgrims or Plymouth. There was, remarkably, "no mention of the colonists in presidential proclamations until 1905," and they were not invoked by name until 1939.[28] In other words, the Plymouth planters may have given thanks, and America may have repeatedly given thanks, but the two phenomena were not seen as especially connected. "Until the 1940s, the Thanksgiving holiday was as often represented in popular culture by accounts of 'old time Thanksgivings' of the late eighteenth and early nineteenth century or stories of contemporary holiday events as it was by the 1621 story."[29]

The Modern Traditions of Thanksgiving

As the true epitome of an invented tradition, Thanksgiving emerged out of colonial (and pre-colonial, medieval, and ancient) practices, took on many forms, adapted to each historical moment, and eventually wrapped back around itself to link the present with a selected and imagined moment in the past. But the invention of Thanksgiving goes much further than that, in directions that the Plymouth planters never foresaw and that many modern-day Americans decry. For instance, one of the most beloved Thanksgiving traditions was composed in 1844 as a poem for children; originally titled "A Boy's Thanksgiving Day" and written by Lydia Maria Child, most Americans probably know it by its first line:

> Over the river, and through the wood,
> To Grandfather's house we go;
> The horse knows the way to carry the sleigh
> Through the white and drifted snow.
> Over the river, and through the wood,
> To Grandfather's house away!
> We would not stop for doll or top,
> For this is Thanksgiving Day.

It continues for ten further verses and, legend has it, was later set to the tune of an English song, "Over the Hills and Far Away." Interestingly, most Americans sing "To Grandmother's house" rather than "To Grandfather's house."

At any rate, parades have also been a common component of Thanksgiving observances. For about a century (from the 1840s until nearly the 1940s), New Yorkers held parades of "fantastics" or "fantasticals" on Thanksgiving Day. According to Appelbaum,

> The fantasticals were neighborhood-based organizations of young men whose sole purpose for existence was so that their members could dress in flamboyant costumes and parade through the streets on Thanksgiving . . . To this author, it seems most

likely that the fantasticals were a high-spirited extension of Guy
Fawkes Day customs . . .

The fantasticals awakened their fellow citizens every Thanksgiving morning with loud blasts on their chosen instrument,
the fish horn . . .

[When the parade was over], for these fantastical revelers the
fun was just beginning at rowdy picnics in parks and amusement
halls on the city's edge.[30]

In addition, "target companies," or men's shooting societies, gathered to
compete for prizes, and "Ragamuffins," or city children in race-bending
make-up (black children in white-face and white children in black-face),
begged for pennies from people on the streets.

Meanwhile, the residents of Norwich, Connecticut, built Thanksgiving
bonfires, and various sporting events began to fill the day—which would
have horrified the pious Pilgrims. Appelbaum discovered bicycle and foot
races, as well as baseball games after 1860 and college football games after
1880; local rivalries like Harvard versus Yale or Tulane versus Louisiana
State were saved for the auspicious holiday. As today's football fans know,
the Detroit Lions have been a "traditional" part of Thanksgiving since
1934, and the Dallas Cowboys have played on Thanksgiving Day since
1966; to satiate the hunger for sports, the National Football League
recently added a third game to the holiday tradition.

As indicated, parades have become an element of Thanksgiving
celebrations, as of other American celebrations. However, these processions have hardly been spontaneous. In 1920 or 1921 (depending on the
source) Gimbel Brothers Department Store in Philadelphia organized
a parade to entice customers to their business and to kick off the
Christmas shopping season. In 1924 J. L. Hudson's Department Store
in Detroit followed suit, adding nursery rhyme and fairytale characters,
clearly aiming at children. The State Street Council of Chicago promoted a parade in 1934 for the benefit of all of the downtown vendors,
which was taken over by McDonald's in 1984, Brach's candy in 1990,
and Target in 2002.[31] But the granddaddy of them all is the Macy's

parade in New York City. Begun in 1924 and originally called Macy's Christmas Parade, it was entirely planned and staged by the Macy's department store, with Santa Claus officially coronated on the balcony of Macy's 34th Street store entrance (hence the name of the famous Christmas movie *Miracle on 34th Street*). The first parade featured live animals, but a new tradition was added in 1927—large inflatable versions of famous characters such as Felix the Cat. Since then, characters have been continuously updated or changed, such as Snoopy (from the *Peanuts* comic strip), Buzz Lightyear (from *Toy Story*), and SpongeBob SquarePants—none of whom were present at the "first Thanksgiving." Marrying two American traditions, Uncle Sam became a balloon character in the 1938 Macy's parade.

The commercialization of Thanksgiving, and its linkage with Christmas, reached a high (or low) point in 1939, when President Franklin Roosevelt moved the date of Thanksgiving to the next-to-last Thursday in November rather than the last Thursday, at the bidding of the National Retail Dry Goods Association, for the purpose of creating a longer Christmas shopping season. And so it was for two years, although only half of the states observed the change (23 Democratic states shifted with Roosevelt, but 23 Republican states kept the older "tradition"—and Texas and Colorado celebrated both). But after two years of popular complaint, the holiday was reset to the fourth Thursday in November.

In 1947, President Harry Truman introduced an odd but poignant tradition, the pardoning of the presidential turkey (although some historians trace the custom all the way back to Lincoln). Also in 1947, the historical exhibit known as Plimoth Plantation, Inc. was opened "to serve as a 'memorial to the Pilgrim Fathers'."[32] Today it includes learning programs for schools, families, adults, and homeschoolers. Not to be outdone, in 1958 Virginia opened its own rival Richmond Thanksgiving Festival, to promote its rival claim to the first Thanksgiving back on December 14, 1619. Since then, Thanksgiving has continued to change with the times, giving us a folk Thanksgiving in Arlo Guthrie's memorable 1969 song, "Alice's Restaurant," not to mention a Peanuts Thanksgiving in the 1973 animation *A Charlie Brown Thanksgiving*.

Finally, one person's tradition is another person's tragedy. Americans may choose to remember Thanksgiving as a day of great happiness in

Macy's Thanksgiving Day Parade, 1979.

the present and of great generosity and peace in the past. The native peoples of Massachusetts beg to differ. In 1970, during the height of the political mobilization of Native Americans, the Wampanoag people declared Thanksgiving Day as their National Day of Mourning. The United Indians of New England protested then and have continued to protest: for instance, in their flyer for the 39th National Day of Mourning (November 27, 2008), they pleaded, "Help us in our struggle to create a true awareness of Native peoples and demonstrate the unity of Indigenous peoples internationally. Help shatter the untrue glass image of the Pilgrims and the unjust system based on racism, sexism, homophobia, and war."[33]

No doubt part of the appeal of Thanksgiving and its romantic, if not saccharine, image of the happy planters and welcoming Indians is the notion that Americans' ancestors came in peace and even meant well for the natives. Thanksgiving is a collective conscience-washing. But as Appelbaum concluded, "The landing of the Pilgrim Fathers [and Mothers, presumably] did not become the honored myth of our nation's birth because of a realistic understanding of who these people were—after all, they themselves were intolerant religious fanatics—but because of who their descendants became."[34] Or better yet, the myth of Thanksgiving is a myth precisely because it is *not* who we are but who we would like to be, or at least how we would like to be imagined. Andrew Smith may insist that "the Pilgrims and their proverbial First Thanksgiving are origin myths, tracing America to its beginnings,"[35] but as with all myths, their value is not their truth but their consequences.

SIX

Honor Thy Mother and Father, etc.: Mother's Day and Father's Day

★ ★ ★

F
amily is a building block of all societies, although the specific forms of family vary tremendously across cultures; the Na or Mosuo of western China traditionally did not even practice marriage or possess a concept or term for "husband" or "father."[1] The American family and its attendant institutions and roles—marriage, household, husband and wife, parenting, and so forth—have also changed significantly over time. In her aptly titled *The Way We Never Were: American Families and the Nostalgia Trap*, Stephanie Coontz wrote that the "traditional" American family that we associate most closely with the 1950s

> was a qualitatively new phenomenon. At the end of the 1940s, all the trends characterizing the rest of the twentieth century suddenly reversed themselves. For the first time in more than one hundred years, the age for marriage and motherhood fell, fertility increased, divorce rates declined, and women's degree of educational parity with men dropped sharply. In a period of less than ten years, the proportion of never-married persons declined by as much as it had during the entire previous half century. At the time, most people understood the 1950s family to be a new invention.[2]

Family is so diverse and changeable for one very simple but important reason: as anthropologists such as W.H.R. Rivers declared almost a century ago, family is not a mere physical fact of blood relations, and even fatherhood and motherhood "depend, not on procreation and parturition, but on social convention, and it is evident that blood-relationship is quite inadequate as a means of defining kinship."[3] As with other social conventions, family was transformed in America in the nineteenth century, in response to the same social forces that fostered enthusiasm and anxiety about the flag, the Pledge of Allegiance, and Thanksgiving. Out of that era came new traditions celebrating and lauding family—first mothers, then fathers, and then just about every kin relation—that evinced similar enthusiasms and anxieties.

Mother's Day

Coontz and others have contended that the early American family was surprisingly like family in pre-modern societies, with parents having a great deal of influence on marriage choices and with love as a rather minor consideration in such choices. Dorothy Mays found that "love was not a prerequisite for marriage, nor did girls grow up expecting it"; in fact, love was viewed with some suspicion, "considered to be a fickle emotion, liable to skew a girl's judgment."[4] Furthermore, the extended family was often as important as, if not more important than, the so-called nuclear family. Divorces and separations, as well as domestic violence, were hardly unknown, and women were not exempt from the hard labor that was entailed in running a family farm.

By the middle of the 1800s, a social revolution was under way in the United States, as in Europe, characterized by urbanization, industrialization, immigration, and what many perceived to be the breakdown of traditional society. Men were more frequently than in the past employed outside the home, and married couples with their children were more often detached from their extended kin group. One reaction was what has been dubbed a nineteenth-century "cult of domesticity," with special pressure on women to play a specific and limited role in integrating the family and ultimately the wider society.

According to a seminal essay by Barbara Welter in 1966, the cult of domesticity largely functioned through a "cult of true womanhood," which assigned women to (she went so far as to say, held women hostage

in) the family home. True womanhood, Welter argued, had four features or "cardinal virtues"—namely, "piety, purity, submissiveness,
and domesticity."[5] Naturally, religious piety was expected of women,
on the presumption that religion came more easily to women than
men and that religion "did not take a woman away from her 'proper
sphere,' her home."[6] Purity, especially sexual purity, went along with
piety. Submission, that is, obedience to her husband, "was perhaps the
most feminine virtue expected of women,"[7] which meant, of course,
that true womanhood was best or only achieved through marriage and
in the home. "The true woman's place was unquestionably by her own
fireside—as daughter, sister, but most of all as wife and mother."[8] The
role of mother was urgently emphasized: "America depended upon her
mothers to raise up a whole generation of Christian statesmen who could
say, 'all that I am I owe to my angel mother'."[9] As evidence, an essay
contest held by the women's magazine *The Ladies' Wreath* on the topic
"How May an American Woman Best Show Her Patriotism" awarded
the prize to an entry that answered, "by staying at home, where she
brings her influence to bear upon the right side for the country's weal."[10]

British settlers brought with them to America a sixteenth-century
holiday known as Mothering Day, originally in honor of the quintessential pure and pious mother, the Virgin Mary, but gradually extended to

"The Cult of True Womanhood," from Myer Solis-Cohen's *Woman in Girlhood,
Wifehood, Motherhood: Her Responsibilities and Her Duties at All Periods of Life;
A Guide in the Maintenance of Her Health and That of Her Children* (1906).

ordinary mothers. On that day, the fourth Sunday of Lent, the servants of the upper class were allowed a day off to visit their mothers, who were presented with cakes and flowers.

The American tradition of Mother's Day is generally traced back to a West Virginian woman named Ann Reeves Jarvis, who organized "Mother's Day" events as early as the 1850s to teach proper mothering and parenting skills to local women and, during the Civil War, to offer nursing care to injured soldiers.[11] Jarvis apparently did not conceive of a holiday based on her activities, but others after her did. Two of the most prominent were her daughter Anna Jarvis and Julia Ward Howe, the latter also renowned for composing "The Battle Hymn of the Republic." In 1870, Howe published her "Mother's Day Proclamation," demanding not a holiday for mothers but rather a movement of women for peace. The proclamation read in part

Arise, then, women of this day!
Arise all women who have hearts,
Whether your baptism be that of water or of tears
Say firmly:

. . . "Our husbands shall not come to us reeking of carnage,
For caresses and applause.
Our sons shall not be taken from us to unlearn
All that we have been able to teach them of
Charity, mercy, and patience . . ."

In the name of womanhood and humanity, I earnestly ask
That a general congress of women without limit of nationality
May be appointed and held at some place deemed most convenient
And at the earliest period consistent with its objects
To promote the alliance of the different nationalities,
The amicable settlement of international questions.
The great and general interests of peace.[12]

Howe had in mind a Mothers' Peace Day, which she originally promoted on June 2, 1873. Allegedly she even briefly advocated that the Fourth

Anna Jarvis, *c.* 1930.

of July should be Mother's Day, but that plan came to naught, and the various celebrations that were held at her own expense ceased "once she stopped footing the bill."[13]

Mother's Day as it would come to be known and practiced was the brainchild of Anna M. Jarvis, the daughter of Ann Reeves Jarvis, who ironically never married or had children of her own. When the senior Jarvis died in 1905, Anna championed the holiday to remember and honor her mother and for others to do the same. History records the first actual observance of Mother's Day as May 10, 1908, in Jarvis's hometown of Grafton, West Virginia, and a few other regional locations. After this single event, Anna Jarvis

resolved to see her holiday added to the national calendar. Arguing that American holidays were biased toward male achievements, she started a massive letter writing campaign to newspapers and prominent politicians urging the adoption of a special day honoring motherhood. By 1912 many states, towns, and churches had adopted Mother's Day as an annual holiday, and Jarvis had established the Mother's Day International Association to help promote her cause.[14]

But what was her cause exactly? A leading scholar and author of *Memorializing Motherhood: Anna Jarvis and the Struggle for Control of Mother's Day*, Katharine Lane Antolini holds that Jarvis intended "a 'thank-offering' from sons and daughters and the nation 'for the blessing of good homes.' 'This is not a celebration of maudlin sentiment. It is one of practical benefit and patriotism, emphasizing the home as the highest inspiration of our individual and national lives.'"[15] In that sentiment, we can hear the echoes of the cult of domesticity and of the true woman, which was also enshrined by other nascent holidays such as Thanksgiving.

In 1914 Jarvis's holiday was legitimized by President Woodrow Wilson, who proclaimed the second Sunday in May as Mother's Day, interestingly implicating it with the flag and the nationalist movement of the day by requesting government buildings and private homes to fly the flag "as a public expression of our love and reverence for the mothers of our country." However, the simple day for writing letters and giving flowers to your mother quickly morphed in directions she neither intended nor approved. First, as Antolini claims, "Jarvis considered it her intellectual and legal property, and not part of the public domain"; moreover, she did not want the occasion "to become the 'burdensome, wasteful, expensive gift-day'" that it eventually became.[16]

In the cases of the flag, the Pledge of Allegiance, and the national motto, we discovered opposition and resistance to the traditions from certain quarters of society. Mother's Day represents a singular case in which the very founder of the tradition turned into its harshest critic. By 1920 "she became disgusted with how the holiday had been commercialized. She outwardly denounced the transformation and urged people to stop buying Mother's Day flowers, cards and candies."[17] For instance, Hallmark Cards had begun purveying Mother's Day cards in the early 1920s, replacing the simple (and free) letters that Jarvis advocated. Jarvis's remonstrations against her own holiday were legendary:

> Media sources chronicled her frequent public condemnations of those she denounced as copyright infringers, trade vandals, and blatant profiteers. In 1922, Jarvis endorsed an open boycott against the florists who raised the price of white carnations every May. The following year, she crashed a retail confectionery convention to protest the industry's economic gouging of the day. In 1925, she interrupted a national convention of the American War Mothers in Philadelphia because she believed the majority of the money raised by the organization's white carnation sales went into the pockets of professional organizers rather than going to aid World War I veterans.[18]

Particular animus she reserved for an upstart competing holiday designated as Parents' Day, which she threatened with a lawsuit in 1923. But by this time Mother's Day was a monster that was beyond any one person's control, even its creator's. She fought to erase the holiday that she birthed until her death, destitute and institutionalized, in 1948. In a final twist of irony, her end-of-life care was financed anonymously by The Florist's Exchange.[19]

Father's Day

West Virginia has the pride of claiming not one but two kin-based American holiday traditions. By most accounts, the first celebration of American fathers was held at Williams Memorial Methodist Episcopal Church in Fairmont, West Virginia—just a few miles from the Jarvises' hometown of Grafton—on July 5, 1908. Late the previous year, as was all too common in the state then and since, a mine explosion nearby had killed 360 men and left a thousand children without fathers.[20] A local woman named Grace Golden Clayton prevailed on the minister to include a remembrance of fathers in his sermon. As in the case of Mother's Day (and the original Pledge of Allegiance, as seen in Chapter Four), this event was planned as a one-time occasion, and the people

Flier for Father's
Day, 1913.

involved did not immediately take credit for inventing a new annual
holiday tradition. (Decades later, in 1985, a marker was raised in West
Virginia proclaiming Fairmont as the home of Father's Day.[21])

If a tradition was not born in that time and place, the model of
Mother's Day made Father's Day a likely idea, and the following year
a Spokane, Washington, woman named Sonora Louise Smart Dodd
hatched the notion after hearing a Mother's Day speech. According to
www.fathersdaycelebration.com (yes, every holiday or potential holiday
has its own website, often more than one), Dodd was to Father's Day
what Anna Jarvis was to Mother's Day—if not its originator, then its
most ardent promoter.

Ms. Dodd began a rigorous campaign to celebrate Father's Day
in the U.S. The Spokane Ministerial Association and the local

Young Men's Christian Association (YMCA) supported Sonora's cause. As a result Spokane celebrated its first Father's Day on 19 June 1910. Though there was initial hesitation, the idea gained gradual popularity all over [the] U.S. and Father's Day came to be celebrated in cities across the country.[22]

Portland, Oregon, picked up the practice in 1911, and by 1915 Father's Day had spread as far east as Chicago.

Having already put his stamp of approval on Mother's Day, Woodrow Wilson endorsed Father's Day in 1916, although Congress was not behind the idea. However, it was another president, Calvin Coolidge in 1924, who suggested that it be elevated to a national holiday in order to "establish more intimate relations between fathers and their children and to impress upon fathers the full measure of their obligations."[23] The recommendation was met with disdain by some American men, though, who "scoffed at the holiday's sentimental attempts to domesticate manliness with flowers and gift-giving, or they derided the proliferation of such holidays as a commercial gimmick to sell more products—often paid for by the father himself."[24]

Whatever else they felt about the proto-tradition, critics were correct about its commercialization. Timothy Marr added that during the Depression era of the 1930s,

> Father's Day was seized upon by the New York business community as a means of promoting sales by creating a "second Christmas" halfway through the year. Separate campaigns in the tobacco, neckware, and shirt industries ("Give Dad Something to Wear") were coordinated when businessmen founded the Father's Day Council in 1935. The advocacy of its first leader, Alvan Austin, combined with honors bestowed upon fathers defending the "home" during World War II, contributed to the holiday's increasing popularity.[25]

Perhaps because it did not fit the norms of masculinity nor contribute to the cult of domesticity, Father's Day was considerably slower to catch on than Mother's Day. In 1956, at the same moment that the legislature was formalizing the motto, Congress also passed a joint resolution in support of Father's Day. It took another ten years for President Lyndon Johnson to issue a proclamation setting the date of Father's Day as the third Sunday in June. It was only in 1972 that President Richard Nixon completed the codification of Father's Day by recognizing it as a permanent national holiday (although not one carrying a day off from work for dad).

Parents' Day?

In the dash to honor mothers and fathers in the early twentieth century, it made sense that someone would conjure a combined holiday in commemoration of both parents. As early as 1916 a letter-writer to the *New York Times* had suggested a "Home Day" to recognize mothers, fathers, and children too. The best-known sire of Parents' Day, though, was Robert Spero (sometimes spelled "Spere") of New York. Ralph LaRossa and Jaimie Ann Carboy assessed the struggle for Parents' Day as "essentially a debate about the cultural position of parents in American society"[26] and a literal, even legal, struggle it was.

Spero was an elderly entertainer of children and philanthropist in the 1920s who was also known as "Uncle Robert" around New York City. In retrospect, he recalled being moved by Mother's Day and the poor families he encountered in the city, but LaRossa and Carboy, as well as Antolini, also emphasized his frustration at a failed attempt to organize a Mother's Day celebration in 1923. Anna Jarvis interfered with his plans, asserting that he "had no right to hold a parade, indeed 'had no right to celebrate Mother's Day' at all, because Mother's Day was *her* holiday."[27] The governor of New York himself, Alfred Smith, prevailed upon Spero to abandon his plans.

In response, the following year Spero assembled a Parents' Day festivity for the second Sunday in May. By 1929 Parents' Day had a promoter in *Parents* magazine publisher George Hecht, who used the journal to endorse collapsing Mother's Day and Father's Day into Parents' Day. The idea gained some traction in New York State, where the state government actually proposed legalizing the holiday in 1930; the organization American War Mothers also threw their support behind the notion. A major Parents' Day event was held in May 1931, attended by Spero, the mayor of New York City, the superintendent of New York City schools (signaling the collaboration with schools also seen in the Pledge and various flag ceremonies), and thousands of parents and children. President Herbert Hoover even sent his well-wishes in a statement that included the sentiment, "you are at liberty to use the following message for the celebration of Parents' Day in Central Park on May 10th 'The love and respect of parents and children are the root of a very large part of all the happiness in the world.'"[28] The next year, Governor Franklin Roosevelt, who would become president in 1933, similarly commended "in the highest terms" the initiative to establish Parents' Day.

Parents' Day grew through the 1930s, and Spero tried to proselytize it beyond New York, but the last celebration occurred in 1939. Spero retired in 1940, stepping down from the leadership of Parents' Day and handing that responsibility to Hecht, who curiously neglected the holiday in 1940, basically leaving it to die.

Jarvis can take some small credit for crushing the nascent holiday, but LaRossa and Carboy maintained that Parents' Day never reached "a point where it could be considered a full-fledged social movement. The idea of merging Father's Day and Mother's Day never really caught on with the public."[29] Part of the explanation is Spero's departure from the cause when it was still young and weak; another part was Hecht's abandonment, jumping ship to lead the National Committee on the Observance of Mother's Day. Timing was also critical: America became involved in the Second World War soon after Spero's retirement, and "All signs indicate that the war helped boost Father's Day and Mother's Day as national observances."[30] And we cannot ignore the business interests that were advanced by having two card-and-gift buying holidays instead of one. Finally, LaRossa and Carboy speculated on how Parents' Day may have related to the gender and family politics of the day.

> It is important to consider the possibility that the Parents' Day campaign may have been not so much a direct assault on Mother's Day as it was a veiled attack on mothers. At different points in history, women have been deemed to be inadequate caregivers, criticized for making sons "soft" and for smothering children in general. The Boy Scout movement was founded at the turn of

the 20th century "to rescue boys from their mothers and reunite them with a virile ideal," while the "unmanliness of those rejected by the military" during World War II was attributed to "mothers' overprotectiveness." The Parents' Day campaign was not manifestly anti-mother, but more than coincidence may have been behind the campaign reaching its zenith during the Depression, when, in the wake of wholesale unemployment, women were regularly blamed for men's travails.[31]

Be that as it may, and despite the fact that President Bill Clinton signed a unanimous congressional resolution in 1994 adopting Parents' Day and setting the fourth Sunday of July for its observance, and despite the fact that there is a National Parents' Day Coalition in the United States today, Parents' Day is not widely known or celebrated by Americans and has not achieved the status of a real American tradition. Maybe next year.

All Our Kin: The Proliferation of Family Holidays

Potentially, there could be as many kinship-related holidays as there are kinship relations. In fact, LaRossa and Carboy reported that at least one New Yorker prophesied an explosion of family days, asking in a letter to the *New York Times* in 1914 "if there was to be a Father's Day, why should there not also be an Uncle's Day, or Brother's Day, or Household Pet Day?"[32]

If that sounds silly, then note the promotion of, for instance, Grandparents Day by, among other entities, the American Grandparents Association. According to the AGA, National Grandparents Day falls on the first Sunday after Labor Day. Also advertised as Intergenerational Day, it is attributed to Marian Lucille Herndon McQuade of West Virginia (what is it about West Virginia and family holidays?), mother of fifteen, grandmother of 43, and great-grandmother of ten. The American Grandparents Association explains that Mrs McQuade "wanted Grandparents Day to be a family day. She envisioned families enjoying small, private gatherings, perhaps even a family reunion, or participating in community events."

McQuade launched her effort to celebrate grandparents in 1970, and she became the impetus for Grandparents Day (AGA notes that there is no apostrophe in Grandparents Day as there is in Mother's Day and Father's Day):

> her unending work to establish and publicize the holiday marks her as a true community leader. She spent much of her life advocating for older adults. In 1971 she was elected Vice-Chair of the West Virginia Committee on Aging and appointed as a delegate to the White House Conference on Aging. In 1972, Mrs McQuade's efforts resulted in President Richard Nixon proclaiming a National Shut-in Day. She served as President of the Vocational Rehabilitation Foundation, Vice-President of the West Virginia Health Systems Agency, and was appointed to the Nursing Home Licensing Board, among many other involvements.[33]

Since her death in 2008, the torch of Grandparents Day has been carried by AGA and a group called Generations United, whose avowed mission is "to improve the lives of children, youth, and older people through intergenerational collaboration, public policies, and programs for the enduring benefit of all." Accordingly, AGA sees three goals for National Grandparents Day—naturally to honor grandparents, but also "to give grandparents an opportunity to show love for their children's children" and "to help children become aware of the strength, information and guidance older people can offer." For that purpose, AGA, through its Legacy Project, has expanded the scope and formality of Grandparents Day far beyond the vision of McQuade. The organization publishes planning guides, sells "Across Generations" kits (the starter kit priced at $59.90), and certificates to award to grandparents and what they call "grandfriends." Their materials suggest two hundred different activities from reading together to games and crafts, many of them focused on the school and the community rather than the home. In 1985, the state government of Michigan passed an Act establishing Grandparents' and Grandchildrens' Day, except it designated March 18, not September, as the occasion.

While all of the attention so far has been focused on (grand)parenting, there are those who also push for a recognition of those who get parented. Thus we have National Son's and Daughter's Day, scheduled annually for August 11. No one seems to know who originated this idea, nor has it institutionalized itself as a national holiday tradition, but the National Day Calendar website encourages Americans on National Son's and Daughter's Day, "if it is possible, spend time with the joys of your life, your sons and/or daughters." "Do something special for your children today," the site admonishes us; "If they are at home, go for a walk or enjoy a local park. If your children are grown, give them a call and remind them how special they are to you. Use #SonsAndDaughtersDay on social media." By the way, on the day of writing this chapter (August 24), the National Day Calendar informs us that it is also National Maryland Day, National Peach Pie Day, and National Waffle Day.

Lest the reader think that the 1914 *New York Times* letter mentioned above was utterly frivolous, there apparently actually is an Aunt's and Uncle's Day, identified by the National Day Calendar as July 25. Although the National Day Calendar cannot identify a source for this holiday either, Melanie Notkin takes credit for it in her blog "25 Reasons Why Aunts Deserve a Day"—without any reference to uncles, asserting that she founded it in 2009 "to celebrate and honor maternal women in a child's life" including "aunts by relation, aunts by choice, great-aunts, godmothers, and all women who love the children in their lives."[34] There is also a National Cousins Day, appointed for July 24, of unknown origin. Indeed, it seems that the multiplication of family days in America is limited only by imagination and the number of days on the calendar. Not all of these proposed holidays have made it or will make it onto the list of heartfelt American traditions, but then not all candidates for tradition status succeed.

By the way, National Pet Day, April 11, was invented in 2005 by Colleen Paige "to celebrate the joy pets bring to our lives and create public awareness about the plight of many different kinds of animals awaiting a forever home in shelters and rescues all across the nation."[35] After all, pets are members of the American family.

SEVEN

Lest We Forget:
Patriotic Holidays

★ ★ ★

"Remember the Alamo."
"Remember the Maine."

A
mericans, as citizens of other countries are, are admonished
to remember the great moments of their history, both the glorious and the tragic. Significantly, the tragic moments—the
defeats in war, the losses of life—are often the strongest memories.
They stir the most emotion, they demand the most respect, and they
are the most motivating. Indeed, it is regularly the painful episodes in
a country's history that are particularly suitable for what scholars have
called the "usable past" (see Introduction).

All countries inscribe their national memory in time and space.
Spatially, certain places—frequently, places where important things
happened, such as the Battle of Gettysburg—become sites of commemoration (literally, "remembering together"). Societies can also
consecrate places that have no inherent historical significance: Japan has
its Yasukuni Shrine where the spirits of the Second World War soldiers
are housed, revered, and placated, and the United States has Arlington
Cemetery and, in recognition of anonymous war casualties, the Tomb of
the Unknown Soldier (created in 1921). Temporally, societies put days
on the calendar to pause and remember the past and perform respectful
actions for those who lived (and died in) those events.

Yet Americans did not actively cultivate national political-military
holidays until after the Civil War. As we have seen repeatedly and will

see again, the Civil War altered America's self-perception dramatically and permanently, and it was in the aftermath of that conflict that the United States really got about the business of building a nation and a full set of national traditions. The Civil War itself was the focus or subject of many traditions, and its survivors and veterans—such as the Grand Army of the Republic—were key players in the formation and propagation of other traditions, such as the flag and the Pledge of Allegiance.

According to a congressional report in 2014, the first four official federal holidays were decreed in 1870 (five years after the conclusion of the Civil War)—namely, New Year's Day, Independence Day or the Fourth of July, Thanksgiving Day, and Christmas Day.

> Since 1870, numerous proposals have been introduced to Congress to establish permanent federal holidays. Only 11, however, have thus far become law . . . In several instances, Congress created federal holidays after a sizeable number of states created state holidays. In other instances, Congress took the lead. Additionally, each holiday was designed to emphasize a particular aspect of American heritage or to celebrate an event in American history.[1]

Only one of those original federal holidays was political, and the other three were in no way unique to the U.S. Subsequently, more—and more political and more specifically American—holidays were added, including George Washington's Birthday (1880), Decoration Day (1888), Labor Day (1894), Armistice Day (1938), Inauguration Day (1957), Columbus Day (1968), and Martin Luther King, Jr's Birthday (1968). Some of these occasions have changed names, and many of them their dates of observance, since their origin. Four such holidays will be discussed in this chapter, and a fifth (Columbus Day) will feature in the next chapter.

Presidents' Day

George Washington, Revolutionary War general, first president of the United States, and esteemed "Father of our Country," was venerated

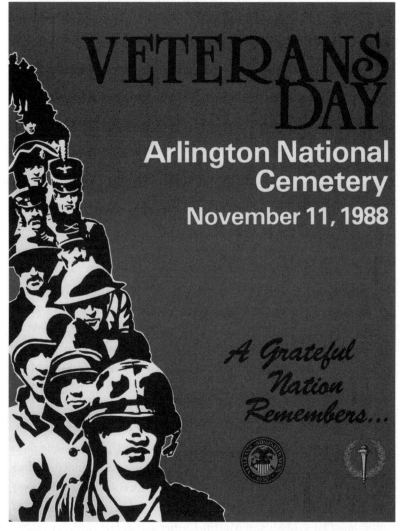

"A Grateful Nation Remembers," poster for Veterans Day 1988.

by the fledgling republic immediately after his death in 1799. Local celebrations of his birth (February 22, 1732) were held as early as 1800, and the centennial of his birth in 1832 was a cause for more extensive festivity. In 1848 construction on the now iconic Washington Monument began, planned and financed by the private Washington National Monument Society. The unlikely obelisk remained uncompleted in 1876, when the government took responsibility and finished the project, dedicating it on February 21, 1885.

Meanwhile, Michael Kammen reported that Henry Tuckerman advocated a national day of remembrance for Washington's Birthday in 1857, believing that such a service would contribute to "a unanimity of feeling and of rites, which shall fuse and mold into one pervasive emotion the divided hearts of the country."[2] Yet despite the deserved adulation of Washington, no official commemoration of his birthday existed until 1879, when President Rutherford B. Hayes proclaimed a Washington's Birthday holiday—but only for the District of Columbia. It was not until 1885 that Washington's Birthday became a national holiday. For a time, the u.s. also observed Lincoln's Birthday (February 12) as at least a state holiday; by 1940, 24 states and the District of Columbia recognized it.

But two paid holidays for federal employees in the same month was apparently too much, so in the 1960s Congress started to contemplate a shift of presidential birthdays and other federal holidays. The Uniform Monday Holiday Act of 1968 reset the date for Washington's Birthday permanently to a Monday, in this case the third Monday in February; several other holidays were also permanently assigned to Mondays, creating a set of three-day weekend holidays in order, according to the History Channel, to organize employee time better and discourage mid-week absenteeism.[3] Although most Americans refer to the holiday as Presidents' Day, bundling Lincoln and Washington together, officially the occasion was never renamed and remains Washington's Birthday on the federal calendar.

As in the cases of Mother's Day and Father's Day, many Americans feel that Washington's Birthday or Presidents' Day has been cheapened by commercialism; it is a prime occasion for sales on all manner of goods. Yoni Appelbaum, writing for *The Atlantic*, contends that Presidents' Day has especially become associated with automobile sales but that it has long been commercial, linked almost from the outset with the bicycle industry. In 1898 bicycle makers promoted Bicycle Day in New York City: "Washington's Birthday, with its cessation of business usually unaccompanied by any extended ceremonies," they determined, "provided the perfect opportunity for a sales event."[4] Allegedly some people actually felt that a good sale would help revive the holiday that had otherwise fallen into obscurity and indifference; no special events or celebrations were ever customary for the holiday. "For several years,"

Appelbaum declares, "the birthday of our first president continued to be observed as Bicycle Day. But after 1900, the bicycle craze abated. Enterprising dealers shifted into newer, more fashionable product lines. Motorcycle stores sprang up between the bike shops, and within a decade, car dealers followed."

Memorial Day

It is perfectly proper to pay tribute to the great men and women whose actions and sacrifices gave life and shape to a society. Among those actions, nothing enters and alters the national consciousness as war does, and for millennia people have been honoring their battlefields and war dead with monuments, cairns, and other markers, while celebrating them in song and story. In fact, Chris Hedges opined that war is a kind of necrophilia, a love and respect of the dead, who are moreover not distant abstract figures like Washington and Lincoln but our own lost sons and daughters.[5] Hedges maintained that war—and the memory of war—gives our individual and collective lives meaning, or at least we feel compelled to make those sacrifices meaningful.

Curiously, America's first war (the Revolutionary War) did not spawn a lot of memorializing and traditioning; the country's sights were set then more to the future than to the past. The country's second war (the War of 1812) inspired a bit of traditioning, notably the eventual national anthem. But it was the trauma of the Civil War that touched off a spree of traditioning, much of it in an especially patriotic vein.

Who better to tell the official version of the origin of Memorial Day than the U.S. Department of Veterans Affairs? Its website states,

Three years after the Civil War ended, on May 5, 1868, the head of an organization of Union veterans—the Grand Army of the Republic (GAR)—established Decoration Day as a time for the nation to decorate graves of the war dead with flowers. Maj. Gen. John A. Logan declared that Decoration Day should be observed on May 30. It is believed that date was chosen because flowers would be in bloom all over the country.[6]

The website continues saying, suspiciously, that the ceremony was centered on the former home of Confederate general Robert E. Lee, an odd choice for a Union celebration, and acknowledges, "springtime tributes to the Civil War dead already had been held in various places" at least two years prior, with "cities in the North and the South claim[ing] to be the birthplace of Memorial Day in 1866." Of all those candidates, for some reason President Lyndon Johnson in 1966, long after the fact, singled out Waterloo, New York, as the original site of Memorial Day.

If some aspects of this official account sound dubious or contradictory, many historians have insisted that the roots of Memorial Day are actually "a mystery or a matter of irresolvable dispute," and as of 2014 Daniel Bellware and Richard Gardiner could assert that "No comprehensive historical analysis of the evidence pertaining to the emergence of the Memorial Day holiday is presently available."[7] Even soon after the birth of Memorial Day, an 1899 newspaper editorial admitted the problem of assigning the practice to "a particular locality, some claiming that it sprang up spontaneously in almost every section of the country at once, while others say it was the women of the south who first went to the graves of their fallen soldiers and placed flowers upon the mounds."[8]

As for the role of Major General Logan and the illustrious GAR, Bellware and Gardiner are adamant that he and they "did *not* originate it" and that Northerners were well aware of that fact.[9] Although the History Channel would have it that Logan proposed a national day of remembrance as early as 1862,[10] Bellware and Gardiner counter that the first explicit suggestion for an annual day of commemoration appeared in a March 1866 letter published in two Columbus, Georgia, newspapers. The letter was authorized by the Ladies Memorial Association of Columbus, Georgia, and authored by Mary Ann Williams, the widow of Confederate Colonel Charles J. Williams. According to the archives of the *Calhoun County Courier*, the letter read in part,

> The ladies are now, and have been for several days, engaged in the sad but pleasant duty of ornamenting and improving that portion of the city cemetery sacred to the memory of our gallant confederate dead . . . Therefore we beg the assistance of the press and the ladies throughout the South to aid us in

the effort to set apart a certain day to be observed, from the
Potomac to the Rio Grande, and be handed down through time
as a religious custom of the South, to wreath the graves of our
martyred dead with flowers, and we propose the 26th day of
April as the day . . . The proud banner under which they rallied
in defense of the holiest and noblest cause for which heroes
fought, or trusting women prayed, has been buried forever. The
country for which they suffered and died has now no name or
place among the nations . . . but the veriest radical that ever
traced his genealogy back to the dock of the Mayflower could
not refuse us the simple privilege of paying honor to those who
died defending the life, honor and happiness of the Southern
women.[11]

Note, in addition to the revisionist history of the Confederacy being
"the holiest and noblest cause" any army had ever fought for (a matter
that Americans are still fighting over in 2017 in regard to Confederate
statues and monuments), that this commemoration was intended for
Southern graves, for the "gallant confederate dead," and not as an
event for the reunited United States of America. In fact, it is probably
not coincidental that the proposed date was also the anniversary of the
surrender of the last Confederate army still in the field, thus bringing
the war to its final close.

Yet, for a remarkable reason, we may still accept this call to commemoration as the first all-American day of memorial, since during that
maiden Memorial Day, "many of the Southern participants graciously
honored both the graves of the Confederate soldiers as well as those of
their former enemies who fought for the Union"; it would be tempting
to dismiss this inclusive claim as retrospective romanticism, but "the
evidence is strong, and this is perhaps the most dramatic and meaningful feature of this entire narrative. This element resulted in the national
embrace of the annual Southern tradition."[12]

As for the place of origin, Bellware and Gardiner insist that the question may not be relevant, as the idea of decorating graves was taken up
in many different towns at roughly the same time, although not always
on the same date—some paying their respects on April 26, others as late

as May 30. For instance, being farther north and therefore having a later spring, Richmond, Virginia (the capital of the old Confederacy), held its first grave-decoration day on May 10, 1866 (which happily for them was also the third anniversary of the death of the great Confederate officer Stonewall Jackson).

Thus contrary to the opinion that Northern general Logan single-handedly invented Memorial Day, even at the time "it was common knowledge that General Logan adopted the South's Memorial Day observance for the entire United States in 1868. The obscurity later associated with the history of the holiday was nonexistent."[13] Nor were

"BUT GRANDPA FOUGHT WITH A SWORD!"

Cartoon from 1919 of a view of Memorial Day, with Civil War and First World War soldiers.

Southerners, or all Northerners, pleased with the appropriation of the practice, a Texas journal criticizing it as "stealing Confederate thunder with a vengeance."[14] Nevertheless, Logan and his organization, the oft-mentioned Grand Army of the Republic, issued their "General Order Number 11" on May 5, 1868, pronouncing May 30 of the same year as a day

> for the purpose of strewing flowers or otherwise decorating the graves of comrades, who died in defense, of their country during the late rebellion, and whose bodies now lie in almost every City, Village, and hamlet, church yard in the land. In this observance, no form of ceremony is prescribed, but Posts and comrades will in their own way arrange such fitting services and testimonials of respect as circumstances may permit.[15]

Marc Leepson told, though, that the GAR was instrumental in having what was until then dubbed Decoration Day renamed to Memorial Day in 1882.[16]

David Blight resurrected another forgotten dimension of the foundation of Memorial Day in writings such as "Decoration Days: The Origins of Memorial Day in North and South" and *Race and Reunion: The Civil War in American Memory*.[17] He passionately insisted that the real roots of the occasion trace back a year before Mrs Williams's letter, to Charleston, South Carolina, where, after the city was largely abandoned by its white residents, "Thousands of black Charlestonians, most former slaves, remained in the city and conducted a series of commemorations to declare their sense of meaning of the war."[18] On a horse-racing track that had been commandeered as an open-air prison for Union prisoners of war, the freed African Americans held a parade on May 1, 1865, carried flowers and wreaths to a mass grave, sang patriotic songs and spirituals, held a picnic, and attended speeches. "The war was over, and Decoration Day had been founded by African Americans in a ritual of remembrance and consecration"—one mostly forgotten, some say suppressed, by later history.

Be that as it may, the rebranded Memorial Day plugged along for some eighty years, although the Department of Veterans Affairs reminds us that the holiday was dedicated specifically to Civil War soldiers until after the First World War, when it was stretched to embrace the casualties of all American wars. As mentioned above, in the midst of another war, this one on distant Asian soil, Lyndon Johnson issued his May 26, 1966, proclamation asking Americans to observe Memorial Day "as a day of prayer for permanent peace and designating a period during each such day when the people of the United States might unite in such supplication" and unexplainably awarding the first Memorial Day to Waterloo, New York. As in the case of Washington's Birthday or Presidents' Day, Memorial Day was moved from May 26 to a Monday (the last Monday in May) in the Uniform Monday Holiday Act of 1968, and because that was not enough, in December 2000 the government passed The National Moment of Remembrance Act and backed it up with the White House Commission on the National Moment of Remembrance, commissioned "to 'encourage the people of the United States to give something back to their country, which provides them so much freedom and opportunity' by encouraging and coordinating commemorations in the United States of Memorial Day and the National Moment of Remembrance."[19]

It is worth noting that, while all Americans are welcomed and urged to acknowledge Memorial Day, nine Southern states will celebrate some variation of Confederate Memorial Day, including Georgia (April 26), Mississippi (the last Monday in April), Alabama (the fourth Monday in April), North and South Carolina (May 10), and Virginia (the last Monday in May). Two states, Louisiana and Tennessee, celebrate Confederate Decoration Day on June 3, and Texas observes Confederate Heroes Day on January 19. Finally, Alabama, Arkansas, Florida, Georgia, Mississippi, and Virginia honor the birthday of Robert E. Lee.

Flag Day

Americans are proud of—some have said obsessed with—their flag, but most are relatively unaware that there is a Flag Day on the political calendar. This is because no high-profile events are held on that day, nor is it a day off from work. Flag Day is not on the congressional list of official federal holidays.

Elks Flag Day Resolution, 1919, banning anarchists, Bolsheviks, unionists, and "who does not give undivided allegiance to our Flag."

We have already told as much of the story as is known of how the flag was invented and how it evolved over time, along with the "cult of the flag" beginning with the Civil War and growing through the late nineteenth and early twentieth centuries. The story of Flag Day is naturally a continuation of the story of the flag, with many of the same players involved in both (and in other traditions too, as with Memorial Day).

It will be recalled that the original Flag Resolution stipulating the stars and stripes was enacted on June 14, 1777. Subsequently, it became an allied tradition to add new stars to the flag, representative of new states, on June 14 following the admission of the state(s); further, the National Flag Code was published on June 14, 1923.

Although June 14 was thus built into certain flag-related customs, the Department of Veterans Affairs stresses that only one instance of anything akin to an actual Flag Day happened within a century of the 1777 Flag Resolution, and that was a local event in Hartford, Connecticut, in 1861.[20] The editor of the *Hartford Evening Press*, Charles Dudley Warner, actually submitted two potential new holidays, Flag Day (June 14, obviously) and Constitution Day (September 17).[21] No action was taken at the time.

Not surprisingly, the impetus for an official Flag Day rose after the Civil War, specifically in the 1880s as part of the wider "flag movement." Most resources credit the holiday portion of the movement to Bernard John Cigrand (or CiGrand), a young teacher in Wisconsin, who assigned an essay on the flag to his students and organized flag-related exercises on June 14, 1885, resulting in what is commonly recognized today as the first Flag Day. (As discussed in Chapter Four, this was the era of designing patriotic activities for schoolchildren, which gave birth to the Pledge of Allegiance.) Cigrand made his first public pitch for an annual flag-based holiday in June 1886 in a Chicago newspaper article,[22] and he became a tireless promoter of the new holiday, composing numerous articles, pamphlets, speeches (he claimed to have given 2,188 talks on the flag and patriotism),[23] and entire books on the flag and historical characters and symbols, such as *Story of the American Flag*, *The Real Abraham Lincoln*, *The Life of Alexander Hamilton*, *Story of the Great Seal of the United States*, and *Story of American Emblems*. He used his later positions as a contributing editor of the *Encyclopedia Americana* and editor of *American Standard* magazine to rally support for a federal law establishing Flag Day.

Interestingly, Leepson claimed that the Grand Army of the Republic at first opposed the idea of Flag Day, competing as it did with Memorial Day in May and Independence Day in July. Nevertheless, a Flag Day ceremony was conducted at the Betsy Ross House in 1891, and at least one local branch of GAR, in Iowa in 1892, joined the Flag Day movement—proposing Washington's birthday of February 22 as the ideal timing. Other patriotic organizations were soon on board, including the Pennsylvania Society of Colonial Dames, who urged the mayor of Philadelphia in 1893 to declare a Flag Day. (Pennsylvania would become the first state to adopt Flag Day as a holiday in 1937, before it was a national holiday.) Slowly, cities and states started holding flag-related ceremonies on June 14, while simultaneously other figures such as George Balch and Francis Bellamy were at work on their own flag celebrations and salutes.

During the presidential campaign of 1896, candidate and victor William McKinley's campaign manager, Mark Hanna, stirred up patriotic fervor by proclaiming a Flag Day—but on October 31 and to opposition from his rival, who condemned the idea as a political stunt (even allegedly tearing down and burning flags at McKinley rallies!). As the twentieth century brought war once again to the United States, President Woodrow Wilson issued a Flag Day proclamation in 1916 but did not establish an official Flag Day holiday. "In 1918," the final year of the First World War, "responding to a plea by the National Security League, a private organization made up primarily of bankers and industrialists, nationwide Flag Day celebrations took place in an effort to boost patriotism."[24] Nor did Calvin Coolidge make the holiday official in his 1927 proclamation. It was only in 1949, after yet another world war, that Harry Truman finally designated Flag Day, June 14, as an annual national tradition. Much more recently, on June 14, 2004, Congress officially recognized Waubeka, Wisconsin, as the birthplace of Flag Day, where a bust of Cigrand honors the tradition's greatest agent.

Veterans Day

Although Americans take the occasion of Veterans Day to remember and honor living and dead veterans of all American wars, the event was originally intended specifically to recognize the end of the First World War in 1918 and therefore could not have a history older than that date. The First World War, at the time dubbed the Great War or, more hopefully, "the war to end all wars," erupted in southern Europe in 1914 and did not drag in the United States until 1917. The conflagration ended indecisively with an armistice or ceasefire (rather than a surrender by any party) on November 11, scheduled to take effect at 11 a.m. on that day (the eleventh hour of the eleventh day of the eleventh month). A peace treaty, the Treaty of Versailles, was not signed until a year later, the harsh terms of which contributed to the German resentment that would lead to a second world war.

According to the United States Army's website on Veterans Day, President Wilson proclaimed the first Armistice Day in 1919 with these words:

> To us in America, the reflections of Armistice Day will be filled with solemn pride in the heroism of those who died in the country's service and with gratitude for the victory, both because of the thing from which it has freed us and because of the opportunity it has given America to show her sympathy with peace and justice in the councils of the nations.[25]

Wilson's vision was a two-minute period of silence at eleven o'clock in the morning accompanied by parades and public events. Two years later, in 1921, an anonymous soldier from the war was interred at Arlington National Cemetery, establishing the Tomb of the Unknown Soldier, mentioned at the outset of the chapter.

It was only in 1926 that Congress officially labeled November 11 "Armistice Day," acknowledging that 27 states had already created a legal holiday on the occasion and requesting the President to order all government buildings to fly the flag and all Americans "to observe the day in schools and churches, or other suitable places, with appropriate ceremonies of friendly relations with all other peoples." Armistice Day was still not quite a federal holiday, until a congressional Act on May 13, 1938, founded it legally by that name. The u.s. Department of Veterans Affairs explains that Armistice Day "was primarily a day set aside to honor veterans of World War I," but after two more wars and many more casualties, the tradition's name was changed to Veterans Day in 1954 by Public Law 380, signed by President Eisenhower.[26] On October 8, 1954, Eisenhower made his Veterans Day Proclamation, instructing that Veterans Day was an anniversary for "all veterans, all veterans' organizations, and the entire citizenry."

Veterans Day is another federal holiday that was moved to Monday in the 1968 Uniform Monday Holiday Act. However, veterans and their associations were displeased with the change, and, in fact, several states over the next few years drifted back to a permanent November 11 observance. Bowing to public pressure, in 1975 President Gerald Ford restored Veterans Day to its original date, effective in 1978. Even so, if November 11 happens to fall on a Saturday, the holiday is marked on the previous Friday, and if it falls on a Sunday, then it is observed on the following Monday. Part of the ceremony entails the laying of a wreath at the Tomb of the Unknown Soldier.

Other patriotic holidays fill the calendar in the United States, most prominently Independence Day or the Fourth of July (which was the date in 1776 that the U.S. *declared* its independence, not the day or year when independence was actually achieved, which occurred with the signing of the Treaty of Paris on September 3, 1783, giving this subsequent date a justifiable claim as the real American independence day) but also the little-noted Constitution Day, the anniversary of the signing of the U.S. Constitution on September 17, 1787. The American people can and will continue to add and modify holidays as further historical events and figures merit. Some current and recent suggestions for holidays, honoring other worthy individuals or constituencies in America, include Cesar Chavez Day (last Monday in March), Susan B. Anthony Day (third Monday in February), Malcolm X Day (third Monday in May), which became an actual holiday in Illinois in 2015, and Native Americans' Day (third Monday in September). A couple of former holidays, specifically Victory Day (in recognition of the end of the Second World War) and The Eighth (celebrating the Battle of New Orleans on January 8, 1815, which ended the War of 1812), have meanwhile been expunged from the calendar. But no matter when and for what reason, patriotic holidays will continue, in the words of Dwight Eisenhower, to "renew our conviction of individual responsibility to live in ways that support the eternal truths upon which our Nation is founded, and from which flows all its strength and all its greatness."[27]

EIGHT

We Are the World:
Ethnic American Holidays

★ ★ ★

The United States is an immigrant society, even if, as previous chapters have illustrated, it often struggled with and against this fact (and continues to do so). But despite—or because of—America's inherent ambivalence about cultural and racial diversity, immigration has been a particularly productive force for traditioning. On the one hand, as has been abundantly clear, the invention and promotion of traditions in the late 1800s and early 1900s was closely linked to assimilation and "Americanization" of immigrant populations. On the other hand, dislocation of the immigrants themselves from their homelands and the friction caused by coexistence with the WASP majority and with other minorities contributed to an intensified communal identity and to acts of traditioning on the part of the immigrants themselves.

Immigrants, of course, brought many traditions with them to American shores, but they also invented traditions in America that are distinctly American because they did not exist in the same form—or did not exist at all—before their arrival. Here are two such whimsical examples: Chinese meals did not traditionally end with a "fortune cookie" (in fact, most sources suggest that fortune cookies are probably based on a Japanese cracker called *senbei* and were popularized in San Francisco in the early twentieth century), nor do Mexican meals always start with chips and salsa. Both of these practices are Americanizations of "traditional" foreign cuisines; indeed, much of the standard menu of Chinese and Mexican (and other ethnic) restaurants is Americanization of ethnic dishes, if not made up altogether to suit American tastes. In an especially amusing yet telling case from outside the U.S. of how ethnic items get reinterpreted and reintroduced into a culture, Yuson Jong tells that Chinese food has been welcomed into contemporary Bulgaria precisely because it is valued as a *Western* food choice, something that modern middle-class Americans and Europeans eat.[1]

In this chapter, we will focus on ethnic holidays that are not only *in* America, but, like fortune cookies or chips and salsa, *of* America. These are occasions that were conceived or elaborated in the United States and which, in some instances, flowed *back to* the ethnic homeland thereafter. And while the celebrations may refer to a foreign country, the events were as much about the immigrant experience in America as about the pre-migration land and culture and were often a message to the wider American society. Finally, while the celebrations may have originally been for the immigrant community itself, in most of the cases discussed here, many, if not most, Americans have embraced the holiday as their own, if not as thoroughly American. After all, don't they say that on St Patrick's Day everyone is Irish?

St Patrick's Day

The perfect place to start, then, is St Patrick's Day, which is arguably the granddaddy of ethnic American holidays. St Patrick's Day, as the name announces, was initially one of many saint's days on the Catholic liturgical calendar. As Mike Cronin and Daryl Adair, who drafted a most complete history of the holiday, wrote,

> Like other saints' days and national anniversaries, the evolution of 17 March as a special day can be understood as an "invented tradition" with a particular starting point, the evolution of distinct patterns of observance, and their annual repetition . . . St Patrick's Day was not only invented in Ireland; it was (re) discovered and shaped anew among the diaspora abroad.[2]

St Patrick's Day was indeed recognized in Ireland long before the nineteenth century—but not in anything like its current form. Nor was it particularly special in its native land: besides being only one of dozens of annual saint's days, it was merely one of a multitude of holiday customs in the country—both Christian and pre-Christian—with no pre-eminence among them.[3]

Obviously, St Patrick's Day is dedicated to a Catholic saint named Patrick, but despite Philip Freeman's biography of the man, much of Patrick's life is wrapped in obscurity and legend.[4] Sources tend to agree that Patrick, or Patricius, was a real person, born in Roman Britain in perhaps Wales or Scotland—but almost certainly not in Ireland—and originally named Maewyn Succat (and St Maewyn Succat's Day just does not have the same ring to it). His birth is typically ascribed to the early 400s or late 300s, although religious historian Josiah Cox Russell argued in a 1956 essay that two different Patricks—one in the fifth century CE and one in the third century—are confused with each other.[5] Patrick did eventually missionize Ireland for Catholicism, although he was neither the first nor the last proselytizer, and his death date is recorded as March 17. He may well have used a shamrock to demonstrate the principle of the trinity, but the legend of chasing the snakes out of Ireland is dubious, since sources concur that there were never snakes on the island.

Although the legend-building around St Patrick commenced within a couple of centuries of his death—Cronin and Adair explained that a scribe in the late 600s wrote a life of Patrick that "ensured that the [saint's] cult was elevated to that of a 'national' apostle'"[6]—a "feast of St Patrick" was apparently not placed on the Roman Church calendar until a thousand years later, in 1631. By 1681 an English visitor named Thomas Dineley recorded a series of St Patrick's Day practices which, in one form or another, became standard markers for those celebrating the day. Dineley observed that the Irish wore Celtic crosses, had green ribbons in their hats, pinned shamrocks to their clothes, and, after demanding St Patrick's groat [alcohol] from their master, drank so that "very few of the zealous are found sober at night."[7]

Such Irish religious revelry naturally traveled with Irishmen as they settled in the Western Hemisphere, and one of the early historians of the holiday, John Crimmins, asserted in a 1902 book that the first organized St Patrick's Day celebration in the American colonies occurred in

1737.[8] Such festivities tended to include an evening feast with toasts and speeches. The parade tradition, which we today associate with the celebration (see below), was slower to evolve, with early occurrences in New York in 1762 or 1766, depending on the source, and Boston in 1775. So the first century of St Patrick's Day in America was mostly an indoor affair, sponsored by Irish fraternal and charitable organizations such as the Sons of St Patrick.[9]

One essential fact for understanding the development of St Patrick's Day is the immigration history of Irish to the U.S. Contrary to assumptions, Irish immigrants did not all arrive after the potato famine of 1845–60, nor were the first generations all poor or even Catholic. Instead, as Kenneth Moss contended in his history of the crucial formative period of St Patrick's Day, before the mid-1800s "the Irish community in America was small, relatively wealthy, and dominated by merchants of both Catholic and Protestant extraction."[10] At this stage, Irish celebrations in America, in the same way as Irish identity in America, were not overtly nationalistic or Catholic, and St Patrick's Day was typical. The basically middle- and upper-class Irish held their respectable evening banquets, often in the company of British and Yankee Protestants, complete with "toasts hailing the memory of Ireland, Irish unity, and the glory of the United States."[11] For instance, in her study of St Patrick's Day in Lowell, Massachusetts, Sallie Marston asserted that the Hibernian Moralizing and Relief Society was founded in 1833, which, renamed in 1836 as the Irish Benevolent Society (IBS), "played an important political role in the wider Irish community particularly by way of its adoption of an accommodative stance toward Yankee values and expectations."[12] The IBS kept a tight rein on St Patrick's Day activities in the city for almost thirty years, "with their solemn, respectable processions and their inordinately patriotic banquets," distinguished by toasts and speeches lauding "the local government officials, the local corporations, the cause of temperance, the friendship of native [i.e., native-born Anglo] Americans, and the benefits of living under a republican form of government."[13]

It was only with the new wave of Irish immigrants—poorer, more desperate, and more Catholic—that the Irish American community, and with it their traditions, began to transform. The result was, in Moss's words, a "sea-change," in which "the old Anglo-Irish character of the pre-Famine enclave was wholly eclipsed by an emerging Irish Catholic nationalism."[14] Consequently, St Patrick's Day in America became what Moss characterized as a "memory-site," where "the majority of Irish Americans, for whatever reason, came to believe that the ceremonies of the day could and should serve as reflections of Irish memory and culture, even—perhaps especially—when they disagreed over what form these ought to take."[15]

One of the most visible and lasting changes to St Patrick's Day was the growth of its associated parade. As Susan Davis has contended, the mid- to late nineteenth century was the great era of parades, which were a common type of street theater well suited to the dense urban centers of the period.[16] Unsurprisingly, Moss concluded that during the 1850s and 1860s "the St Patrick's Day Parade became the undisputed centerpiece of St Patrick's Day festivities," unseating the more patrician evening banquet.[17] Reportedly the first modern St Patrick's Day Parade was held in Boston in 1841, and pageants in Boston and New York remained comparatively small and insignificant through the 1840s.

The parade tradition took off as—and partly because—middle-class associations such as Lowell's IBS started to lose their grip on the holiday; one sign was the organization's willingness to permit the Young Men's Catholic Library Association to march in the parade.[18] As more clubs and organizations joined the event, the parades not only got larger but shifted in character: in Lowell, processions of two hundred grew into marches of more than one thousand (with 40,000 taking part in the 1870 New York City parade by some accounts), while an increasing number of militantly nationalist and exclusively Catholic organizations marched in the streets, with names like "Erin's Guard" and "Irish Rifles." The parades were an embodiment of Irish pride and defiance of English rule of their homeland, but they were also a display intended for an American audience: "the parades presented the Irish community as a social and political force to be reckoned with," promoting at once "an image of respectability" and of "community solidarity and strength"[19] and "the development of a full-fledged Irish American identity which involved the reworking of the multiple immigrant identities in nationalist terms."[20]

That St Patrick's Day with its dramatic parade was an *Irish American* tradition rather than an Irish one is signaled by Cronin and Adair's

St Patrick's Day gathering in Cleveland, Ohio, 2012.

observation that in the 1860s many Irish in Ireland began to feel that there should be an organized festival for the occasion in their own country.

> In 1869 a National Anniversary Celebration Committee was formed to organize a grand celebration of St Patrick's Day in Dublin. The Committee, and the resultant celebration in 1870, were a product of the city's trade guilds . . . The Committee had a twofold objective: to encourage a decidedly "Irish" form of festivity on St Patrick's Day, and to promote dignified behavior among those who commemorated 17 March.[21]

However, this effort to institutionalize St Patrick's Day in the American style was not immediately successful:

> Instead, St Patrick's Day reverted to a more traditional pattern of loosely organized spectacle, disparate events and localized custom. Over the next three decades St Patrick's Day was never again established as a major public event in Ireland. It was unquestionably an important religious day, and for many had also become a day free from work, but Patrician observance

did not become, as it had in North America and Australia, a day
for street parades and ostentatious public celebration.[22]

In its true home, the United States, St Patrick's Day as we know it
caught on in the 1860s, with several states holding parades and related
events, although their popularity did lag somewhat in the 1880s. They
were revived and became fixtures in the 1890s through the initiative of
organizations such as the Knights of St Patrick and the Irish American
Society, which were expressly formed for the purpose of coordinating
"elaborate and impressive St Patrick's Day banquets."[23] The Second
World War and city politics in places with large Irish American populations such as Chicago gave further energy to the tradition; Chicago's
iconic mayor Richard Daley promoted the St Patrick's Day Parade as a
major civic occasion, and television after the 1950s brought St Patrick's
Day into the homes of more Americans—with Ed Sullivan leading a
1955 parade.

As the trade guilds in Ireland had done, so too has commerce driven
St Patrick's Day (and many other traditions, as we have seen, from
Thanksgiving to Mother's Day) in the United States, and "plastic green
hats, green-colored beer, cheap souvenirs and gaudy marketing have
been part and parcel of America's St Patrick's Day experience for most
of the twentieth century."[24] Two of the most notable traditions are green
beer and corned beef and cabbage—the latter of which, according to the
History Channel, is an Irish dish that only recently became connected
to St Patrick's Day. Simultaneously, the religious or even specifically
Irish quality of the day has evaporated for the reportedly 39 percent
of Americans who celebrate St Patrick's Day in some form or another,
mostly by wearing green, which few Americans know or care is the color
of Irish *Catholics*, not Irish *Protestants* (who use the color orange).

Columbus Day

Despite the concerning propensity for drunken partying, who doesn't
love St Patrick's Day? Columbus Day, while much more central to the
history of America or at least the Western Hemisphere, is a considerably
more controversial and contested matter. No one to my knowledge has

tried to disrupt a St Patrick's Day parade—if anything, the greatest disruption to the tradition was the demand for inclusion by gay and lesbian groups, which was only achieved for the first time in Boston in 2015 with the welcome of OutVets, an LGBT veterans' organization—but protests have frequently sought to shut down Columbus Day celebrations and parades, if not to end the observance completely.

As every American schoolchild is taught, "In fourteen hundred ninety-two, Columbus sailed the ocean blue." Fewer people remember or ever learned that Columbus's voyages were a moment in a vast geopolitical struggle, essentially between the West and Islam. As David Boyle stresses in his *Toward the Setting Sun: Columbus, Cabot, Vespucci, and the Race for America*, the proximate motivation for his (and others') journeys was the fall of the ancient capital of the Eastern Roman Empire, Constantinople, to the Turks in 1453, cutting off the eastern overland trade routes to Asia.[25] Directly related to the fact that it was Spain that sponsored the first successful westward exploration was the completion of the *Reconquista*, the defeat of the Muslim Moors in the Iberian Peninsula, who had ruled at least parts of present-day Spain for seven hundred years.

With that conquering vitality suddenly liberated, and with visions of great wealth from a monopoly of trade by "sailing west to reach the east," the Spanish crown financed Christopher Columbus (1451–1506), an Italian from Genoa, to captain a small fleet across the Atlantic Ocean. Contrary to popular belief today, it was fairly widely recognized in the 1400s that the earth is round, although its size was vastly underestimated; no Europeans knew that there were continents to the west between Europe and Asia—which is why Columbus assumed that he had reached "India" and gave the inhabitants of the Americas the fateful name "Indians" (one of the more unfortunate American traditions). At any rate, Columbus's crew (whether it was Columbus himself or one of his sailors is a matter of debate) first sighted land on October 12, 1492, specifically one of the islands of the Bahamas (possibly San Salvador, Samana Cay, or Grand Turk Island). Sailing on, his fleet landed on Cuba in late October, and then stepped onto what they called La Española (Hispaniola), today's location of Haiti and the Dominican Republic, in early December. Columbus left a company of men to form a settlement called La Navidad and set off for Europe in mid-January, arriving at Lisbon, Portugal, on March 4.

What happened on that voyage—and before and after—is hotly contested. One thing is sure: Columbus never set foot, during this maiden voyage nor in the subsequent three trips he made, on soil that would someday be the United States. Whether he was even the first European to "discover" the Americas is questionable: it is reasonably certain that Norsemen under Leif Erikson visited the northern shores of North America five hundred years before, although without founding lasting colonies, and there is good evidence that fishermen from England were trawling the Canadian coast for cod by 1482, if not earlier. (Of course, there are indications, too, that non-Europeans may have reached the western shores long before.) In the midst of Columbus's four journeys to the Caribbean and South America (1492, 1493, 1498, and 1502), John Cabot—another Italian, born Giovanni Caboto in Genoa and a colleague of Columbus, according to Boyle—who sailed for England, made landfall in 1497 in North America somewhere along the Newfoundland, Labrador, or Maine coast. A short time later, in 1513, Ponce de León touched the southern coast of what he christened La Florida. Yet none of these men left their name on the new continents; that honor fell to Amerigo Vespucci, a version of whose personal name—America—was inscribed on the famous early map by Martin Waldseemüller.

Given Columbus's rather small role in the history of the Americas—and lack of *any* role in the history of North America and the United States of America—Lakshmi Gandhi poses the reasonable question, "So why Columbus Day?" instead of "Cabot Day," "Bristol Fishermen Day," "Vespucci Day," or even "Leif Erikson Day"?[26] (Actually, there is a minor holiday called Leif Erikson Day in the U.S., designated as October 9.) During the first century of English colonization of the Americas, Columbus was mostly irrelevant, if not anathema: Spain was, after all, a major rival of England in the colonial enterprise, likely to gain little respect from English settlers. English North America had its own intrepid heroes, such as the Pilgrims and Puritans of New England, who are celebrated at Thanksgiving. It was only in the late eighteenth century, after independence and therefore maybe as an insult to the former British colonial master, that Columbus began to attract attention. The first

Columbus Day celebration was reportedly held in 1792 in New York, on the 300th anniversary of his original voyage. As noted in Chapter One, the United States in this era commonly even referred to itself as Columbia and named its new capital region the District of Columbia.

The lore of Christopher Columbus was greatly advanced by Washington Irving's 1828 *A History of the Life and Voyages of Christopher Columbus*, a "highly fictionalized" chronicle of the navigator and "the source of much of the glorification and myth-making related to Columbus today,"[27] But, as with St Patrick's Day, the evolution and institutionalization of Columbus Day in America had very much to do with immigration and the contrary forces of ethnic pride and Americanization. Americanization took the front seat initially: recall from prior chapters that much of the impetus for popular flag displays and salutes was oriented towards Columbus Day 1892, fatefully the 400th anniversary of his arrival. Indeed, Bellamy composed the Pledge of Allegiance as part of a program for Columbus Day—or what was then known as Discovery Day and scheduled for October 21, not October 12. On the occasion, President Benjamin Harrison issued a proclamation (shortly after eleven Italians were lynched in New Orleans) of Columbus Day, which "directly linked the legacy of Columbus to American patriotism, with the proclamation celebrating the hard work of the American people and Columbus equally" but with "no real references to Columbus' life, work, or nationality."[28] Rather, in Harrison's words, the day was set aside for Americans to "express honor to the discoverer and their appreciation of the great achievements of the four completed centuries of American life"—although there had not, to that point, been four centuries of United States of American life.

In an interesting defense of Columbus Day, William J. Connell argues that the idea, "lost on present-day critics of the holiday, was that this would be a national holiday that would be special for recognizing both Native Americans, who were here before Columbus, and the many immigrants—including Italians—who were just then coming to this country in astounding numbers."[29] As proof, he offers the following account of the first Columbus Day Parade in New York in 1892:

> It consisted mostly of about 12,000 public school students grouped into 20 regiments, each commanded by a principal.

The boys marched in school uniforms or their Sunday best, while the girls, dressed in red, white and blue, sat in bleachers. Alongside the public schoolers there were military drill squads and 29 marching bands, each of 30 to 50 instruments. After the public schools, there followed 5,500 students from the Catholic schools. Then there were students from the private schools wearing school uniforms. These included the Hebrew Orphan Asylum, the Barnard School Military Corps, and the Italian and American Colonial School. The Dante Alighieri Italian College of Astoria was dressed entirely in sailor outfits. These were followed by the Native American marching band from the Carlisle Indian School in Pennsylvania.

Of course, despite the title of Connell's essay ("What Columbus Day Really Means"), traditions and symbols do not "really" mean anything but instead have different meanings for different people. Italian Americans were quick to embrace Columbus Day, Native Americans not so. As in the case of St Patrick's Day for Irish Americans, "many in the community saw celebrating the life and accomplishments of Christopher Columbus as a way for Italian Americans to be accepted by the mainstream."[30] Indeed, historian Christopher Kauffman saw Columbus playing exactly the same role for Italian immigrants as Patrick for Irish: "Italian Americans grounded legitimacy in a pluralistic society by focusing on the Genoese explorer as a central figure in their sense of peoplehood."[31]

The institutionalization of Columbus Day proceeded apace, with Colorado the first state to make it an official holiday in 1906, partly due to the efforts of the Italian American newspaper man Angelo Noce. Within five years, fourteen more states had joined the celebration. Columbus Day was apparently not without competition, though, as President Calvin Coolidge spoke in 1925 in favor of Leif Erikson as the discoverer of America, and in 1930 Wisconsin, a state with a large population of Scandinavian immigrants, founded Leif Erikson Day. But with the support of the Catholic organization the Knights of Columbus, Columbus Day was made an official federal holiday in 1934, although it was one of the holidays moved to a Monday in the Uniform Monday Holiday Act of 1968.

Indigenous Peoples Day celebration, Seattle, Washington, 2016.

As for Native Americans, many of them do not perceive the honor
in Columbus Day that proponents such as Connell allege was intended.
Some U.S. states with particularly large indigenous populations—South
Dakota, Alaska, and Hawaii—do not participate at all. South Dakota
went so far as to declare Native American Day in 1990, and the famously
liberal city of Berkeley, California, announced in 1992 that Columbus
Day would be observed as Indigenous Peoples Day; Los Angeles made
the same shift only recently, on August 30, 2017.

In 1994, in the birthplace of modern Columbus Day—Denver,
Colorado—the politically activist American Indian Movement (AIM) published a notice in the *Rocky Mountain News* titled "Goodbye Columbus!"
in which they asserted, "From a Native perspective, Columbus' arrival
was a disaster from the beginning":

> Although his own diaries reveal that he was greeted by the
> Tainos with the most generous hospitality he had ever known,
> he immediately began the enslavement and slaughter of the
> Indian peoples of the Caribbean . . .
>
> Columbus Day is a perpetuation of racist assumptions that
> the Americas were a wasteland cluttered with dark skin savages
> awaiting the blessings of European "civilization" . . .
>
> To dignify Columbus and his legacy with parades, holidays,
> and other celebrations is repugnant. As the original peoples of

this land, we cannot, and we will not, tolerate social political festivities that celebrate our genocide. We are committed to the active, open, and public rejection of disrespect and racism in its various forms—including Columbus Day and Columbus Day parades.[32]

Since then, AIM and other Native groups have periodically protested Columbus Day, held their own parades or events and/or tried to disrupt the official events, and attempted to sway public opinion to "rethink Columbus Day." The result has often been to pit one minority's pride against another's.

Cinco de Mayo

In Denver, Colorado, where I live, there are three major annual street festivals—the People's Fair (early June), which began as a neighborhood craft fair; the Taste of Colorado (Labor Day weekend), which is a celebration of local restaurants; and Cinco de Mayo (the weekend closest to May 5). In its place of birth, Mexico, Cinco de Mayo is a relatively small affair.

Cinco de Mayo (Spanish for "Fifth of May") is a commemoration of a historic event in Mexico, but that does not make it a "Mexican holiday." Indeed, David Hayes-Bautista, who has written one of the most comprehensive histories of the day, asserts,

If Cinco de Mayo were primarily a Mexican holiday, then the U.S. version ought to be a pale imitation of the Mexican original, yet it is the other way around. This fact provides the key. Although the holiday celebrates a Mexican victory over the French at Puebla on May 5, 1862, the answer to the question is not to be found in Mexico. It is found instead in California, Nevada, and Oregon during the Gold Rush and the American Civil War—for the Cinco de Mayo is not, in its origins, a Mexican holiday at all but rather an American one, created by Latinos in California in the middle of the nineteenth century.[33]

Fundamentally, separating an "American" tradition from a "Mexican" tradition in this case is problematic because, until 1848, a chunk of the western United States was Mexico. The United States annexed Texas in 1845 (after the defeat at the Battle of the Alamo), and the two countries went to war in 1846, culminating in the U.S. invasion of its southern neighbor and the occupation of Mexico City. In the 1848 Treaty of Guadalupe Hidalgo, Mexico ceded territory to the U.S. that would become California, Nevada, Utah, most of Arizona, and parts of Colorado and New Mexico. In this way, many Mexicans suddenly and involuntarily became Mexican Americans.

The U.S. is thus indirectly implicated in the origin of Cinco de Mayo. Joanna Kaftan instructs that the expenses of the Mexican–American War drove Mexico to withhold its debt payments to England, Spain, and France, and the three countries sent soldiers to punish the country.[34] While the English and Spanish withdrew, France sent a force towards the capital city, which was intercepted and defeated by a much smaller and poorly equipped Mexican contingent at the Battle of Puebla on May 5, 1862. Within days, Mexicans in Mexico and north of the border were cheering the unlikely win. It is overlooked that the next year, France successfully conquered Puebla and Mexico City. "Despite the ultimate victory of the French at Puebla," Kaftan writes, "the victory and courage of the Mexican resistance at the first battle of Puebla are celebrated during Cinco de Mayo. The idea of overcoming insurmountable odds may be especially salient and appealing to Mexican Americans"[35]—even if the triumph was temporary.

As appealing as the narrative might be, the Battle of Puebla and its attendant holiday are relatively minor subjects in Mexico, and Cinco de Mayo has historically been at most a regional holiday in the vicinity of Puebla. The fifth of May is *not* Mexican independence day, as many Americans assume, as Mexico had been independent since 1821, issuing its own Declaration of Independence from Spain on September 28 of that year. Curiously, though, Mexicans generally recognize September 16 as their independence day, commemorating the so-called *Grito de Dolores* ("Cry of Dolores") in 1810, which inspired the independence struggle. (Remember that "independence day" in the United States is also not the actual date on which independence was achieved but rather the date on which it was "declared.")

So, as Hayes-Bautista notes, the story of Cinco de Mayo as a holiday is really an American story and a typically murky one at that. The commander of Mexican forces at the original battle, Ignacio Zaragoza, was born in what is today Goliad, Texas, and that town was claimed in 1999 as the site of the first Cinco de Mayo celebration. Hayes-Bautista, on the other hand, focuses on the development of the holiday in southern California, where Cinco de Mayo was commemorated in Los Angeles at least from 1877. He describes a flag-raising (of both Mexican and American flags), an artillery salute, patriotic songs, and speeches on the occasion. A junta or committee of first-generation Mexican Americans and veterans of their great war (which he refers to as "the French Intervention") kept the memory of the victory alive, not unlike the Grand Army of the Republic in the United States. However, later immigrants and descendants of the first generation did not remember Cinco de Mayo in the same way, if at all. He reports that a new organization, the Sociedad Hispano-Americana, was formed in the early twentieth century "to better institutionalize the public memories they had been shaping," usurping what Hayes-Bautista aptly terms the "summoning power" of the older committee.[36]

Accordingly, Cinco de Mayo soon became entangled in the experiences and struggles of the growing and evolving Mexican American community. By the 1940s and the outbreak of the Second World War, "the celebration of the Cinco de Mayo seemed too important to leave in the hands of independent community organizations. Its summoning power could be harnessed to assist the war effort," and the mayor of Los Angeles, along with the governor of California—neither of them Hispanic—took an interest in promoting the holiday to emphasize the shared commitment of the two countries to defend democracy.[37] But if anything, the 1960s were even more formative of the holiday, as Mexican immigration accelerated and the farm workers' movement of Cesar Chavez and the wider Chicano movements emerged. This new generation and its cultural and political issues also challenged previous definitions of and ways of celebrating the Cinco de Mayo. A 1970 event at the University of California, Irvine, was described as "a five-day

Cinco de Mayo celebration, Washington, DC, 2015.

program by Mexican-American students at UC Irvine on trends and problems of Chicanos in California."[38]

Yet many Mexican Americans in the southwest were unfamiliar with the holiday through the 1940s and 1950s, and in a 1998 study Alvar Carlson found that in the 1960s

> only a few Cinco de Mayo festivals could be found in the United States, entirely in the American Southwest including California. Their numbers did not increase substantially and geographically until the 1980s when they became significant enough to be included in the lists of festivals as well as in the tourism literature of not only southwestern states, but also that of several other states. Today, the country's more than 120 Cinco de Mayo festivals can be found in at least 21 states.[39]

Local and state governments along with private ethnic organizations were crucial in promoting the day, but Carlson also stressed the role of the media—especially Spanish-language radio—and of course corporations. He revealed how Anheuser-Busch, the giant beer company, sponsored two hundred Cinco de Mayo events (whether out of a love of Mexican culture or a desire to sell beer, the reader may speculate), and other businesses from Miller Brewing to Pepsi-Cola, and RJR Tobacco to the California Lottery got in on the act.

At the turn of the century, Cinco de Mayo was still a mostly south-western American holiday, with two-thirds of festivities held in the four states of Arizona, California, New Mexico, and Texas; nevertheless, Carlson identified 36 celebrations in seventeen other states—and half as many Cinco de Mayo festivals as St Patrick's Day parades.[40] And while Cinco de Mayo certainly expresses Mexican historical and cultural pride, the occasion is already showing a pan-Hispanic appeal, with Cuban Americans, Puerto Ricans, and other Latinos not only participating in but identifying with the tradition. That the fiesta is catching on with the wider American public is evinced by the fact that some 400,000 people attend the two-day fair in Denver, with 300,000 enjoying the Portland, Oregon, event and 200,000 showing up for Chicago's version; Cinco de Mayo weekend 2014 was apparently among the top five holidays in America for consuming alcohol,[41] and in Denver, in addition to the downtown festival, Latino cars—customized "low-riders" with Mexican flags and other symbols, occupied by Mexican revelers—cruise Federal Boulevard.

Cinco de Mayo has attained such acceptance that President George W. Bush actually held a celebration at the White House in 2005. But with this mainstreaming of the ostensibly Mexican holiday has come criticism that it is being watered down and corrupted. Carlson passed along the complaint that the historic day has morphed into "a tamale-and-cerveza version of St Patrick's Day" and a party for gringos as much as, if not more than, for Chicanos.[42] But that only goes to prove that Cinco de Mayo "is a genuine American holiday":

Far from being foreign or un-American, it originated in a devoted adherence to the basic American political values [of freedom and democracy, and the little guy triumphing against great odds] by the majority of Latinos in the United States . . . It should be remembered that from the beginning, Cinco de Mayo parades have flown the United States and Mexican flags side by side as symbolic of this fact. That tradition is still followed today, although the reasons are largely forgotten.[43]

Kwanzaa

Kwanzaa is by far the newest of the holiday traditions discussed in this chapter, invented—quite overtly—only in 1966. It is also different, according to Keith Mayes, one of the main analysts of the holiday, because it is part not only of a parallel and largely unheralded African American holiday calendar but an intentional counter-tradition or even anti-tradition to the mainstream American holiday system.[44]

To understand Kwanzaa and the history of black holidays, it is necessary to go back more than a century, to a speech given by Frederick Douglass in 1852. Douglass was one of the most celebrated and articulate of the freed slaves and abolitionists, and on the occasion of Independence Day 1852 he gave a memorable talk titled "What to the Slave is the Fourth of July?" Noting the irony that Africans in the U.S. were far from independent, he said, in part,

What have I, or those I represent, to do with your national independence? . . . I say it with a sad sense of the disparity between us. I am not included within the pale of this glorious anniversary! Your high independence only reveals the immeasurable distance between us. The blessings in which you, this day, rejoice, are not enjoyed in common. The rich inheritance of justice, liberty, prosperity and independence, bequeathed by your fathers, is shared by you, not by me . . . This Fourth [of] July is yours, not mine. You may rejoice, I must mourn. To drag a man in fetters into the grand illuminated temple of liberty, and call upon him to join you in joyous anthems, were inhuman mockery and sacrilegious irony.[45]

Like many other non-whites in America then and since, Douglass felt that American holidays, and America itself, fundamentally excluded them, if not celebrated events (such as Columbus Day) that directly contributed to their oppression. Indeed, we can agree with Mayes that the holidays that were created and promulgated between the Civil War and the Second World War, most notably the ones presented in this chapter, were projects aimed at integrating mostly white (Irish and Italian) ethnics into mainstream society and at "quieting old disputes and erasing sectional, white ethnic, religious and class rifts."[46]

None of the official American holidays spoke to African American identity or interest, and until Martin Luther King, Jr Day (established in 1983), none explicitly honored an African American individual. Thus, as in many other areas of life such as religion, music, and food, African Americans created their own parallel culture, including "an entire black holiday tradition [that] can be seen as an alternative tradition to mainstream American observances."[47] Among these were various versions of Freedom Day, recognizing for instance the end of the slave trade on January 1, 1808, or the signing or enactment of the Emancipation Proclamation (September 22, 1862, and January 1, 1863, respectively). In present-day Denver, one of the most prominent African American festivities is Juneteenth, commemorating the freeing of the slaves of Texas on June 19, 1865, by order (General Order Number 3) of Union general Gordon Granger. Subsequently, Juneteenth became something of an "independence day" for American blacks, and in 1980 Texas adopted it as an official state holiday.

Nevertheless, the segregation and repression of African Americans persisted and was institutionalized (and legitimized by the highest law of the land) throughout the late nineteenth and early twentieth centuries. One of the first efforts to recognize African American contributions to the republic was Carter G. Woodson's proposal for a Negro History Week in 1926. Designated as a week in February because both Lincoln's and Douglass's birthdays fell in that month, it has been argued that "Woodson was up to something more than building on tradition. Without saying so, he aimed to reform it from the study of two great men to a great race."[48] Even then, promoters of black rights and consciousness such as Woodson appreciated the political power of calendars and annual events for changing society. Half a century later, during America's bicentennial year of 1976, Negro History Week was renamed and expanded to Black History Month.

Mayes reasonably contends that Kwanzaa is another practice of reforming through study and ritual, set in the more recent context of the civil rights struggle and especially the Black Power movement. Maulana Karenga, the founder of Kwanzaa, was active in this movement. Born Ronald McKinley Everett in 1941, in the late 1950s or early 1960s he was attracted to Black Power or black nationalist ideology, changing his name first to Ron Karenga, and then adding the title "Maulana" (Swahili for "great teacher") before adopting the name Maulana Karenga. In 1965 he started a group called US (not to be confused with the abbreviation for United States but rather "us" as in "not-them") as an organization by and for African Americans, to recover their African identity and culture.

> Inspired by the continent of Africa, US's organization structure, the oath, rules, African attire, and name changes of members from English to Swahili were all preparatory for the coming cultural revolution. US promoted the idea of returning to what its leader and members saw as the source of cultural blackness.[49]

A crucial element of Karenga's cultural revolution was the creation of separate black holidays with ties to Africa. In 1966 Karenga introduced Kwanzaa as a black alternative to—in fact, a substitute for—Christmas, which he condemned as white and racist. But Kwanzaa was only one piece of a greater philosophy that he called Kawaida, Swahili for "custom" or "tradition," with its Seven Criteria of Culture (mythology, history, social organization, economic organization, political organization, creative motif, and ethos), Three Ends of Black Power, Four Areas of Political Power, and Six Character Types of White Liberals, among other doctrines. But, as Karenga fully understood in his own 2008 book *Kwanzaa: A Celebration of Family, Community and Culture*, Kawaida and its building blocks such as Kwanzaa were invented traditions, borrowing freely from Africa while also reinterpreting those practices and sometimes devising them for a local African American audience.[50]

Kwanzaa was Karenga's most widely accepted innovation. The name derives from the Swahili term *matunda ya kwanza* or "first fruits," *kwanza* literally meaning "first." The official Kwanzaa website, based on Karenga's book, describes it as "an African American and Pan-African holiday which celebrates family, community, and culture," held over seven days from December 26 to January 1.[51] It was conceived as a time to gather people together and (re)form social bonds, to honor and give thanks to the creator, to remember the past and African Americans' African roots and ancestors, and to recommit to "our highest cultural ideals in our ongoing effort to always bring forth the best of African cultural thought and practice" for the purpose of establishing the good life. In a word, Kwanzaa "was created to reaffirm and restore our rootedness in African culture."

Key to the philosophy and practice of Kwanzaa are the *Nguzo Saba*, or Seven Principles:

- *Umoja* or unity;
- *Kujichagulia* or self-determination;
- *Ujima* or collective work and responsibility;
- *Ujamaa* or cooperative economics;
- *Nia* or purpose;
- *Kuumba* or creativity; and
- *Imani* or faith.

In terms of representing and performing Kwanzaa, Mayes notes five central symbols or objects, including the mat (*mkeka*), the candleholder (*kinara*), the seven candles (*mishumaa saba*), the ear of corn (*muhindi*), and the gifts (*zawadi*). The Kwanzaa website adds the unity cup (*kikombe cha umoja*) and the crops (*mazao*), but this only highlights that Kwanzaa has evolved since its inception, with the original five symbols shifting in meaning. For instance, Mayes suggests that the *kinara* initially represented the South African creator-god but later was adjusted to stand for the parents of the family and the ancestors of the nation. Further, the flag (*bendera*) in the African colors of black, red, and green (also associated with Rastafarianism, another Western Hemisphere Africanist invented tradition) and the poster of the Seven Principles (*Nguzo Saba* poster) are mentioned as "supplemental symbols."

According to Mayes, the first Kwanzaa celebration was held in Los Angeles, with the opening hours dedicated to "a lost African past" and the next hours redirected to the African American experience.[52] As

A Kwanzaa celebration, 2003, attended by Ron (Maulana) Karenga.

with every tradition—holiday or otherwise—the success of Kwanzaa, however, depended on many people, who often competed to define and control the doctrine and practice. Crucial for the spread and institution-alization of Kwanzaa were the Committee for a Unified Network in New Jersey, the EAST organization in Brooklyn, and other groups around the country, as well as what Mayes calls "the Black Public Sphere Collective" of neighborhood groups, black schools and student unions, black theater troupes, and local Kwanzaa committees.[53] Especially important were the Western Regional Black Youth Conference in 1967 and the early acolyte of Karenga, Harriet Smith (renamed Sister Makinya), who carried the holiday to the San Francisco Bay Area. Kwanzaa soon began to feature all the accoutrements of an American tradition such as parades, concerts, and feasts but also the signs of a political and consciousness-raising movement such as workshops and lectures.

Since its founding, Mayes notes that Kwanzaa has developed into two streams or traditions, one the "black cultural nationalist" holiday envisioned by Karenga and the other a "multicultural" holiday embraced by mainstream America and particularly by corporate America. Purists may bemoan corporate sponsorship of Kwanzaa events by the likes of General Motors, Kraft Foods, Philip Morris, and AT&T, or Hallmark

Kwanzaa cards and a u.s. postage stamp of Kwanzaa issued in 1997—not to mention reconciliations between Kwanzaa practitioners and Christian churches—but this merely shows that traditions, even nationalist or separatist ones, are living and evolving things under no one's control, not even the National Coalition to Preserve the Sanctity and Integrity of Kwanzaa.

On the other side, critics of Kwanzaa (mostly white conservatives such as Ann Coulter[54] and William Bennett[55]) delight in pointing out that Kwanzaa is not an authentic African holiday and that, for example, corn is not indigenous to Africa and that Swahili is a composite language of Bantu, Arabic, and other sources spoken by a minority of Africans on the southeastern coast, far from the ancestry of most African Americans. But such attempted discrediting misses the point—willfully or otherwise—about Kwanzaa in particular and traditions in general. All traditions are invented and thus questionably "authentic," including those presumably loved by Coulter and Bennett, and Karenga understood and admitted that Kwanzaa "was only inspirationally African and not African in fact. Due to the growing confusion in Kwanzaa's early years, Karenga was forced to level with black America, clarifying: 'Nowhere on the African continent is there a holiday named Kwanzaa.'"[56]

So it is fair, and obligatory, to say that Kwanzaa, as in the case of all holidays and other traditions, is *aspirational*—that is, it aspires to be traditional and authentic, and if it succeeds, it *becomes* traditional and thereby authentic. Kwanzaa also joins other aspirational black American (counter)holidays such as Umoja Karamu (alternative Thanksgiving, which some black nationalists reject as Misgivings Day), Black Solidarity Day (alternative Election Day), Black Love Day (February 13, alternative Valentine's Day), A Day of Praise (March 26, alternative Easter), and African Holocaust Day (October 12, alternative Columbus Day).

AMERICAN
LIFESTYLE
TRADITIONS

NINE

America in a Word:
"OK"

★★★

O
f all of America's gifts to the world, perhaps none is greater, at least in sheer volume of use, than the word "OK". Already in 1941, Woodford Heflin could brag that "O.K. is king of all American abbreviations. It is uttered probably one billion times a day in the United States, more or less, and is undoubtedly the most popular of all abbreviations."[1] Not only is it one of the most common words in the English language (and now in other languages too), but it is one of the most versatile: it functions most often as an adjective or an adverb, but it can also be a noun (as in "She gave her OK for the project"), an interjection (as in "OK, let's go"), and even a verb (as in "He OKed the proposal"). It can be spelled in various ways (OK, O.K., okay) and has a hand gesture to go along with it (the thumb-and-finger circle).

Not surprisingly, any word that is so universal yet so diverse can generate a lot of confusion and conjecture. Most Americans never think about where "OK" first came from, and Heflin went on to state that "it is not known for certain what the two letters stand for, or why the expression ever arose. Interest in its origin has aroused speculation and hard work by many a common man and historian; and theories about it have been about as plentiful as sunshine in New Mexico."[2] Accordingly, a startling body of literature has grown up to analyze the origin and evolution of these two simple letters.

One of the most committed students of OK and of the American use of the English language in general was H. L. Mencken. In his magisterial 1919 *The American Language*, he noted how an American "likes to make his language as he goes along, and not all the hard work of his grammar teachers can hold the business back"; in particular, Americans exhibit "the habit of reducing complex concepts to the starkest abbreviations."[3] Thus Americans are forever inventing new, clever words and especially abbreviations and acronyms: Mencken quoted a man named John Farmer who judged that "Americans, as a rule, employ abbreviations to an extent unknown in Europe . . . This trait of the American character is discernible in every department of national life and thought."[4]

By almost a century ago, the word OK had acquired not only wide usage but a folklore of its own about its source, meaning, and history. Mencken summarized a number of these claims, many of which were still in circulation decades later although most of them are whimsical at best and absurd at worst. One of the more persistent explanations is that the word derives from the Native American language of the Choctaw, specifically from their word *ok* or *okeh* for "it is." Interestingly, one of the main proponents of this theory was America's most scholarly president, Woodrow Wilson (served 1913–21), who practiced the custom of writing "Okeh" on documents to express his approval. According to his wife, "Someone asked why he did not use the 'O.K.' 'Because it is wrong,' Mr Wilson said. He suggested that the inquirer look up 'okeh' in a dictionary. This he did, discovering that it is a Choctaw word meaning 'It is so.'"[5]

OK has been given other non-English origins as well. David Dalby apparently attributed it to African languages in a 1969 lecture, along with other Americanisms such as "jive," "hep," and "rap." Some potential African correlates have been found, such as Wolof *waw-kay* and Mandinka *o ke*, both of which are expressions of affirmation. Some have thought that it came from the Greek *ola kala* (another affirmative), the French *Aux Cayes* (after a port in Haiti), the German *Ober Kommando* (for "High Command"), or maybe Scottish or Latin. However, similarity alone does not indicate kinship, and these suggestions are rejected by most contemporary linguists and folklorists.

Two homegrown and persistent theories on the first OK relate it to an alleged usage in 1815 or to an allegedly illiterate president. Andrew Jackson was indeed one of America's least formally educated chief executives, and some of his critics made the most of the accusations of his boorishness and lack of sophistication. One story went that he could not spell simple words and phrases such as "all correct," thinking that the words were spelled "oll korrect" leading to the abbreviation OK. However, there seems to be no authority for this claim, and formal education was a rather rare commodity for all Americans in the early 1800s, so Jackson was probably no more illiterate than most. The 1815 claim is more interesting. In the diary of William Richardson, the letters "ok" appear on one page, but it is uncertain what he meant by them, and it is fairly certain that other people did not imitate his use, so whatever his "ok" was for, most scholars do not regard it as the first appearance of the modern OK. (Heflin reproduces the original handwritten entry from Richardson's diary on page 88 of his essay, so examine it for yourself.)

How a Joke Became the World's Most Common Word

After Mencken, the other leading historian of OK is Allen Walker Read, who wrote a series of articles in 1963 and 1964 for the journal *American Speech* on the birth and rise of the word. He rejected all of the speculative theories mentioned above, resting his case instead on an odd habit of early nineteenth-century Americans: "Beginning in the summer of 1838, there developed in Boston a remarkable vogue of using abbreviations. It might well be called a craze."[6] Among the examples he cited were W.O.O.O.F.C. (for "with one of our first citizens"), R.T.B.S. (for "remains to be seen"), O.F.M. (for "our first men"), w.y.g. (for "will you go"), and d.u. (for "done up"). Still more interestingly, many of these abbreviations were based on intentional misspellings, enhancing the humor. Accordingly, by 1838 O.W. for "oll wright" had been featured in print, as well as a.r. for "all right."

Such jocularity and linguistic sport was almost bound to lead to OK. Read ultimately found the following paragraph in a March 1838 edition of the *Boston Morning Post*, which contained the earliest-known appearance of the familiar OK:

We said not a word about our deputation passing "through the city" of Providence.—We said our brethren were going to New York in the Richmond, and they did go, as per Post of Thursday. The "Chairman of the Committee on Charity Lecture Bells" [Thomas B. Fearing], is one of the deputation, and perhaps if he should return to Boston, via Providence, he of the [Providence] Journal, and his train-band, would have the "contribution box," et ceteras, o.k.—all correct—and cause the corks to fly, like sparks, upward.[7]

Read attributed this invention to Charles Gordon Greene, "nationally famous for his wit."[8]

The neologism quickly spread along the East Coast, picked up by newspapers and transmitted to the next city; Read located it in New Orleans by 1839. He concluded, then, that the proximal source of OK

> was the fad in the late 1830s for the use of misspelled initials like
> o.w. for "oll wright." In a frolicsome group called the Anti-Bell-
> Ringing Society, in Boston in the spring of 1839, o.k. became
> current as standing for "oll correct," in a slang application of all
> correct, and from there it became widespread over the country.
> Thus the emergence of o.k. is well accounted for.[9]

But OK was merely one of many silly words and abbreviations floating in American publishing and speech, and it would take something more to complete the traditioning of OK.

That something, according to Read in his second essay, was the presidential race of 1840. Martin Van Buren of the Democratic Party (successor to Andrew Jackson) was the incumbent, and despite a lack of enthusiasm for his re-election, social clubs with funny names such as the Butt Enders, the Indomitables, the Huge Paws, and the Simon Pures were organized to support him. Among these groups was the Democratic o.k. Club. However, it seems likely that o.k. here did not have the same meaning as the flippant "oll correct." Instead, Read opined that o.k. to the Democrats stood for "Old Kinderhook," a nickname for Van Buren referring to his birthplace, Kinderhook, a town near Albany, New York. Read offered the following quotation as evidence:

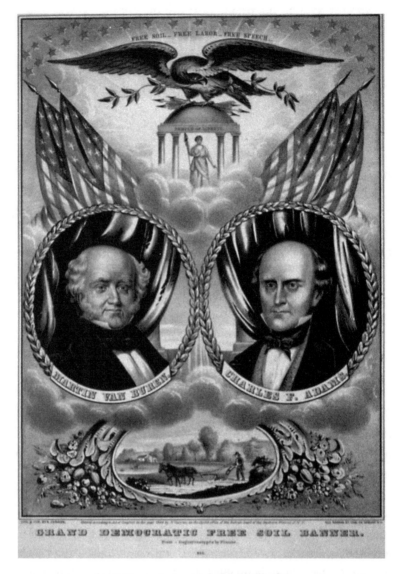

An 1848 campaign poster for Martin Van Buren.

We acknowledge the receipt of a very pretty gold Pin, representing the "old white hat with a crape" such as is worn by the hero of New Orleans [Andrew Jackson, Van Buren's predecessor], and having upon it the (to the "Whigs" [the opposing party]) very frightful letters O.K., significant of the birth-place of Martin Van Buren, old Kinderhook, as also the rallying word of the Democracy of the late election, "all correct" . . . Those who wear them should bear in mind that it will require their most strenuous exertions between this and autumn [election day], to make all things O.K.[10]

Read asserted that the Democratic "rowdies used it as a war cry while rioting and attacking the opposition. This indicates, I believe, that the political use of O.K. was the result of a deliberate decision by certain Democratic politicians."[11] There is also reason to believe, he stated, "that the Democrats did their best to hold O.K. as their own proprietary slogan,"[12] but as with most such attempts to harness and trademark a word, it was not to be.

The political usage of O.K. by one political party induced imitation and parody, especially by the opposing Whig party which tried to establish many witty negative associations with the abbreviation: one Whig sympathizer made the following entry in his diary on May 1, 1840: "But we'll be O.K. by and by, perhaps according to the new Whig interpretation: out of kash, out of kredit, out of karacter and out of klothes; perhaps out of klients may be added, including out of kansas and out of kosts."[13] As a result, OK became known to Americans across the country and across party lines—although what they "knew" by the word differed for some overtly partisan reasons.

OK Takes on a Life of Its Own

The word "OK" was well and truly launched by 1840, but its future and its meaning were not yet secured. It might have died along with other campaign slogans such as "I like Ike" or "Tippecanoe and Tyler Too." Instead, as Read wrote in yet a third article, OK periodically got "booster shots" that perpetuated it in American speech, gave it new meanings or applications, and generally endeared it to America and the world. Mencken, for instance, observed that a song called "O.K. Gallopade" was published in 1840 by John Hewitt;[14] the same year, "O.K. Quickstep" was composed by one "Jos. K. Opl."[15] Allan Metcalf also came across a poem in the *Boston Daily News* from December 15, 1840, the first stanza of which ran as follows:

What is't that ails the people, Joe?
They're in a kurious way,
For every where I chance to go,
There's nothing but o.k.
They do not use the alphabet,
What e'er they wish to say,
And all the letters they forget,
Except the o. and k.[16]

Within a decade, Read posited that OK had made it across the border and as far afield as Jamaica. However, the word was still weighed down by its political and plebeian associations: polite speakers, let alone scholars and novelists, did not accept it as proper English. Curiously, OK occurred in the journals of Henry David Thoreau—"I am for a moment absorbed in thought, thinking, wondering who they are, where they live. It is some Oak Hall, O call, O.K., all correct establishment which she knows but I do not"[17]—but was omitted from the published version of *Walden*. American literature was not ready for OK, yet. The Civil War helped to spread and normalize the word, but it was still street talk until the 1870s, when it made its first documented appearance in literature—namely the 1875 play by Benjamin E. Woolf titled *The Mighty Dollar*. Woolf apparently introduced America to the abbreviation P.D.Q. for "pretty damn quick," along with reviving OK—although some theatergoers remembered him using QK for "quite correct." No one is entirely sure.

At any rate, OK was gathering steam and finding its place in polite American language. A St Louis newspaper in 1888 declared it "grammatically correct," and within three years "an observer in Chicago remarked concerning the use of the verb form that 'the practice has become common in business circles'."[18] It gradually began to appear in commercial use (for instance, an 1893 advertisement for a brand of sardines) and in fiction writing. According to Metcalf, Sinclair Lewis adopted it in his 1914 novel *Our Mr Wrenn: The Romantic Adventures of a Gentle Man*, his 1920 *Main Street*, and his 1922 *Babbitt*. As we have already seen, Woodrow Wilson gave it the imprimatur of the presidency, although in its ostensible Choctaw variation.

As OK diffused through American speech, it also spun off new variants, like "oke" and "okie-doke," both of which materialized around 1930. These led further to "okie-dokie" and forgotten offspring like "okey-poke" and "okey-pokey." In fact, Read mentioned two versions of OK that featured in songs of the 1940s. The first was a Second World War song called "Okie Dokie" by Smoky Okie Rogers, with the following lyrics:

Okie Dokie, I'm a Pale Face Okie,
And a workin' on a 'ssembly line.
Hotsy Totsy, make it tough for the Nazi,
Turn out the planes on time,
Vodeodo, out to get Tojo,
With my Victory Bonds.
Now I'm a patriotic Okie
From back in Muskogee
And proud of this country of mine.[19]

(Notice how the words presage Merle Haggard's famous 1969 "Okie from Muskogee.") The second, a ditty titled "Ok'l Baby Dok'l" from the 1947 musical film *The Big City* by Sidney Miller and Inez James, was even cuter:

Ok'l Baby Dok'l I kelikel baby you,
If you"ll Ok'l Baby Dok'l likel me.
Ok'l Baby Dok'l I kelikel huggel you,
If you"ll Ok'l Baby Dok'l huggel me.[20]

Obviously Americans were not over their playful, almost childlike, treatment of their language.

By the 1940s at the latest, OK had picked up a gesture to accompany or replace the word—the well-known O made by touching fingertip to thumb-tip. It has been claimed that the OK gesture dates back to the 1840s and the "Old Kinderhook" days, but none of the reputable scholarly sources supports the claim. Certainly, Paul Beath in a very short article in *American Speech* from 1946 described the practice of radio producers, who were separated from their on-air talent by glass walls, using the gesture: when everything is correctly set for transmission, "he tells his artists by means of a sign that the show is going 'O.K.' This he does by joining his thumb and forefinger in the shape of an 'O' with other fingers extended."[21] One other possible origin for the sign was among divers, but either way, as with many forms of gestural language, it probably arose when people could not communicate orally due to distance or obstacle. It should be noted, in passing, that the same gesture has quite different meanings in other cultures: in Japan it signifies money, while in Turkey and Venezuela it can mean homosexual, in Australia it means zero (and it can mean that in the U.S. too), and in parts of Germany it is an insult. Finally, Americans can also signal OK with a "thumbs up," which has its own cultural history and other, including derogatory, meanings in other countries.

Read, writing in the heyday of the space program, also reminded us that astronaut Alan Shepard purportedly said "A-OK" during his return to earth in 1961. "The public, assuming that A-OK, for 'all O.K.,' was part of the ordinary vocabulary of the astronauts, picked it up immediately, and within a few days the *New Yorker* satirized the new vogue with a cartoon that pictured a waiter in a fashionable restaurant obsequiously asking a patron, 'Is everything A-O.K., sir?'"[22] And despite the fact that journalists later "disclosed that Shepard had not used A-OK at all, but it had been put into his mouth merely in the reports of a publicist, Lieutenant Colonel John A. Powers,"[23] A-OK lives on.

Is OK the American Philosophy?

Whatever the facts of OK, its birth and course are definitely dependent on the spirit of Americans, particularly their humor but also their politics and their attitudes toward life. The invention, survival, and elaboration of OK—not to mention all of the incredible folklore that has grown up around it—are products and effects of American wit. Yet, as Read concluded, the "effect of these exercises in wit was to mask completely the true historical information about OK. When serious inquirers came along, they found a mass of wild fabrications."[24] But either way, the story "of O.K. serves well as a laboratory for observing linguistic attitudes."[25]

In a recent return to the exploration of America's word, Allan Metcalf goes further yet, asserting that "those two letters encapsulate a whole view of life—the American philosophy, if two letters can be said to embody a philosophy, and if Americans can be said to have one."[26] OK is unrelentingly upbeat—it means "all correct," after all—but Metcalf adds that OK is "not necessarily wonderful. Or terrible either. About the value of the affirmation, OK just doesn't say."[27] It is neutrally positive, good enough; it passes, but we do not know whether it is A-OK or D-OK. It is "noncommittal": just because it is OK does not mean that the speaker is for it or against it. And it is rather lukewarm: "Most adjectives can express greater intensity with the modifying adverb *very*, as in *very good* or *very satisfying*. But you can't say *very OK*; something is either OK or not."[28] Therefore, OK as such "is value neutral. Whenever there are different degrees of acceptability, OK doesn't point to any particular one. By default, that permits mediocrity as well as excellence."[29]

Metcalf extracts great meaning out of this philosophy of OK, and it is hard to judge if he is wrong. The fact that OK is positive but ambiguously, even unenthusiastically, so makes it practical—after all, we approve documents and plans often without much excitement—but also makes it undesirable for things that really excite us or that others want us to be excited about. Interestingly then, just as Uncle Sam is noticeably absent in government, so OK "remains practically nonexistent in the names of products and rare in the names of businesses. OK affirms, but without the enthusiasm that a product or business would want."[30] Accordingly, OK is not quite appropriate for advertisement, one of America's grand traditions. But it is just right, indeed "oll korrect," for two of America's other grand traditions—pragmatism and tolerance.[31] Americans are practical people, people who like things that work but perhaps do not expect perfection; good enough is good enough. We also like things simple and brief—"short and sweet," we say (or worse, "keep it simple, stupid")—because we move fast; we are always on the go. Finally, we try to be accepting of other people's ways of life, even if we do not much care for those ways: we tolerate other people's habits, beliefs, and manners not because they thrill us (they may actually irk us) but because it is the only way to get along and because we want to be tolerated too. Other people's ways of life are OK, although we might not think that they are great.

As Metcalf reminds us, OK literally did become a philosophy in the 1950s and 1960s. In 1950 Stephen Potter wrote one of those self-help books that Americans so enjoy, titled *Some Notes on Lifemanship*. Rather humorous, as Americans are also wont to be, Potter coined terms such as "OK-words" and "OK-names." However, this striving for OK-ness became more serious, almost scientific and therapeutic, in Thomas Harris's 1967 bestseller, *I'm OK—You're OK*. Part of the "transactional analysis" movement that tried to help people understand the relationships—and ruts—that they were in, Harris offered OK-ness as the goal for mental and social health. Individuals did not need to be or try to be perfect. Being OK "doesn't imply or demand perfection, nor does it imply disappointment. It's just . . . perfectly OK,"[32] Metcalf holds. Years later, the *Saturday Night Live* television character Stuart Smalley, played by Al Franken, beautifully summed up the OK philosophy with his self-affirmation, "I'm good enough. I'm smart enough. And doggone it, people like me."

Why, the very fact that OK began as an intentional misspelling, a deliberate imperfection, and a mockery of America's own language conveys the philosophy at the heart of the word. "Best of all," Metcalf closes, OK "exemplifies imperfection successfully, blatant misspelling not holding it back from becoming America's most successful invention."[33] OK is the voice of America, and America is just OK.

TEN

I'd Like to Teach the World:
Coca-Cola

"The history of Coca-Cola is a story of special moments—times with family and friends and special occasions when Coke was naturally there. Every person who drinks a Coca-Cola enjoys a moment of refreshment—and shares in an experience that millions of others have savored. And all of those individual experiences combined have created a worldwide phenomenon."[1] So says the Coca-Cola Company itself, which we could probably dismiss as myth (it is, after all, given on a page of "Coke Lore"), hype, and self-promotion if it were not largely true. In Mark Pendergrast's weighty tome on the history of Coca-Cola, he quoted one Coke operative as saying, "Coca-Cola is the holy grail, it's magic . . . Wherever I go, when people find out I work for Coke, it's like being a representative from the Vatican, like you've touched God. I'm always amazed. There's such a reverence towards the product."[2] Roberto Goizueta, CEO of The Coca-Cola Company in the 1980s, felt that "working for The Coca-Cola Company is a calling. It's not a way to make a living. It's a religion."[3]

Maybe many employees feel this way about their employer—or at least employers wish that they did. But the public too has treated Coca-Cola as if it were part of the American fabric, an American tradition, almost a sacred object. As we will see below, this became clearest when Coke changed the taste of its century-old drink; among the protest letters received, one cried, "Would it be right to rewrite the Constitution? The Bible? To me, changing the Coke formula is of such a serious nature."[4] And if Coca-Cola is a tradition, verging on a religion, then it is a specific and intentional one. Another earlier Coke CEO, Robert Woodruff, and his ad man Archie Lee, who were together responsible for some of the most viral marketing in American history, "wanted the public to view Coke as a facet of American life, an icon as American as the Fourth of July."[5] Finally, as with Robert Bellah's American "civil religion" that was not Christianity but was neither just "generic religion,"[6] the tradition and religion of Coca-Cola has very particular characteristics, including perennial values such as love, peace, and universal brotherhood; most powerfully, Coke drinkers are encouraged to think—or to feel—that they "belong to a warm, loving, accepting family, singing in perfect harmony . . . We'll build a better world for you, and me, and everyone."[7]

Every tradition naturally wants to saturate its world, if not *the* world, and every tradition tries to associate itself with positive if not supreme forces, but Coca-Cola is different from anything we have met so far in our journey. It is not only an icon but a singular product; after all, a hamburger is more a concept than a unique item (in other words, you can make a hamburger in various ways), while Coca-Cola is one single thing, that particular brown liquid. Coca-Cola is much more, though; it is a corporation; nobody *owns* the hamburger, but somebody owns Coke. Therefore, the story of Coke is the story of a product, a company, *and* a tradition.

Inventing Coca-Cola

Coca-Cola does not grow on trees or flow in streams, so someone had to invent it, more obviously than some traditions that just appear "to happen." But no one invents a tradition like Coke singlehandedly, so the Coke tale is a tale of many contributors, direct and indirect. Long before there was Coca-Cola or any "soft drink," there were mineral springs and carbonated water, often believed to have healing qualities; people bathed in hot springs and drank bubbly water millennia before Coke. It took the scientist Joseph Priestley, in 1767, to discover how to make carbonated water in the laboratory, and Joseph Schweppe built a water carbonator soon after, turning it to the production of tonic water and ginger ale.

In the United States, a druggist, Samuel Fahnstock of Lancaster, Pennsylvania, introduced a soda water dispenser in 1819, and his "fountain" was soon dispensing mixtures of carbonated water and flavored syrup. Among the first and most memorable of these flavors was "root beer," sold by Charles Hires in 1876 (although it was initially marketed as "root tea" but sold better as "beer"). Thus, one of the streams leading to Coca-Cola was in place. A second stream was the coca leaf, another substance consumed (at first in South America) for eons; with its energy-inducing qualities, it was a natural winner. By the late 1800s, the wonders of coca were well known in the u.s. (including its derivative, cocaine). One particularly attractive preparation was *Vin Mariani* (Mariani wine), a beverage produced by French chemist Angelo Mariani in the 1860s by combining Bordeaux wine and coca leaf.

Vin Mariani, as Hire's root beer and many another potion of the day were, was offered as a tonic or health drink, and significantly many of their designers were pharmacists. As Pendergrast stressed, the nineteenth century was the age of "patent medicines," often made and sold by amateurs (there was no FDA—Food and Drug Administration—in those days), some of them deserving their pejorative label of "snake oil." He called Americans of that era (and only that era?) "a nation of neurotics" disturbed by the rapid social changes around them and seeking relief or cure from almost any quarter.[8] Thus the field was full of hucksters flogging their cure-all concoctions and blending in tasty and psychoactive ingredients to get an effect. The patent medicine entrepreneurs, he commented, "were the first American businessmen to recognize the power of the catchphrase, the identifiable logo and trademark, the celebrity endorsement, the appeal to social status, the need to keep 'everlastingly at it.' Of necessity, they were first to sell image rather than product"[9]—inaugurating another tradition that still plagues us today.

With three streams thereby in place, all we need is a hero, and that hero was John Stith (spelled "Styth" and even "Smyth" by various sources but "Stith" by the official company website) Pemberton of Atlanta, Georgia. The myth, even retold in Pat Watters's 1978 history of Coca-Cola, is that the intrepid but humble Dr Pemberton brewed up a batch of Coke in his backyard, stirring a brass kettle with an oar, and thus inventing a never-before-known taste sensation.[10] However, Pendergrast rejected this as the log-cabin legend that it is. First, as we noted, coca drinks, including "wine of coca," were already popular, and there were lots of inventors tinkering with formulas; in fact, "Pemberton's French Wine of Coca, first advertised in 1884, was a direct imitation" of Mariani's blend.[11] Further, Pemberton was no bumbling amateur but a pharmacist who spent considerable money on chemicals and technology, who knew the science of the day, and who developed more than a few alleged medicines, such as Globe Flavor Cough Syrup, Extract of Stillingia (a blood tonic), and Sweet Southern Bouquet (a perfume). In short, he was aggressively and systematically searching for a concoction that would make a big hit.

Sometime around 1886, Pemberton had his breakthrough: adding kola nut, a caffeine-carrying African plant, to the coca-leaf drink while removing the wine. Thus he stumbled on a recipe for a coca and kola hybrid, which he sold through a local soda fountain of Willis E. Venable, located at Jacob's Pharmacy. To be precise, what Pemberton provided was a syrup, to be mixed with carbonated water in and sold from the soda fountain dispensers. His drink was reportedly not a huge success at first, selling only 50 gallons (190 l) in the first year.[12]

Inventing the Coca-Cola Tradition

There is a big difference between inventing a product and inventing a tradition. No product is a tradition on its first day, and tradition requires more than inventing; it requires work, the *work of traditioning*. There is perhaps no product that has been more and more-effectively traditioned than Coca-Cola, and no company better at traditioning than The Coca-Cola Company. Of course, in 1886, no Coca-Cola Company existed (the name "Coca-Cola" was patented in 1887). But one of the signs of the traditioning to come was an ad in the Atlanta *Journal* on May 29, 1886, that read, "Coca-Cola, Delicious! Refreshing! Exhilarating! Invigorating!" No doubt this was true, given its combination of coca, caffeine, and a trace of alcohol. But here was the initial irony of Coca-Cola: Pemberton considered it a medicine, not a beverage, and for many years the marketing was schizophrenic, touting both its medicinal qualities and its pleasant recreational character.

Additionally, Pemberton was not much of a businessman, selling the rights to the name, the formula and/or his business (Pemberton

Chemical Company) to multiple parties; worse yet was the fact that he was in desperately ill health, which is one reason why he made so many deals. Among the buyers of Pemberton's properties were Mr and Mrs J. C. Mayfield, who purchased the company but not the rights to Coca-Cola; instead, they sold their own Chero-Cola, and after they divorced, Mr Mayfield went on to sell Koke. But the disparate parts of Coca-Cola were reunified by Asa G. Candler, a rich pharmacist and savvy investor who bought other people's discoveries rather than finding his own. He acquired Electric Bitters, Everlasting Cologne, Bucklen's Arnica Salve, King's New Discovery, and De-Lec-Ta-Lave, in addition to Coca-Cola in 1888.[13] At this point, the modern story of Coke really begins.

Candler soon pinned all of his ambitions on Coca-Cola, continuing for a time to promote it as both medicine and soft drink; for instance, an 1891 ad credited it as "the ideal brain tonic . . . Relieved mental and physical exhaustion. Specific for headache."[14] Another problem was that Coca-Cola was still a local product, native to Atlanta. The solution was pitch man Samuel Candler Dobbs, Asa Candler's nephew, who "hired

COCA-COLA
SYRUP ✣ AND ✣ EXTRACT.

For Soda Water and other Carbonated Beverages.

This "INTELLECTUAL BEVERAGE" and TEMPERANCE DRINK contains the valuable TONIC and NERVE STIMULANT properties of the Coca plant and Cola (or Kola) nuts, and makes not only a delicious, exhilarating, refreshing and invigorating Beverage, (dispensed from the soda water fountain or in other carbonated beverages), but a valuable Brain Tonic, and a cure for all nervous affections — SICK HEAD-ACHE, NEURALGIA, HYSTERIA, MELANCHOLY, &c.

The peculiar flavor of COCA-COLA delights every palate; it is dispensed from the soda fountain in same manner as any of the fruit syrups.

J. S. Pemberton;
↩ Chemist, ↪
Sole Proprietor, Atlanta, Ga.

An early promotion for Coca-Cola, signed by Pemberton.

Six classic Coca-Cola bottles.

a small army of salesmen to blanket the Midwest," offered free samples through coupons distributed to fountain operators, and commissioned a banner with the Coca-Cola trademark and slogan "Delicious and Refreshing," thousands of which "were to be placed on drugstore awnings nationwide."[15] But that was only the beginning. Coca-Cola got into what we call today cross-marketing or merchandising, producing and selling—or giving away—"outdoor posters, painted wall and barn signs, blotters, calendars, serving and change trays, Japanese fans, bookmarks, and marble paperweights, and streetcar cards. All across the nation the red-and-white or red-and-green signs with the cursive trademark were becoming as familiar as—well, a Coca-Cola sign today."[16] Less successful were Coca-Cola cigars and chewing gum.

Coca-Cola was still at this juncture a point-of-sale product, offered only by the glass at soda fountains, and the business model of the company was to sell Coca-Cola syrup directly to soda fountains, which blended and served the drink. Joseph Biedenharn saw another possibility: selling Coke in bottles, which could theoretically be bought, carried, and consumed anywhere, including at home. And Biedenharn, of Vicksburg, Mississippi, already had the state-of-the-art delivery system: four men with mule-drawn wagons! Candler was actually opposed to the idea of bottling the liquid, for quality reasons as well as from concerns about losing central control. But two lawyers, Benjamin Franklin Thomas and Joseph Brown Whitehead, convinced Candler to grant them the exclusive rights to bottle Coke; in a famously terse (six-hundred-word) contract, Candler agreed to sell Coca-Cola syrup to no other entity (except Biedenharn) and to allow them to use the trademark, while leaving them with all the costs and liabilities of bottling. Eventually, the two men divided the country between them, Thomas serving the East Coast and West Coast, while Whitehead bottled for the middle of the country. By 1905, 119 Coke bottling plants were in operation, and by 1910 there were 379. According to Pendergrast, soda bottling was a tough industry that often hired child labor; "the tedious manual labor in Coca-Cola bottling plants never commanded a decent salary. In later years, because of the noise and monotony, many plants hired deaf employees at minimum wage."[17]

Bottling reasonably enough requires a bottle, and here is another place where Coca-Cola business genius shined. Bottles were fairly standard in the 1800s (basic cylinders), although the narrow neck was introduced around 1900. Then in 1916 Coca-Cola sought the perfect bottle for their beverage, and the Root Glass Company of Terre Haute, Indiana, created the design. As the founding story goes, Alex Samuelson researched the main ingredients of Coke (coca and kola) in an encyclopedia and got the idea to model the bottle after the coca nut; however, what he actually saw was a cocoa bean, rounded and ridged, so he instructed machinist Earl Dean to blow what came to be called the "hobbleskirt" bottle, named after a tight dress of the day. "Someone looking at this bosomy first effort called it a Mae West bottle," and others described it as "aggressively female" with "twenty cleverly concealed devices [the bevels or twists] to lure and satisfy the hand."[18]

In a very real way, the recognizable bottle was a form of advertising, but it was in print and graphic advertising that The Coca-Cola Company truly distinguished itself—and established itself as a key American tradition. As early as 1892 the company had issued a calendar among its many promotional materials, complete with "a femme fatale" that earned the item the name "the 'pretty girl' calendar."[19] But in the twentieth century the company took its advertising up a notch or two, beginning with the hiring of the D'Arcy Advertising Agency in 1906 to manage all of the Coca-Cola marketing. In 1908 Samuel Candler Dobbs and William Cheever D'Arcy unveiled the world's largest animated ad, along the railroad between New York and Philadelphia, with colored water pouring through a pipe into a glass being filled by a more than 30-foot-tall soda jerk.

However, when Robert Winship Woodruff came to the helm of the company in the 1920s, he and ad man Archie Lee unleashed a storm of thirst-quenching and eye-catching advertising, including a string of slogans. As Gyvel Young-Witzel and Michael Witzel put it, "Each slogan proclaimed that Coke was not just a product, it was the path to enjoyment, fulfillment, and success—a path to a better life!"[20] Among their mind-worms were "Enjoy Thirst," "Pause and Refresh Yourself," "Refreshment Time," "Around the Corner from Anywhere" (epitomizing their intention to make Coke truly omnipresent), "Stop at the Red Sign," "It Had to Be Good to Get Where It Is," "The Shortest Distance Between Thirst and Refreshment," and then finally in 1929 the timeless "The Pause that Refreshes."

Woodruff and Lee did not stop at the wording but crafted many never-forgotten images. Lee, for instance, designed the familiar logo with the white cursive letters in a red circle. He also cashed in on archetypal themes in American culture, not least of which was the conventional love story; fatefully, "for the first time, ads not only showed boy-meeting-girl, but suggested pointedly that boy and girl somehow were meeting *because* of Coca-Cola."[21] In fact, as far back as 1910 a Coke ad had flatly proclaimed, "Nothing is so suggestive of Coca-Cola's own pure deliciousness as the picture of a beautiful, sweet, wholesome, womanly woman."[22]

To deliver their message, they utilized the latest media, such as movies, radio, and eventually television. For example, a 1927 radio show about "Vivian, the Coca-Cola Girl" featured a soap-opera style story about Vivian and her beau Jim. The Coca-Cola Company sponsored other shows, too, such as 1934's "The Pause That Refreshes on the Air" and 1935's "Refreshment Time." Movie-star endorsements followed, with the likes of Buster Keaton, Rudolph Valentino, Stan Laurel, Clark Gable, Joan Crawford, and Jean Harlow all helping to pitch Coke to a thirsty—and increasingly depressed—America. The Great Depression shaped the 1930s, but as far as Coke was concerned life was still good. Moreover, in hard times, comforting images were especially valuable, and who could be more comforting than Santa Claus? Accordingly, in the 1930s Saint Nick became a spokesman for the soda, in the process helping to settle the image of Santa in the American mind. Santa's Coke career commenced in December 1930 in the pages of the *Ladies' Home Journal*, with Kris Kringle surrounded by children at a soda fountain; the headline read, "The busiest man in the world comes up smiling after . . . 'the pause that refreshes'," and elsewhere in the ad it told readers that "even Old Santa, busiest man in the world, devotes a minute now and then to 'the pause that refreshes'."[23] The next year, artist Haddon Sundblom started drawing Santa, further suggesting that children leave the old elf a Coke instead of milk and cookies; in the process, Sundblom and Coca-Cola profoundly affected the Christmas tradition, since they "not only changed the nation's perception of how Santa looks, from jolly dwarf to the way we envision him today (big, fat, kindly), but also managed to associate Coca-Cola with the most delicious memories of everybody's childhood."[24]

The ubiquity of Coke was aided by two other developments around the same time. The six-pack was introduced in 1924, urging folks to buy several bottles, take them home, and drink them later. A decade later, Everett Worthington constructed a cooler for Coca-Cola, so that people could buy an ice-cold soda on any street corner.

The Second World War was a national emergency for the United States, but it was also a marketing windfall for Coca-Cola, since no one needed a reminder of home and a pause that refreshes more than our men in uniform. The company convinced the army and the government that Coke was essential for troop morale, even supplying a pamphlet, "Importance of the Rest-Pause in Maximum War Effort," that offered expert testimony that pausing and refreshing were crucial not just for soldiers but for workers in state-side factories: "In times like these," it bragged, "Coca-Cola is doing a necessary job for workers . . . bringing welcome refreshment to the doers of things."[25] And what American, after all, is not a doer of things? So General Dwight Eisenhower ordered Coke for his men in Europe, while General George Marshall had the government pay for bottling equipment "as an essential military priority."[26] And of course it was no contradiction to the patriotism of the Coca-Cola Company, or the fundamental American-ness of Coke, that Nazi Germany drank Coke too and that the Company did business with the enemy during the war. Be that as it may, the conflict was also an opportunity to construct bottling plants in Europe and Asia.

Battling Traditions

The course of true tradition never does run smooth, and Coca-Cola had to fight a number of challenges. The first two were its own negative image and its copycats. For starters, Coke was not always the popular and blithely accepted icon that it is today; indeed, in its early days, "Coca-Cola was plagued with a rather unsavory reputation."[27] The charge that it contained coca, perhaps even cocaine, drove moralists crazy; already in 1898 a Baptist preacher named Lindsay "launched a hellfire attack on Coca-Cola, the ingredients of which were, he asserted, fully two-thirds cocaine; imbibing would lead to 'morphine eating'."[28] Four years later, a doctor claimed that "the excessive use of Coca-Cola" had caused a suicide, while another medical expert accused the company of creating "Coca-Cola fiends" whose "cravings rivaled those of opium addicts."[29] The temperance movement opposed Coke for supposedly containing alcohol, and the government pursued the company repeatedly, particularly over the safety of ingredients such as cocaine, caffeine, and saccharine. In fact, in 1911, after seizing forty barrels and twenty kegs of Coke as evidence, the court case of *The United States v. 40 Barrels and 20 Kegs of Coca-Cola* went to trial, which was eventually settled, allowing the company to carry on with its product.

At least as annoying to the company were imitators and copyright infringers. Admittedly, Coca-Cola was not the first drink to contain the ingredient or the name coca. A few years before Pemberton, Henry Downs had placed coca in a syrup and called it Imperial Inca Coca; this was soon followed by "Coca-Coffee, Coca-Malta, Cocacaffeine, Burgundia Coca—and of course—Coca-Cola."[30] And after Coke's success, the copycats proliferated; by 1916 there were already

153 of them to be fought down in the courts, including Koca-Nola, Fig Cola, Candy Cola, Cold Cola, Gay Ola, and Coca and Cola. The names down the years are a study in unethical ingenuity: Caro-Cola, Kola, Kota-Nola, Kola-Nola, Co Kola, King-Cola, Coke Ola, Kos-Kola, Toca-Cola, Sola Cola, Kel Kola (It Has the Kick), Kaw-Kola (Has the Kick) Dope, Ko-Co-Lema, to mention but the closest to the original.[31]

But the most persistent threat of all was Pepsi-Cola. Pepsi was born around the same time as Coke and is attributed to another pharmacist, Caleb Bradham of New Bern, North Carolina, around 1893. Bradham's Pepsi company almost folded three times by the 1930s, and he even tried to sell out to The Coca-Cola Company in 1922, the rejection of which offer Coke no doubt regrets. But new management at Pepsi in the 1930s gave Coca-Cola its first and most stubborn competition, especially when Pepsi made the wild move of cutting its price in half in 1934. Coca-Cola became so alarmed that it sued Pepsi for illegal use of the term "cola," but the suit failed, meaning that "Coca-Cola had irrevocably lost the exclusive right to 'cola'."[32]

Pepsi proved an adroit rival, securing a full third of the American cola market by the end of the 1950s. It also proved to be more daring and experimental, offering more serving sizes and better prices. But most critically of all, Pepsi responded more effectively to the social climate of the 1960s and beyond. Coca-Cola was very committed to its established image and clientele, while Pepsi saw the "baby boomer" generation as a new and different demographic. Thus in 1963 when Coke debuted a new slogan, "Things Go Better With Coke," Pepsi responded with "Come Alive! Come Alive! You're in the Pepsi Generation!" Pepsi seemed comparatively young and hip, its ads "brash, loud, overtly sexy, centering not on the product but on the consumer. Through lifestyle advertising, Pepsi sought to woo the 75 million baby boomers."[33] Pepsi also brought out new products such as Teem, Mountain Dew, and Diet Pepsi and even acquired the snack company Frito-Lay in 1965, a brilliant synergy of thirst-making and thirst-quenching goods. Pepsi's home run, though, was the 1975 "Pepsi Challenge," a head-to-head taste test in which consumers seemed to prefer the taste of Pepsi. And while this did not destroy Coke, it changed the basic rules of the game: taste had become the main issue, and Coca-Cola felt the need to address the taste deficit.[34]

Managing—and Messing with—Tradition

Coca-Cola continued to pervade American society in the 1950s and '60s. The company sponsored a television special for Thanksgiving 1950, with ventriloquist Edgar Bergen and his dummy Charlie McCarthy; the next year, it joined with Disney to do a Christmas special. However, The Coca-Cola Company had always had two authoritative business principles: make one product and one product only, and never tamper with that product. Coke was to be as eternal as the heavens themselves.

Then in 1960 The Coca-Cola Company merged with Minute Maid Corporation, so that for the first time it was in another business besides the soda business. (In 1977, it even dabbled in the alcohol industry, briefly owning The Wine Spectrum.) Soon it was adding new soft drink brands such as Sprite, Mr. Pibb, Fanta, and Tab (also TAB or TaB); Fresca followed in 1966, after which the company bought Belmont Springs Water Company (1969), getting into the new trendy market for bottled water. In 1982 The Coca-Cola Company responded to popular demand with diet Coke (with a lower-case "d" to remind people that Coke, not diet, was still king). But again Pepsi beat them to the punch, unveiling Pepsi Free one day before diet Coke's big announcement.

Coke and Pepsi continued to play dueling commercials, and dueling celebrities, through the 1960s, '70s, and '80s. Coca-Cola signed up Tom Jones and the Supremes, as well as Bill Cosby, Michael Jordan, and Elton John, while Pepsi eventually got Michael Jackson and Madonna. Coca-Cola introduced new slogans such as "Things Go Better with Coke" and "It's the Real Thing." In 1979 Coke premiered one of its most iconic ads, the "Mean Joe Greene" commercial in which the fearsome football player traded his jersey to a boy for a sip of Coke. In 1993 it introduced us to a friendly family of animated polar bears enjoying Coke. But without doubt the most memorable moment in Coca-Cola history, and the most indicative of its era, was the 1971 "I'd Like to Teach the World to Sing" campaign, featuring two hundred handsome young people on a hilltop, singing a song that became a hit for the New Seekers.

But good enough is never good enough, so The Coca-Cola Company did something it had never done and ended up regretting. On April 23, 1985, it announced a change to the formula and thus the taste of Coke. This was not a *second* Coke, since there could be only one. This new formula *was* Coke, meaning that the tradition was no longer traditional. Despite tens of thousands of pre-release taste tests, the reaction against the new Coca-Cola (despite the fact that it was never called "the new Coca-Cola") was swift and ugly. Consumers demanded the traditional Coke in the strongest possible language:

"Changing Coke is like God making the grass purple or putting toes on our ears or teeth on our knees."

"I don't think I would be more upset if you were to burn the flag in our front yard."

"Monkeying with the recipe is akin to diddling with the U.S. Constitution."[35]

Duly chastened for monkeying with tradition, The Coca-Cola Company returned to the old formula within three months, calling it at first "Coca-Cola Classic" until the whole painful memory faded.

It's Not Just a Drink; It's a Feeling

While the Coca-Cola tradition has returned, there are still some sour aftertastes toward the company and its product. In the 1970s the company became mired in a controversy about the working conditions of migrant orange pickers in its Minute Maid orchards; after a television documentary called "Migrant: A White Paper," Cesar Chavez threatened a boycott of Coke and won a union contract for the workers in 1972.[36] Similar bad press has followed the company overseas: it has been linked to anti-labor violence in Colombia (including the assassination of Isidro Gill,[37] the secretary-general of the labor union SINALTRAINAL on December 5, 1996), as well as anti-labor activity in Turkey and Guatemala and the diversion of water supplies in Mexico and India.[38] The Greek Olympic Committee felt that The Coca-Cola Company exploited its wealth and influence to bring the 1996 Olympic Games

Oxfam supporters outside ABF headquarters, calling for the company to tighten its supply chain and ensure that the sugar it produces is not grown on land that has been grabbed from poor communities.

to Atlanta, when they should have been held in the birthplace of the ancient and modern Olympics.[39]

At home in America, Coke has been implicated, along with other sugary drinks, in the obesity epidemic. It has also been criticized for inordinate power in the city of Atlanta and the state of Georgia. And more than a few people are offended by the recent practice of placing soda vending machines in schools and, worse, of exclusive contracts between The Coca-Cola Company and schools that block the availability of non-Coca-Cola products, including healthier juices. Many schools, unfortunately, support these contracts, as they generate considerable financial gain for cash-strapped institutions. According to Michael Blanding, "By 2000, according to the Centers for Disease Control and Prevention, 92 percent of high schools had long-term soda contracts, along with 74 percent of middle schools and 43 percent of elementary schools."[40] Coca-Cola also often makes contracts with restaurants and other outlets for exclusive sale of Coke (but then so does Pepsi). Perhaps the tackiest thing that Coca-Cola does is maintain a museum/theme park, the World of Coca-Cola, where teachers can bring their classes and even download social studies study guides—with the Coke logo and some tasty mentions of Coke in world history.

In the end, no tradition becomes a tradition without a lot of work, even a little coercion, even a little chicanery. Maybe we have to admit,

> Man does not live by bread alone. Out of sugar and water and other good things, Coca-Cola gave to the world, in its drink and the promotion of it, an essence of the moonbeams of southern romanticism, the frivolous and harmless myths which Southerners, when defeat most haunted them, held onto for self-satisfying, self-respecting pleasure. The most recent chapter of promotional history carried this to the ultimate.[41]

ELEVEN

Meals on Wheels:
Hamburger

★ ★ ★

A society is what it eats, and for better or for worse what America eats is hamburgers. What America encourages the rest of the world to eat as well is hamburgers, and the hamburger experience has spawned an entire "fast food" industry—with the hamburger model applied to fried chicken, tacos, pizza, and (through new chains like Garbanzo and Bombay Bowl) even falafel and curry. That is to say, the hamburger and its philosophy are universal and ubiquitous. If speaking of a "hamburger philosophy" seems a bit grandiose, then consider how the modern hamburger experience (from making one to eating one—or more than one) is fast, casual, standardized, portable, and infinitely adaptable. We might say the hamburger is the "OK" of cuisine, just as OK is the hamburger of language.

In probably the most thorough study of the history of the hamburger, Josh Ozersky writes that a hamburger

> isn't just a sandwich; it is a social nexus. Even before the hamburger became a universal signifier of imperialism abroad and unwholesomeness at home, it had a special semiotic power—a quality not shared even by other great American sandwiches like the hot dog, the patty melt, the Dagwood, the Reuben, the po'boy, or even such totemic standards as fried chicken and apple pie. At the end of the day, nothing says America like a hamburger.[1]

As with every tradition, the hamburger tells a story or *is* a story. Unlike many of the traditions we have seen, the story of the hamburger is not a particularly political one, but it does bring together many themes and characters—the sandwich, the beef industry, immigration, industrialization, urbanization and suburbanization, the automobile and highway system, a number of key figures such as Walter Anderson, the McDonald brothers (Maurice and Richard), and Ray Kroc, and, like Coca-Cola, big business and advertising. Along the way, more than a bit of myth-making has transpired as well.

Burger Lore

Nobody knows who first put ground meat to bread. Besides, as John Edge insists, "The history of a proletarian dish like hamburgers is rarely explained by a linear progression of events."[2] The folklore of the hamburger customarily begins with the Mongols, horse-riding marauding nomads of eastern and central Asia during the 1200s and 1300s. The standard story goes something like this, according to Ronald McDonald (yes, seriously):

> Ground meat was the perfect choice for the Mongols. They could use scrapings of lamb or mutton, which were formed into flat patties. They placed these uncooked patties in rolled skins and carried them under their saddles until it was time to eat. The constant pressure mashed the meat between the saddle and the horse, tenderizing it as they rode.[3]

Always on the move and usually on horseback, the Mongol patty was convenient for one-handed eating. Of course, even if this tale is true, it is a long way from a hamburger, as the patty was neither beef nor cooked, nor on a bun. Furthermore, it is unlikely that the Mongols were the first people ever to flatten a meat patty: in fact, John Edge reported that the ancient Romans prepared chopped meat dishes and even wrote about them in at least one cookbook.[4]

The Mongols in this picture sound a lot like a modern commuter, clutching a burger in one hand as she speeds off to conquer her office job

A "Hamburger steak" or "Salisbury steak."

or child's soccer practice. Perhaps the story sticks because it sounds so familiar. Be that as it may, the Mongolian pre-burger then travels in lore to Russia, where raw chopped meat becomes "steak tartare" ("Tartar" being another name for Mongol). Andrew Smith, however, in his short history of the hamburger, rejects both of these episodes as "fakelore,"[5] and he minimizes the significance of the next stop on the hamburger trail—namely, the German town of Hamburg. Hamburg is obviously the putative origin of the term "hamburger," just as Frankfurt is the source of "frankfurter" and Vienna is the source of "wiener" (and, so you would think, Hawaii is the land of "Hawaiian punch" and England the land of "English muffins"!).

John Edge does indicate that by the end of the 1700s, the British were stuffing minced beef into "Hamburg sausages," and Ozersky even mentions a 1763 recipe in a book called *Art of Cookery, Made Plain and Easy* that instructed chefs to make Hamburg sausage by mixing minced beef with suet, cloves, nutmeg, garlic, vinegar, red wine, and rum[6]—not quite the modern formula for hamburgers. Germans did apparently cook with chopped or minced beef too, even shaping the meat into patties or cakes, but sources suggest that Germans did not call the result "hamburger" or even "Hamburg steak" but merely "steak."[7]

Jeffrey Tennyson in his history of the hamburger argued that German immigrants brought their Hamburg steak with them to America,[8] although Ozersky claims that the dish preceded the main wave of immigration from Germany in the mid-1800s; instead, they "arrived in America to find Hamburg steak ready to greet them,"[9] the English and Americans being already familiar with Hamburg sausage and other ground-meat delights. (No one seems to mention that Germans were in the U.S. long before the 1840s, including Hessian troops in the Revolutionary War.) There is even a famous item on an 1834 menu from Delmonico's restaurant in New York, a hamburger steak, although Smith stands out from his fellow burger historians in dismissing the Delmonico's menu as a fake.[10]

So we have little idea what to believe about the prehistory of the hamburger. But, whatever the case, as Tennyson cautioned us, "a Hamburg Steak is not a hamburger."[11] As a steak, it was usually served on a plate with side items like mashed potatoes and gravy. It much more closely resembled meatloaf or "Salisbury steak" than today's hamburger. Indeed, one Dr James Salisbury, a nutritionist, began to warn the public of the risks of consuming raw meat in the 1860s and "suggested as an alternative that the scraped beef should be pressed into patties about an inch thick and grilled . . . By 1889, recipes for 'Salisbury Steak' appeared in medical works and in cookbooks. Similar recipes appeared under other names, such as the more common phrase 'Hamburg steak'."[12]

Hamburg steak took another great leap forward in 1876, when Philip Lauber opened a German restaurant that served the dish at the Philadelphia Centennial Exposition. Gradually (the Delmonico's story notwithstanding), Hamburg steak did begin to show up on other, including non-German, restaurant menus, and by 1896 it appeared in Fannie Farmer's *Boston Cooking-school Cook Book* which informed cooks to "shape, cook, and serve as meat cakes."[13] These instructions became much easier to follow with the introduction of the home meat-grinder; home cooks, restaurant chefs, and butchers alike

could now use unsaleable or undesirable scraps and organ meats that might otherwise have been tossed out. It also became possible to add non-meat ingredients to the ground beef, and it was very hard for the consumer to know what was actually in the mixture. Ground meat was cheaper, ideal to sell to the working classes, and by adding even cheaper fillers, such as gristle, skin, and excess fat, the butcher could enhance his already substantial profit.[14]

Interlude #1: The Sandwich

No one knows for certain who first assembled the "hamburger sandwich"—quite possibly it was some person who built one alone in his own home and did not therefore contribute to the public tradition of the hamburger—but before there was a hamburger sandwich, there was a sandwich. A sandwich is simply "two or more slices of bread, or the equivalent in rolls, flatbread, or other baked goods, used as a structure to contain a filling of some other food, whether hot or cold, to make a meal, such that no utensils are necessary."[15] The naming rights to what seems like an obvious serving idea go to John Montagu, the fourth Earl of Sandwich (1718–1792) "who, too busy to stop for dinner, called for some beef between two slices of bread."[16] The first documented mention of such an innovation is found in the journal of the great historian Edward Gibbon, who also wrote *The Decline and Fall of the Roman Empire*, which refers to a gathering of prominent men who dined on "a bit of cold meat, or a Sandwich."[17] And so the Earl of Sandwich's creation apparently not only caught on and bore his name but became a treat for the nobility, theater-goers, travelers, and other posh people on the go. But the sandwich did not remain the province of the respectable; soon people of all classes, especially the working class with little money or time and with hands often occupied with other tasks, joined the sandwich line.

When Burger Met Bread

Like every other step in the prehistory of the hamburger, the burger-to-bread transfer is steeped in mystery and controversy. The story probably relates to nineteenth-century urbanization and industrialization. Urban factory workers, many of them European immigrants, suffered from low pay and long working-hours, so cheap, fast, and portable food would have suited their needs. Near factories and other workplaces (then as today), food carts and lunch wagons opened for business, hawking all sorts of prepared foods. The credit for first conceiving the idea of putting hamburger on bread sometimes goes to Charlie Nagreen of Seymour, Wisconsin, who in 1885 reportedly put "a meatball" on bread at the Outagamie County Fair.[18] At least the good people of Seymour, Wisconsin, consider that the birth of the hamburger, so they constructed a Hamburger Hall of Fame in their town in 1990.

But when is a ground beef sandwich a hamburger? In, of all places, Hamburg, New York, Frank and Charles Menches also sold a ground beef sandwich in 1885 at the Erie County Fair, but allegedly beef was not even their first choice. Ozersky asserts that they were selling pork sandwiches and ran out of pork, so they switched to beef; he also describes their filling as more meatloaf-like than burger-like.[19] Still another candidate is Louis Lassen of Louis' Lunch in New Haven, Connecticut, who offered a ground beef sandwich on toasted bread in 1895. Finally, many historians give Fletcher Davis of Athens, Texas, the glory as the first hamburger maker; at the 1904 St Louis World's, Fair he put his hamburger steak on Texas toast with raw onion. In the end, though, Edge concludes that "the telling of such tales is an exercise in fiction, for none of these accounts is truly verifiable. (Each is, however, commemorated by a proclamation of primacy from its respective state legislature.)"[20] And many observers emphasize that the hamburger was not the brainchild of any one person but was rather a gradual—and inevitable—evolution of two American staples. "Who was the first lunch wagon proprietor to sell the Hamburg steak between two pieces of bread is unknown, but, by the 1890s, it had already become an American classic" and already featured in a cookbook by 1901.[21]

Interlude #2: Beef, It's What's For Dinner

One could theoretically make a hamburger out of any kind of meat, as the Mongols supposedly did with lamb or mutton (or even out of non-meat, like a "veggie burger"), but the American classic is premised on beef. So

Ozersky also tells the tale of the American beef industry, which was essential to the future of the hamburger (and the hamburger industry). According to Ozersky, pork was the more common meat in America through the nineteenth century; since pigs were easier to raise (requiring less space) and pork was easier to preserve, pork "was the American meat par excellence."[22] Three critical variables collided to replace pork with the more expensive, and therefore higher status, beef. The first was the conquest of the Great Plains of North America (including the elimination of the Native peoples and the native buffalo) for grazing cattle. The second was the development of the meatpacking industry, centered in Chicago. Beef became such big business in the United States that there was "a 'beef trust' in place by the 1880s that controlled the burgeoning traffic from the Midwest to the cities of the East"[23]—some of the horrors of which were described in Upton Sinclair's 1906 novel *The Jungle*. Finally, the beef industry awaited the construction of the railroads for moving cattle and packed beef. Ozersky calls the decade of the 1880s "the Golden Age of Beef, when Gustavus Swift developed an infrastructure that linked Chicago's vast meatropolis with the East Coast via refrigerated railroad cars."[24] Subsequently, beef became widely available and affordable for almost everyone—even if the lower classes had to eat their beef in the form of scrapings and grindings, with who-knows-what additives. Unable to afford real steak, "Hamburg steak was the cheapest way for the poorest Americans to eat beef. It was the rock-bottom entry point to the American beef dream."[25]

The Burger Business

The hamburger is not so much a food as a phenomenon, and it would not be an iconic item if it were merely something that people fried up at home or if it were just one more option on a restaurant menu. The hamburger's place in American culture has much more to do with the way it came to be produced and sold than with the (questionable) virtues of a fried beef sandwich as such. And becoming a cultural icon in America and around the world depended on the effort and ingenuity of a series of food entrepreneurs or impresarios, virtual circus ringmasters and culture heroes, who managed the transformation of the hamburger from a lowly street food to a food system, a big business, and a way of life.

Central to the story is Walter Anderson, a fry cook in Wichita, Kansas. Anderson did not invent the patty-on-bread, but he pioneered many of the specifics that turned the hamburger sandwich into the modern mass-produced hamburger. Prior to his improvements, the hamburger steak was generally a thick meat cake, cooked slowly over a low heat. In order to speed the preparation, he altered the process, cooking thin patties at high heat. Additionally, he decided that sliced bread was not a suitable delivery system for the meat, preferring instead the more substantial bun (which was already in use for hot dogs). So "he developed a bun specifically for the hamburger sandwich. The dough he selected was heavier than ordinary bread dough, and he formed it into small, square shapes that were just big enough for one of his new flat hamburgers."[26]

This was hardly the end of Anderson's perfecting of the hamburger process. He next designed a custom rectangular gas grill, which became "the forerunner of the commercial flat grills that are used today in most of the hamburger restaurants around the world."[27] And he had to solve one more problem—the justified concern among customers about freshness and cleanliness. Many other and older burger joints and diners deserved the nickname "greasy spoons," and Anderson set out to make his place a model of hygiene and quality. He located the grill next to the window of his restaurant so customers could actually see the cooking process. He had fresh meat and buns delivered to his store twice each day, and he kept the space and the servers spotless. For all this, he charged five cents for a burger.

Anderson opened his first location in 1916, and by 1920 he had three restaurants in the Wichita area. However, no one fashions a tradition alone, and his partnership with Edgar Waldo "Billy" Ingram forever changed the course of hamburger culture. Out of that relationship, a new chain of burger restaurants (White Castle), a new kind of burger (the mini or slider), and a new system for making and promoting burgers (the White Castle System) was born. With Ingram, a real estate investor, White Castle embarked on an aggressive campaign of expansion, standardization, and self-promotion. By 1931 there were

115 White Castle outlets throughout the Midwest and Northeast. Each restaurant was built on exactly the same design—a white castle, signaling cleanliness and high quality, staffed by young men in white uniforms and even white paper hats designed by Anderson himself. It is fair to say that, by 1930,

> a standard White Castle restaurant was an exquisite machine, dynamically engineered to allow one man to sell coffee and hamburgers, supremely efficient and gleaming with chrome and white enamel. Its frame was a prefabricated steel structure . . . built of 149 pieces of steel . . . All its paper products were made by a White Castle subsidiary. Soon enough its buns and burgers were too, as Ingram decisively replaced the fresh meat that was WC's reason for being with the pre-portioned frozen patties we know and dread today.[28]

Equally important was advertising. White Castle advertised in newspapers and even circulated its own news: in 1930, to allay fears about the nutritional value of hamburgers, the company actually reported the results of an "experiment" in which a medical student lived for thirteen weeks on a diet of White Castle burgers and water. According to Ingram, a food expert certified

> that a normal, healthy child could eat nothing but our hamburgers and water, and fully develop all its physical and mental faculties if we were to do two things: increase the percentage of calcium in the buns to aid in the development of bone structure, and maintain a specific proportion of bun and patty to provide the correct balance of proteins, carbohydrates, and fat.[29]

The success of White Castle encouraged many imitators, who often literally aped the chain's name and look. Among the more memorable examples were White Tower, White Diamond, and White Manna. Other followers were less shameless, like Wimpy Grills (started in 1934 by Edward Vale Gold in Bloomington, Indiana, and named after the character J. Wellington Wimpy from the *Popeye* comic strip who loved but could never pay for hamburgers) and In-N-Out Burger (founded in 1948 by Harry and Esther Snyder of Baldwin Park, California).

The next step in the evolution of the hamburger tradition was the "drive-in" restaurant, linked intimately with the rise of the automobile culture, the highway system and suburb, and youth/adolescent culture. The first drive-in is widely attributed to J. O. Kirby of Dallas, Texas, who opened Pig Stand in 1921 when he noticed that people liked to eat in (or were too lazy to get out of) their cars. One modification required for a drive-in was a server who came out to your car, and soon these "car-hops" became young women, often on roller skates (for faster movement) and in short skirts (for other obvious reasons). The drive-in phenomenon spread, especially to car-happy places like California, where Mel's, Stan's, Carpenter's, Simon's, Delores's, and Tiny Naylor's soon popped up. Eventually Steak 'n Shake opened in Normal, Illinois (1934), followed by Sonic in Shawnee, Oklahoma (1959). But the big daddy of the drive-ins was Bob's Big Boy, with an oversized burger created by Bob Wian in 1937, apparently as a joke. Big food is no joke in America, though, and by the 1940s Big Boy locations were sprouting around the country under various names, including Bobs, Kips, Shoney's, JB's, Abdow's, and Elby's.

However, if there is one name indelibly associated with the hamburger, and the business of hamburgers, it is McDonald's. After trying their hand at a hot dog and orange juice stand in Hollywood, Maurice and Richard McDonald opened McDonald's Brothers Burger Drive-In in San Bernardino, California, in 1940, with many of the ordinary conventions of a contemporary drive-in such as carhops, in-door seating, and a menu that included but did not emphasize hamburgers, also featuring barbecued pork and spareribs. But when the brothers decided to break the mold of the burger drive-in in 1948, they changed hamburgers, business, and America forever.

The first thing they did was simplify the menu, dropping the barbecue and focusing on the burger. They also eliminated carhops, turning their place into a "self-service" restaurant where customers had to walk up to the counter to order, as well as bus their own tables. This apparently caused some confusion and consternation among consumers accustomed to car-side service: they would sit in their cars and honk

A classic McDonald's restaurant, with golden arches and pre-Ronald McDonald "Speedy" Mascot.

their horns for a server. The McDonalds also did away with indoor seating, encouraging their customers to pay and leave. To save money on cutlery and dishwashing, they replaced plates and silverware with disposable paper and plastic. Burgers became smaller and flatter, as standardized as the condiments—one shot of ketchup and mustard, some onion, and two pickle slices—with no options and measured out by a special condiment dispenser. Finally, they developed an assembly-line approach to food production, with young unskilled workers performing simple repetitive tasks. Smith describes this as "a militarized production system,"[30] which has been copied by so many businesses, not just burger joints, that George Ritzer saw fit to announce "the McDonaldization of society."[31]

Two other factors are part of the archetype of the McDonald's system. The first is the classic restaurant look, with its "golden arches." According to Tennyson, Richard McDonald and architect Stanley Meston designed a new McDonald's restaurant with a flared roof, the enormous gold arches, and a neon sign in front featuring the store mascot, Speedy, a cartoon chef with a hamburger patty for a head and with feet suggesting constant motion.[32] The second was the grand impresario Ray Kroc, who has claimed to be the inventor of McDonald's but who bought several franchises in the 1950s, acquired the chain in 1961 (when it had 228 locations), and turned it into the burger behemoth that it has been ever since.

Interlude #3: Would You Like Fries with That?

Today, it is hard to imagine burgers without fries. Even in the days of hamburger steaks, fried potatoes were often a side dish. Of course, French fries, or potatoes in any form, are not a very old American or European tradition; the potato is not indigenous to Europe, and no European ever saw one until they reached Central and South America, where it was first domesticated and long cultivated. Spaniards no doubt encountered it during their conquests, and the first Englishman to mention it was John Hawkins in 1565. According to Smith in his short history of the potato, the tuber was first used for horse feed in England, although it was grown for human consumption in Scotland and Ireland.[33] The dependence of Ireland on the potato, and the dire consequences of the crop failure in 1845, are well known. Smith insists, however, that frying potatoes was not part of the culinary tradition in South America.

The technique of deep-frying potatoes reportedly developed in France in the late 1700s, and Thomas Jefferson mentioned them in 1801. The term "French fried potatoes" was in use by 1856, when it appeared in a British cookbook, and the aforementioned Fannie Farmer cookbook included a recipe as well. However, Smith also notes that the dish was sometimes called "German fried potatoes" or "German fries."

French (or German) fries were not an obligatory part of every early burger joint menu. They are notoriously difficult to cook: they are labor-intensive (for example, peeling), it is hard to tell when they are sufficiently cooked, and the boiling oil is tricky and dangerous to handle. The Second World War was a turning point, when potatoes were not subject to rationing, and restaurants offered fried potatoes "to round out their downsized or unavailable burgers."[34] Americans soon developed a taste for French fries, although White Castle actually dropped them from the menu. But McDonald's put them back on the menu, and the American agenda; both the McDonald brothers and Ray Kroc experimented with methods of growing, storing, freezing, and frying potatoes. Together with J. R. Simplot, an Idaho potato farmer, Kroc perfected his techniques of freezing and frying potatoes, including the proper heat and oil composition.

Burgers, Burgers, Everywhere

With the hamburger, and the hamburger business model, mature, exponential growth was the obvious result. New players entered the field, such as Keith Cramer, who, after touring the McDonald brothers' initial operation, bought the rights to the new Insta-Burger Broiler that could cook hundreds of burgers per hour in 1952 and launched Insta-Burger King in Jacksonville, Florida, which would eventually become simply Burger King. By 1956 there were 47 Burger Kings in 22 states. Adapting the burger tradition, David Edgarton, a Burger King franchisee in Miami, helped design a new gas-flame broiler and a new bigger sandwich, the Whopper. Other successful chains included Hardee's, Jack in the Box (the first with a drive-through window), and Wendy's. Unlike the original McDonald's business plan, Burger King offered more customization (their slogan for a time was "Have it your way"), while Wendy's boasted a much more extensive menu. And there were other less successful attempts at burger fame too, such as Baron Von Burger, Lone Ranger burgers, Conway and the Twitty Burger, and Li'l Abner and his Yokumburgers.[35]

But the hamburger tradition reaches far beyond the food itself. Crucial to the triumph of the hamburger has been, for instance, the characters and mascots associated with it. No doubt the best known is Ronald McDonald, the hamburger clown, introduced in 1963 and originally played by television weatherman Willard Scott; in fact, McDonald's has the most fully realized mascot world, with the Hamburglar and Mayor McCheese, etc. Burger King's slightly creepy King has been featured in a

Pre-packaged hamburgers in Japan.

series of television commercials in recent years. Bob's Big Boy still hovers over restaurants, inspiring spin-offs such as Lard Lad on *The Simpsons*.

Hamburger restaurants have also used music and slogans that have sometimes become parts of American culture too. "You deserve a break today," "I'm lovin' it," and the rhythmical listing of ingredients in a Big Mac by McDonald's have stuck in the American consciousness, as have Burger King's "Have it your way" and, perhaps most famously, Wendy's "Where's the beef?"—which even became a campaign slogan by presidential candidate Walter Mondale in 1984. Menus have grown and changed with the times, first reaching out to children (for instance, the "Happy Meal" from McDonald's), and then accommodating the tastes of morning commuters (for example, the McDonald's Egg McMuffin or the Burger King Croissandwich) and the health conscious (salads, chicken sandwiches, and many menu innovations).

One of the appeals of the hamburger, as mentioned at the outset, is its nearly infinite variability. Not all hamburgers are even made of beef anymore: there are chicken and turkey burgers, veggie burgers, and tofu burgers. Regional variations abound; in fact, much of John Edge's book about hamburgers is a tour of American regional burgers, from the bean burger of San Antonio (with refried beans and corn chips) to the New Mexico chili burger, and to the Memphis barbecue burger and the Miami Cuban burger, ad infinitum. Internationally the burger is still more flexible. Australians often put fried eggs or slices of beet on their burgers, and Smith asserts that the Australian restaurant "Hungry Jack's" makes a burger with egg, bacon, and cheese but no beef.[36] Japanese chain Lotteria naturally sells teriyaki burgers and shrimp burgers, and Nirula's of India transforms the American hamburger into a nutty paneer burger, a mutton maniac burger, a French flip burger, and a crazy pea burger.[37]

Finally, a cultural tradition has really established itself when it spawns more traditions within the culture. From the hamburger-craving character Wimpy to the *Saturday Night Live* "Cheeseburger" sketch, and from Jimmy Buffet's song "Cheeseburger in Paradise" to the 2004 movie *Harold and Kumar Go to White Castle*, the hamburger has infiltrated American popular culture. As Ozersky concludes,

> There was some symmetry to this. It was, after all, White Castle that created the hamburger from the fabric of immigrant experience and helped make it an American icon; fitting, then, that it should come around again to welcome another group of immigrants into the fold. America was infinite, absorptive, an idea that transcended physical shape and borders. The hamburger, its most universal symbol, could be no less immortal.[38]

TWELVE

America's Individualistic Uniform: Blue Jeans

★ ★ ★

In a 1970s advertising campaign, the soft drink Dr Pepper—another beverage invented in the 1880s, this time in Texas, and originally billed as a "brain tonic" like Coca-Cola—invited Americans to drink the soda and become "part of an original crowd" who identified themselves as "Peppers."[1] The irony of that claim was not lost on those of us who lived through the era. But drinking Dr Pepper is hardly the only case of Americans displaying their individuality in utterly conventional ways. Look down any American street or across any American college campus and you will see a rippling ocean of blue, at least from the waist down. That is the tide of the original crowd of blue jeans-wearers.

Few commodities project Americanness to the world as blue jeans do, and David Little, one of the many chroniclers of the clothing, contends that blue jeans are particularly expressive of American character or at least "what Americans have believed themselves to be: strong, unpretentious, unadorned, informal, comfortable, classless, hard-working, reliable, consistent and improving with time."[2] In a general study of popular culture, John Fiske pinpointed the paradox of blue jeans also contained in being a "Pepper": "The desire to be oneself does not mean the desire to be fundamentally different from everyone else."[3] Equally paradoxical, jeans—especially "distressed" or torn ones—both reflect and resist dominant values . . . or reflect the fact that one of America's dominant values is resistance.

Perhaps most illustrative and ironic is the fact, according to Graham Marsh and Paul Trynka, that the story of blue jeans "nestles snugly against the curves and sinews of American history," most prominently its diverse immigrant history: "a look conceived by the French, a technology perfected by the English, a form of clothing invented by two Americans—one recently arrived from the Baltic, the other from Bavaria. Nurtured by an immigrant culture, it was worn by workers and popularized by American icons from John Wayne to Madonna."[4]

Blue Jeans before Levi's

Most Americans probably recognize the name Levi Strauss as a brand—Levi's—that is virtually synonymous with blue jeans in the same manner that Kleenex is equivalent to facial tissues or Band-Aid to adhesive bandages. However, not only the material from which they are made but the fashioning of that material into trousers long predates Levi Strauss and his company. As Lynn Downey, a historian for Levi Strauss & Company, reminds us, the standard attribution of the term "denim" is to a serge fabric manufactured for centuries in the French town of Nîmes. However, Downey, among others, is skeptical that *serge de Nîmes* gave rise to the English word "denim" or that all denim was a French import.[5] Downey and James Sullivan, another historian of blue jeans, both report that a fabric billed as "serge de Nimes" was also produced in England by the seventeenth century at the latest, and besides, *serge de Nîmes* was made of wool, while the familiar denim is made of cotton. To confuse matters further, Sullivan finds that a cotton, wool, and silk blend was manufactured in Genoa, Italy, even earlier (imported into England in the 1500s) and known for its place of origin as "Gen" or "jean"—"a word which the Oxford English Dictionary dates to 1567."[6]

Amazingly, Sullivan discovers jeans in America almost from its first days: in the 1620s the Massachusetts Bay Company store was already ordering "English jeans," and by the 1760s the United Company of Philadelphia, a textile mill, was producing its own jean material.[7] Downey adds that denim was advertised in the United States in 1789, with a 1792 guidebook suggesting techniques for weaving the material.[8] By the mid-1800s denim and jean (which were not quite identical) were relatively common items, featured for instance in an 1849 catalogue from the New York company Lewis & Handford that offered "blue jean trousers and a 'Fancy Mixt' jean, as well as vests, jackets, and topcoats in jean material dyed in black, white, blue, chestnut, and olive."[9] Finally, "Bib-front overalls, often considered to be a precursor to jeans, were a common workingman's garment by the time they became prevalent in America in the early nineteenth century," worn for example by farmers and their children, like Huckleberry Finn.[10]

Levi Strauss Makes Blue Jeans

Both terminology such as "denim" and "jeans" and specific sartorial uses of those fabrics were thus well established in America before the career of Levi Strauss. Mr Strauss did not invent denim fabric or jeans trousers. Nor did he single-handedly invent the Levi's blue jean, nor did he or his company monopolize the manufacture and design of blue jeans for long after his iconic trousers were first made.

Levi Strauss was born (by the name Loeb Strauss) in Buttenheim, Bavaria, in 1829 and arrived in the U.S. with his widowed mother and two sisters in 1847. As many new and old immigrants did, he trekked west, reaching San Francisco in 1853, where he opened a wholesale "dry goods" store selling an array of ordinary products to local consumers; he was not a manufacturer of anything at this point. Unfortunately, the famous San Francisco fire of 1906 destroyed much of the record of the first decades of Strauss's business, making it especially easy for the company's history to "become a repository for tall tales and dubious anecdotes, some of them possibly embellished by long-ago salesmen, others by the vagaries of old newspapers and biographical resources."[11] Downey writes that for years, the legend "ran like this":

> Levi Strauss arrived in San Francisco, and noticed that miners needed strong, sturdy pants. So he took some brown canvas from the stock of dry goods supplies he brought with him from New York, and had a tailor make a pair of pants. Later, he dyed the fabric blue, then switched to denim, which he imported from Nimes. He got the idea of adding metal rivets to the pants from a tailor in Reno, Nevada, and patented this process in 1873.[12]

Levi Strauss, before
1902.

Not only is this story untrue, but it neglects the crucial contributions of other men in the creation of Levi's blue jeans, as well as of the other companies that were competing to make their own jeans.

In fact, Marsh and Trynka began their modern history of blue jeans not with Levi Strauss at all but with Jacob Davis, a tailor born in Latvia in 1831 and living in Reno, Nevada, in the 1870s. It was Davis who hit upon the idea of reinforcing denim with copper rivets to serve the needs of nearby miners; Davis's riveted denim work clothes were so popular that he sought a business partner to help him secure a patent and to mass-produce his design. In 1872 he reached out to Strauss, who supplied his fabric, with a business proposition, offering "a half-interest in the proposed riveted pants business in exchange for the price of the patent application."[13] It was one of the best business offers of all time.

Although the U.S. Patent Office declined their application twice on the grounds that it was not original (copper rivets having been used in boots for some years), they secured their patent in 1873, and Strauss brought Davis to San Francisco as part of Levi Strauss & Company to manage the production process (recall that Strauss was a wholesaler, not a manufacturer). Davis oversaw the design and production of "copper

Levi's 501 Jeans, with characteristic label and pocket stitching.

riveted 'waist overalls'" (which was the old name for jeans) out of a brown cotton duck, and a blue denim.[14] (Cotton duck, also known as duck cloth or duck canvas, is a heavy, tightly woven material well suited for work wear.) The use of duck cloth was temporary, ending in 1911 at the latest, but blue denim would become legendary.

Levi Strauss's blue jeans were thus definitely not the first denim wear in America, but they soon became the most recognizable. In 1873 the company added its trademark orange double-stitching pattern on the back pockets, which was joined in 1886 by the leather tag on the back of the waist depicting two men and their horse-teams trying unsuccessfully to rip the tough trousers. It was in 1890 that a specific lot number—501—was assigned to the classic "waist overalls"; the name Levi's 501s is still in use today, although those garments no longer feature suspender buttons.[15]

Rivals were quick to enter the lucrative denim jeans market. Indeed, a competitor called Sweet-Orr, based in New York, claimed to manufacture overalls two years before Levi Strauss—including an ad depicting men trying to tear the pants and a caption, "All Goods Warranted 'Never to Rip'."[16] From 1895 OshKosh B'Gosh of Wisconsin sold overalls, and department stores such as Sears & Roebuck, Montgomery Ward, and J. C. Penney offered their own denim clothing lines by the early 1900s. The most enduring challenger, though, was Lee, founded by Henry David Lee in Salina, Kansas, in 1889. In 1913 Lee premiered the "Union-All" neck-to-foot jumpsuit, which was such a hit that the U.S. Army adopted it in 1917. Soon thereafter, in 1924, Lee introduced what would become Lee Riders.

> These were pants made of heavy thirteen-ounce denim (Levi's were made of ten-ounce denim at that time) and were crafted especially for seamen and loggers. The heavy "cowboy pant" was to follow. By 1926, Lee had initiated a remarkable series of merchandising firsts including jeans with zippers, more comfortable styling, and tailored sizing.[17]

Another entry, the Wrangler Company, began life when Blue Bell Overall Company and Big Ben Manufacturing merged in 1926 and quickly became associated with railroad workers. Lee also vied for the railroad market, even using the slogan "Lee, the Jeans that Built America" in the 1930s, despite the fact that much of America was built long before the first pair of Lees came off the assembly line only twenty years before. Interestingly, there is a more obscure maker of denim clothing today that still bears the name of Strauss's partner, Jacob Davis.[18] Many more, including high-fashion, brands were yet to come, as we will see below.

Cowboys, Counterculture, and Couture

Denim overalls, jumpsuits, pants, and jackets were popular among manual laborers of many kinds in the late nineteenth and early twentieth centuries—farmers, miners, loggers, railroad men, and others, but we have so far not mentioned two other highly important markets. These missing consumers of blue jeans are cowboys and the general public, and the path to the latter leads through the former.

The American frontier was unofficially "closed" around 1890, ending the heroic (and for the Native peoples of America, catastrophic) expansion of the United States across the continent. Almost immediately, Americans were struck with a wave of nostalgia for the legendary ridin'-the-range, shoot-'em-up life of the cowboy (which was summarized by historian Frederick Jackson Turner in 1893 as the "frontier thesis" of American society—that is, that the frontier experience had left an indelible mark on the country's personality). The popular culture of the era helped generate and perpetuate romantic images of the American cowboy, such as the 1902 Owen Wister novel *The Virginian: A Horseman of the Plains* and the many books of Zane Grey such as his 1912 *Riders of the Purple Sage*. In 1914 *The Virginian* was made into a very early feature film by Cecil B. de Mille, to be followed by an infinite number of "Western" movies and, later, television programs.

At the same time that the cowboy emerged as a central symbol of American history and character, "Levi's was directing its advertising at cowboys; by the 1920s their jeans were becoming obligatory wear for their on-screen counterparts . . . Before that time, few people outside of California had seen a pair of their trousers."[19] By the 1930s, although various kinds of manual laborers still wore denim, the look became "associated less often with laborers in general, and more as the fabric of the authentic American as symbolized by John Wayne, Gary Cooper, and others. Levi Strauss & Company advertising did its part to fuel this craze, using the West's historic preference for denim clothing to advertise Levi's waist overalls."[20] John Wayne, for example, wore a pair of Levi's 501s in the classic 1939 film *Stagecoach*, and other popular figures such as Gene Autry and Roy Rogers donned their Wranglers. At the same time, Lee was directly involved in the formation of the Rodeo Cowboys Association in 1936, acting as an official sponsor of the rodeo circuit, just as Wrangler continues to do today.

Since few Americans were actually professional cowboys or aspired to be, the blue jeans industry got a big boost from the *amateur* cowboy business, in the form of "dude ranches" that sprang up in the 1920s for city slickers to experience the (tame) Wild West temporarily. And dude ranchers needed dude ranch duds, a need fulfilled by the literally named Dude Ranch Duds line from Levi's in the mid- to late 1930s. Marsh and Trynka opined that fancy items such as the "'High color Rodeo and Fiesta shirts' hardly epitomized the tough, laborers' practicality that Levi Strauss and Jacob Davis had championed. But they signaled the company's unconscious, telepathic ability of being at the center of every new social trend."[21] And again, Levi Strauss & Company got assistance in inventing the Western look from allies such as Rockmount Ranch Wear, founded in Denver in the 1940s by Jack Weil who pioneered the "diamond snap" and "sawtooth pocket" now customary in Western shirts and reputedly uttered the words, "The West is not a place, it is a state of mind."

A signal change came to the jeans industry after the Second World War, marked by Blue Bell/Wrangler's alteration of its slogan from "The World's Producer of Work Clothes" to "The World's Largest Producer of Work and Play Clothes."[22] The 1950s introduced a new icon of rugged American individualism and even anti-authoritarianism, the "biker" or motorcycle rider, who would be the bridge for blue jeans to reach a new generation and a new social category—the teenager. (There are those who contend, with considerable justification, that the concept and social role "teenager" and his associated "youth culture" was an invention of the 1950s.) The year 1951 saw Marlon Brando wearing tight blue jeans in the film version of *A Streetcar Named Desire*. Levi's 501s appeared on Brando two years later in the 1953 biker movie *The Wild One*. Two years after that, 1955's *Rebel Without a Cause* starred James Dean sporting his jeans (whether they were Lee's or Levi's has been hotly debated) for the infamous game of "chicken" in stolen cars, and in 1957 Elvis Presley rocked the jailhouse in a black denim jacket and black jeans.

Jeans became ever more ubiquitous in the youth and rock 'n' roll counterculture of the 1950s and beyond, moving dramatically away from the hardworking denim wear of previous generations. Gene Vincent's 1956 rock 'n' roll album was actually titled *Blue Jean Bop* (although he wears all leather in a recorded performance of the song),[23] and the restless characters in Jack Kerouac's 1957 novel *On the Road* travel with jeans. In fact, Downey maintains that it was only in the 1950s that denim pants with metal rivets, which had previously been referred to as overalls, acquired the name "jeans"—a change emanating from the youth culture and absorbed by the denim industry.[24] But naturally, through this association with bikers, rockers, and such unsavory types, blue jeans gained a disreputable image, with many older Americans believing that the garments were inappropriate for children and teens; some schools actually banned them. Sensing both an opportunity and a threat, Levi Strauss & Company promoted the wholesomeness of their products with the slogan "Denim: Right for School" as far back as 1949,[25] and the Lee Company promoted a photo ad in 1953 contrasting the "right way" to wear jeans in school respectfully versus the "wrong" and disrespectful way.[26]

Blue jeans attained a new dimension of rebellion as American culture entered into new forms of agitation in the 1960s, specifically the civil rights and the anti-Vietnam War movements. Young idealistic civil rights activists from the North "who went south to join the sit-ins traded their chinos, loafers, and short-sleeve Oxford shirts for the everyday clothes of the men and women they came to support."[27] In his study of the 1960s, Todd Gitlin asserted that these proper young people "were powerfully affected by the most impoverished and disenfranchised Negroes [and] . . . picked up the back-country look of Georgia and Mississippi: denim jackets, blue work shirts, bib overalls."[28] As the decade progressed and protests expanded against many aspects of mainstream America, blue jeans were embraced as what Little calls "the perfect uniform for this disenfranchised army of teenagers and young people":

> Denim became as free and colorful as the idealistic "hippies" who wore it during those "summers of love" in the middle and late Sixties . . . Clothing became looser in reflection, even the jeans. The "tapered" and "pegged" skintight jeans of the late Fifties and early Sixties were out.[29]

Jeans continued to evolve and to maintain an association with counterculture and resistance, from the punk rock movement of the mid- and late 1970s (for example, with the Ramones and the Sex Pistols) to the grunge genre of the 1990s. However, at the same time and fascinatingly, jeans began to become *more* mainstream, to be accepted, if not domesticated, and then redeployed by the fashion industry. (Meanwhile, we can never forget, or forgive, that Lee was responsible for the travesty known as the "leisure suit" in 1972.) As early as the 1920s, Levi Strauss & Company had featured a line of denim wear for women, who were, until then, largely excluded from the jeans market. But a remarkable step was taken in the late 1940s by designer Claire McCardell, who turned away from standard fabrics to create fashion designs in unprecedented materials such as denim. Her signature design was the so-called "Pop over" dress, "a simple, wrap-front dress, which even came with a matching oven glove and sold for just $6.95."[30] Soon, Wrangler and Lee were also producing jean fashions for women, and Levi Strauss & Company answered with a line of women's "Ranch Pants" in vivid new colors such as light blue, red, pink, and gold.

It did not take long before other influential designers were working with denim and manufacturing their own lines of jeans—Yves Saint Laurent in 1969, Calvin Klein in 1977, and Gloria Vanderbilt in 1978. Predictably, these were not your grandfather's jeans, simple and functional, but were styled up—or down—in all sorts of fresh ways. One of the most revealing developments in blue jeans was the selling of intentionally aged or damaged fabric. Jeans makers noticed that consumers continued to wear their jeans if they were faded, stained, or even torn; indeed, not only did jeans, unlike virtually all other clothing, in some ways look *better* when they were old and worn, but the wear-and-tear in a sense personalized the items, giving them an individuality, a biography if you will. Owners sometimes deliberately tore them. As always, manufacturers seized on a trend, offering the public jeans that looked like they had already been beaten and abused. And often they had: in 1965 two French designers, Maritime Bachellerie and Françoise Girbaud, started to wash jeans repeatedly to soften and fade them, and then literally scratch the material with sandpaper "to give it a well-worn appearance."[31] No later than 1973, Lee was "prewashing" its jeans to make new clothes look old. Around the same time, denim aficionados such as Adriano Goldschmeid doused fabric with bleach to create stains and holes, and soon Lee and Levi were selling "acid-washed" jeans that were treated with various caustic chemicals. At the extreme, denim was attacked with rocks—specifically, pumice or lava rock—to get the "stone-washed" look. Mark Emelfarb, whose family was in the decorative stone business, provided pumice to Levi Strauss & Company, Lee, Wrangler, and the new manufacturer Guess and "was soon trafficking three hundred ocean containers of lava rock each month" to torture their jeans with.[32]

As jeans became more associated with style, they also became more associated with sex. A prime example was the controversial television ad for Calvin Klein jeans in 1980 and 1981, featuring a fifteen-year-old Brooke Shields who provocatively uttered, "You want to know what comes between me and my Calvins? Nothing" as she whistled the folk song "My Darling Clementine."[33] Calvin Klein became a leader in sexualized print and video advertising, but other companies such as Jordache and Guess followed suit, employing models such as Anna Nicole Smith and Claudia Schiffer. Loeb Strauss could hardly have foreseen where his overalls would go.

But that is the whole point and appeal of blue jeans. Sullivan concludes that "jeans are mutable . . . evolving from function to form, from drudgery to romance"; even more so, and even more so than most traditions, "jeans are an accumulation of history"—the history of the individual owner and wearer, to be sure, but also collective American

Denim has moved from a working-class fabric to being used as a fashion statement—
a trend capitalized upon by many high-end brands.

history.[34] The story of blue jeans follows and reflects the contours of the story of America with special precision. Both have multiple European roots, arose from the immigrant and frontier experience, evolved from nostalgia to popular culture to counterculture and finally to high culture. And both tell the tale of process and paradox.

> America *is* a process . . . The country's history is the process
> of moving into and out of its cities; of moving west, and back
> again; of moving up and down the social ladder. It is also
> the process of reconciling contradictions . . . We've made the
> process, and those contradictions, inherent in our jeans.[35]

At the top of the list of these contradictions, as John Fiske argued, are the paradoxes of individuality and conformity, of naturalness and commodification, and of freedom/equality and hierarchy/status-seeking.

Jeans and a T-Shirt

No American wardrobe would be complete without T-shirts to go with the jeans. Whether or not cowboys, miners, and railroad workers wore T-shirts with their jeans, by the 1950s jeans and T-shirt was a familiar look, at least among the bikers and delinquents (the shirt sometimes worn under a leather jacket), and T-shirts have since become as recognizably American as blue jeans. The story of how what is essentially underwear became outerwear—and even fashion wear—is as rich and informative as the journey of jeans themselves.

People have probably been wearing shirts or tunics of wool or cotton under their clothes from time immemorial, but one of the most enduring and celebrated manufacturers of undershirts is Fruit of the Loom, founded by Robert Knight in Rhode Island in 1851. Fruit of the Loom later acquired BVD, which originally made women's underwear (especially the nineteenth-century treat the bustle) and an item called the "union suit," a one-piece neck-to-ankle undergarment that would be perfect beneath the Lee Union-All. The website www.stolenshirts.com claims that a business called Russell Manufacturing Company made the first T-shirt, allegedly named because its simple design featured sleeves projecting in a perpendicular direction from the body like a "T," in 1902—interestingly, as women's wear and featuring front buttons. By 1910 Fruit of the Loom was manufacturing a sleeveless cotton T-shirt.

Most sources agree that, whatever its prehistory, the modern T-shirt came to life around the time of the First World War, as used by the U.S. Navy. Karl Smallwood explains that the 1905 *Uniform Regulations of the United States Navy* specified the cotton shirt to be worn under the sailors' uniform; not unreasonably, on hot days the uniform top might come off, displaying the plain shirt beneath.[36] Some historians have also suggested that the T-shirt originated in the sports world, under football jerseys for instance (often featuring the name of the team or college), and by 1933 the famed company Lacoste (known for its alligator emblem) was producing short-sleeved cotton shirts for golfers and tennis players.

The Second World War was another giant leap for the T-shirt, as soldiers wore it more prominently and the public accepted it more graciously as outerwear. An iconic image on the cover of *Life* magazine, dated July 13, 1942, showed a strapping man holding a machine gun and wearing a white T-shirt with the logo "Air Corps Gunnery School," which enhanced the profile and prestige of the item. As blue jeans were, T-shirts were promoted by the media and the youth culture in the 1950s, in the exact same films such as *A Streetcar Named Desire* and *Rebel Without a Cause*. Smallwood notes that "Brando's smoldering performance in both the play and 1951 movie [*A Streetcar Named Desire*] caused a nationwide spike in sales of T-shirts, proving to the world that the T-shirt could be a 'sexy, stand-alone, outer-wear garment.'"[37]

The subsequent course of the T-shirt through American culture closely paralleled that of blue jeans, from limited professional use (in this case, by soldiers and athletes as opposed to manual laborers) to counterculture gesture, to mainstream item and ultimately to fashion statement. As denim wear had been, T-shirts were appreciated for their comfort, their freedom, and their individuality: you could tie-dye them, rip them, and—most importantly of all—post your own message on them. As mentioned, particular colleges, universities, teams, and military units printed their names on the chests of T-shirts. In 1948, presidential candidate Thomas Dewey reportedly offered a T-shirt with the slogan "Dew

It for Dewey," which continued a long tradition of campaign items, from buttons to hats to stickers, with candidates' names and mottoes.

Of course, people have customized jeans for a long time too, not only ripping and staining them but sewing on patches or embroidering messages, but nothing provides the sort of billboard space that a T-shirt offers: the website Zani calls the T-shirt "the graffiti wall of clothing," on which individuals can display any information they can find or make.[38] One could always commission a custom T-shirt, but manufacturers were quick and keen to sell print T-shirts with everything from corporate logos (Zani claims that Budweiser was the first, producing a shirt picturing a can of Bud beer) to rock band names and political or personal statements such as "Make Love, Not War" or "I ♥ NY." Some of the most amusing examples are documented by Eric Silverman in his study of Jewish dress, including T-shirts with messages such as "Jesus Saves, Moses Invests," "Sephardilicious," and "What Would Maimonides Do?"[39] Wearers thus became living and moving advertisements for companies and causes—and even when the message was a cause, it still served the company that manufactured and marketed it, such as the Che Guevara T-shirt that was revolutionary at first and now is simply another commodity. Tourist destinations all around the world know that Americans desire T-shirts as souvenirs, and I personally have T-shirts with images and slogans from Mexico, Thailand, Nepal, Bali, and Aboriginal Australia (the Warlpiri tribe of central Australia had their own T-shirts printed!).

It is hard to imagine any sentiment that has not featured on a T-shirt, especially since the shocking logo of the clothier French Connection UK appeared as FCUK after 1991. This quality and history makes the T-shirt the perfect accompaniment to blue jeans for Americans. Both are comfortable but owe their popularity to much more than comfort. Both evolved from professional wear to casual wear, by way of the youth and counterculture. Both are free and hopeful at the same time as angry and rebellious. And both are simultaneously very personal and highly commoditized, avowing an individualized meaning that is mass-manufactured and as marketed as any other consumer product. Accordingly, Lynne Neal aptly lauded and criticized the T-shirt as *the clothing of democracy*. The T-shirt represents the ideal democratic apparel as it symbolized cherished American values—individualism and free speech, sameness and difference. Thus, it is *the* clothing of democracy. However, at the same time, the T-shirt obscures how these same values foster the status quo, cloak injustice, and amplify inequities.[40]

Or we might more accurately say that the T-shirt, like the blue jean, is the clothing of capitalism—liberatory and oppressive, inspiring and offensive, and always for sale.

AMERICAN
TRADITIONAL
CHARACTERS

THIRTEEN

And the American Way: Superman

★ ★ ★

The hero figure is as old as human society. From the Greek *heroe* for a defender or protector, the hero is a person of extraordinary, sometimes divine, strength, courage, skill, intelligence and virtue who accomplishes great things, ideally for the benefit of others. Gilgamesh of ancient Mesopotamia may be the first hero in recorded history, but others from myth, literature, and lore include Samson, Hercules, Achilles, Beowulf, King Arthur, and Dekanawida or Tekana:wita, the Iroquois "Great Peacemaker." They doubly reflect the values of their culture, as personifications and often as founders of those values. According to Ben Saunders, who has written a book on contemporary caped "superheroes," the common message of the hero, "the wish that things were otherwise," is a fantasy reaction "to the distressing mismatch between our expectations of the world and the way the world actually appears to be."[1]

America has spawned its share of heroes, but none has become so perfectly identified with the country and its self-image as Superman. As the nation itself was, Superman was created at a specific moment, and as the nation has, he has changed and grown—and sometimes shrunk—with time. In the words of Glen Weldon, another chronicler of the great Kryptonian,

> Superman's perceived status as a static fixture of popular culture, an unchanging icon of spandex-clad heroism, is an illusion. Examining the Man of Steel during the course of his

seventy-five years reveals that everything about him exists in a state of perpetual flux. The particulars of his origin and his power-set have vacillated wildly. So, too, has his persona continually evolved: in his first few years of life, he was our hot-headed, protective big brother; he spent the forties and fifties assuming the role of our coolly distant father; he morphed in the sixties and seventies into our bemused, out-of-touch uncle; and he even became—mercifully briefly, in the benighted nineties—our mulleted, hillbilly cousin.[2]

Moreover, Superman is a schizoid character, and not only in his alien and human heritage. During most of his career, across multiple media, parallel Supermen with contrasting and even contradictory biographies and qualities have coexisted.

Super Men and Super Menaces

Superman is clearly heir to a long tradition of heroic defenders; he is not even the original American hero. *The Lone Star Ranger* was penned by Zane Grey in 1915, and the Lone Ranger found his way onto radio in 1933, several years before Superman was invented. Zorro, another swashbuckler with a secret identity, originated in 1919 in Johnston McCulley's story "The Curse of Capistrano," published in one of the many pulp magazines of the era. Popeye, with his non-supernatural spinach-given strength, first graced the comic strips in 1929, and Doc Savage emerged in 1933. Before them and outside the United States, Sherlock Holmes was solving crimes with extraordinary perceptiveness and intelligence in 1887, and the Scarlet Pimpernel was imagined by Baroness Emma Orczy in 1903 as a masked champion with a foppish true identity. The very name "Superman" is not entirely original. The German philosopher Friedrich Nietzsche used the term *Übermensch* (translated as "overman" or "superman") in the 1880s to refer to a future higher form of humanity, and playwright George Bernard Shaw composed his *Man and Superman* in 1903.

Thomas Andrae, in an insightful 1980 essay, made the important observation that modern heroes and super men differ from ancient and mythical or religious ones precisely because their powers are *natural*, even "scientific." Thus he claimed that Superman's pedigree owes less to Samson and Hercules than to science fiction in the late 1800s and early 1900s.[3] And the new genre of science fiction was further embedded in a culture of profound and often-unsettling technological advancement and social change. This is why Andrae noted that the super men of those decades were often, intentionally or not, a menace to the population of normals like you and me (an interesting point stressed in the 2015 television series *Supergirl*).

Nietzsche had predicted that the *Übermensch* would be a threat to ordinary people, cruel in his superiority and "evil" by the conventional standards of good and evil. Andrae insisted that many of the supermen, the *Homo superior*, of the turn of the century were at best extralegal—operating outside the bounds of established laws and institutions—and at worst dangers to society and to themselves. Great power could be destructive, certainly alienating, and often seductive; why should superior men help when they could rule? Importantly, "all the stories of mentally and physically superior human beings end tragically and futilely. Whether he becomes an outcast, a pathetically lonely creature who is ostracized, or a tyrannical monster so dangerous that he threatens to enslave the world, convention dictates that he either die or be robbed of his power."[4]

One common manifestation of the sinister superior was (and is) the "mad scientist" whose knowledge drives him to perilous acts of hubris (such as Dr Frankenstein's attempts to create life itself). A proximate influence on the familiar Superman—which we know because his creator, Jerry Siegel, wrote a review of it in 1932—was Philip Wylie's 1930 novel *Gladiator*, featuring such a scientist who deliberately used a chemical serum on his wife to give their unborn child super strength, to make him "a being of steel." The result is an anti-Superman, a lonely character who is isolated and punished for his superiority: for instance,

> When he rescues a clerk trapped in a bank vault, he is brutally tortured and branded as a potentially dangerous criminal. And when he plans to right the wrongs of politics by forcing the

selfish and cynical from office and securing the idealistic and incorruptible in their place, he realizes that he is becoming a tyrant.[5]

The theme seems to be "that there was no longer room in the modern world for the heroic, superior, or unique individual."[6]

Perhaps the only place where a modern hero could survive is in another world, which may explain Edgar Rice Burroughs's *John Carter of Mars*, introduced in 1911 (and made into an unsuccessful movie in 2012). John Carter was an earthling who developed super strength on Mars thanks to the planet's weaker gravity. While there is no direct evidence that Superman's inventors knew Burroughs's work, "the formula for Superman's otherworldly origin and ensuing powers was a simple inversion of Edgar Rice Burroughs's John Carter stories."[7] Superman reverses the direction of John Carter's travels—not *from* Earth but *to* Earth—and more consequentially but never completely reverses the fate of the *Homo superior* among *Homo mediocris*.

The Superman That Almost Wasn't

There were very few new ideas in Superman, but what was unique was that the introduction of this character was the first time that all of these traditional science fiction, pulp, and fantasy elements had been combined into one hero. Superman was the first superstrong, crime-fighting, costumed hero from another world. In other words, he was the first superhero.[8]

If Jeffrey Johnson, yet another student of Superman, is correct, the 1930s was a fertile period for all the previous traditions of supermen to converge, as America found itself in particular need of heroes. The Great Depression, urbanization, immigration, organized crime, and the rumblings of world war merged to form an especially scary time when neither the little guy nor the people in power seemed capable of solving the country's problems. But even if Superman was not created out of thin air but was synthesized from available traditions, he required a synthesizer, and that person would be writer Jerry Siegel, in conjunction with illustrator Joe Shuster.

The first pages of Siegel's 1933 short story "The Reign of the Super-Man."

Siegel (1914–1996) and Shuster (1914–1992) were schoolmates in Cleveland, Ohio, both sons of Jewish immigrants. Even before he finished high school, Siegel wrote and published in late 1932 what Weldon regards as one of the original fanzines, under the title *Science Fiction: The Advance Guard of Future Civilization*. (In the second issue, he reviewed Wylie's novel *Gladiator*.) The third issue (January 1933) featured a short story called "The Reign of the Super-Man," with pictures by Shuster, sure enough about an evil scientist who experimented on a homeless man in a bread line, giving him super powers and then coveting those powers for himself so that he might "rule the universe."[9]

In other words, the first Superman was "the Super-Man," a stereotypical power-mad *Homo superior*. Then Siegel began to tinker with his creation, first reimagining him as a strongman in T-shirt and dress pants. Gradually—or suddenly, as legend would have it—the Super-Man morphed into Superman. The next step in Superman's evolution placed him in "a trapeze-artist's leotard: tights, shorts, belt—and that striking, idiosyncratic cape."[10] Then, almost as epiphany, it happened: one summer night in 1934, sleeping in his mother's house, the superheroic Superman occurred to Siegel in bits and pieces, causing him to jump up repeatedly to record his ideas. The next morning he ran to

Shuster's house to solicit a drawing of his inspiration. Superman was born—but he was not born whole, and he was far from sold.

Siegel and Shuster began to shop their new character around to publishers, with no success. Siegel even approached other, more famous illustrators, and drafted more complete scripts for Superman stories, such as one about a super-scientist from future-Earth who traveled back in time to fight crime in the 1930s. Alternatively, Superman was the baby of the last man of Earth, sent back in a time machine and found by Sam and Molly Kent. Interestingly, while Superman was being rejected again and again, Siegel and Shuster managed to sell two other characters— Henri Duval, Famed Soldier of Fortune, and Doctor Occult, the Ghost Detective—to *New Fun* magazine.

They finally found a buyer in DC (Detective Comics) in 1938, selling their first story, "Superman: Champion of the Oppressed," to businessmen Harry Donenfeld and Jack Leibowitz (who also dabbled in pornography, among other subject-matter) for $130. Superman featured in a thirteen-page segment of the 64-page issue number one of *Action Comics* (dated June 1938 but released on April 18) and also appeared on the cover, in his signature blue-and-red uniform, lifting a carload of criminals off the ground. Apart from his appearance, little about the superhero resembled what readers would come to know and love about him. For instance, his origin story was seriously underdeveloped: in just one page it was revealed that an unnamed scientist from an unnamed dying planet sent his infant son in a rocket capsule to Earth, where he was found by unnamed "passing motorists" who took him to an orphanage, where he discovered his tremendous strength, including his ability to "run faster than an express train" and deflect bullets off his skin. His powers were explained as totally natural, all of the inhabitants of his home planet possessing physiques that were "millions of years advanced of our own," gifted with the proportionate strength of ants and grasshoppers to lift weights and jump distances far in excess of their own size and weight. For unstated reasons, he "decided that he must turn his titanic strength into channels that would benefit mankind. And so was created . . . Superman."

No Ma and Pa Kent, no "leap tall buildings in a single bound," and definitely no "truth, justice, and the American way" in this first issue.

Clark Kent worked for an unnamed editor at the *Daily Star*; the only constant aspect of the tale is Lois Lane. Most distinctive were the kinds of crimes and violations in which Superman intervened. On page two, he breaks into a governor's mansion and tosses the butler around, brandishing written proof of the innocence of some unjustly convicted woman scheduled for immediate execution. In the ensuing pages, "Superman manhandles a wife beater, destroys the car of a group of gangsters, and stops a lobbyist and corrupt senator from pulling the U.S. into the war in Europe."[11] Through the following issues,

> Superman combats political graft at city hall, stops gangsters from fixing boxing matches, battles smugglers, prevents the assassinations of both a senator and a royal family member, shuts down an orphanage that exploited children, prevents profiteers from starting a war, and creates decent public housing. Superman accomplishes all of these things by being a tough hard-nosed fighter that at times even appears to become excessively brutal . . . This early Superman was a superpowered street brawler who fought for the less fortunate and concerned himself more with social ills rather than cosmic threats.[12]

Contrary to the familiar image of Superman as the ultimate patriot, Jeffrey Johnson calls him "a super-strong avenger," and Thomas Andrae judged him a socialist. For example, in *Action Comics* #3 (August 1938), he publicized the unsafe conditions in a coal mine, and in January 1939 (issue #8), "he proceeds to destroy the dilapidated houses of an entire slum area in order to force the government to erect modern, low-cost housing and to undertake a campaign of massive public aid"; even more remarkably, "National Guardmen and a squadron of aerial bombers are ordered to annihilate him,"[13] but of course they cannot, because he is invincible.

So what we had in the early months of Superman's life was a hero of great moral rectitude who often opposed the establishment, "a lawless individual who is wanted by the police,"[14] a *Homo superior* who does not mind—indeed, seems to enjoy—destroying private property and hurting people for the good of the little guy. In a word, Superman was an embodiment of another venerable American tradition, the vigilante (just like the Lone Ranger or Zorro). Interestingly, Andrae claimed, "the publishers were unaware that Siegel had cast Superman as an outlaw. When they discovered this fact inadvertently Siegel was told to make Superman operate within the law and to confine his activities to fighting criminals. All controversial social issues were to be avoided."[15]

The Many Lives of Superman

Superman was an instant success, quickly reaching a circulation of 500,000 copies per month. But almost as soon as he was invented, Superman began to change. Over time, "Siegel's original version of Superman was radically subverted and a vapid, establishment hero substituted in his place which the public, ironically, came to accept as the 'real' Superman. The memory of Superman's existence as an outlaw and champion of the oppressed would be virtually extinguished."[16] Even more significantly, and more so than many traditions, during the course of almost eighty years and multiple media incarnations, Superman would literally multiply into several parallel Supermen, elaborating details neglected in the original while creating serious discontinuities for the great American hero.

As already seen, Superman's origin story was especially abbreviated in the debut comic book; it was simply unimportant where he came from, who discovered him on Earth, or how he honed his superpowers. Many of those minimized or absent facts were expounded in his subsequent incarnations, starting with a dedicated comic book called *Superman* (first issue June 1939) that ran alongside *Action Comics*, and a newspaper comic strip that was inaugurated in January 1939. His origin story, dashed off in one page in *Action Comics* #1, was given two weeks in the newspaper and introduced Krypton as his home planet and Jor-L and Lora as his parents. *Superman* #1 also told how John and Mary Kent handed the infant to an orphanage and then some unspecified time later adopted him; it was after the Kents' deaths that Clark sought a job at the *Daily Star* in the city of Metropolis, which was identified in *Action Comics* #16.

Even more formative for the Superman legend was the radio show that commenced on February 12, 1940. In the demos for the show, Clark's employer was named the *Daily Flash*, his editor was Paris White, and "Miss Lane" was not a reporter but a switchboard operator—and Superman arrived on Earth as a fully grown man, not a baby! Larry Tye, yet another in the long line of Superman watchers, reports that our hero "grew up on his way to Earth and by the time he stepped out of his spaceship, he was ready to save this adopted planet."[17] In that storyline, there is no need for the Kents at all.

The radio show introduced a number of other memorable innovations to the Superman tradition. The announcer opened the first episode with the words, "Faster than an airplane! More powerful than a locomotive! Impervious to bullets." That episode, set on Krypton, named the infant more than once as Kal-L, although apparently Jor-L intended the escape spaceship for his wife rather than his child. The second episode began with the equally famous words, "Up in the sky! Look! It's a bird! It's a plane! It's Superman!" and found Superman landing in a desert, and then hovering over Indiana. By the 30th episode, he was described as "dedicated to the cause of truth and justice"; by the 100th episode, he was waging "a never-ending battle against crime and oppression," which changed to "crime and injustice" by the 130th episode. ("And the American way" would not show up until mid-1942, during the Second World War, and Tye argues that the words were designed "with the help of a child psychologist to ensure they touched the right chords."[18])

Other elements of the radio show that entered the Superman legend were cub reporter Jimmy Olsen, Superman's ability to fly, catchphrases such as "This is a job for Superman!" and "Up, up, and away!" and Superman's bane, kryptonite. Superman was voiced by Clayton "Bud" Collyer, and according to the Superman website kryptonite was conceived to give Collyer periodic vacations from the show: a weakened Superman "would give Collyer a few days to rest and relax."[19]

"Such was the power of the radio program," says Weldon, "that it altered the comic's continuity forever in several ways,"[20] including renaming characters and expanding Superman's powers and origin story. The radio show further cross-fertilized with the animated cartoon shorts produced by Max Fleischer between 1941 and 1943; Collyer also portrayed the animated Superman. Superman would make repeated forays into animation, such as *The New Adventures of Superman* from 1966, again with Collyer, *The Superman/Aquaman Hour of Adventure* from 1967, and

Title screen from a 1941 Max Fleischer *Superman* animated film.

Super Friends from 1973. His most unlikely—and forgettable—role was in a 1972 episode of *The Brady Kids* cartoon, in which he joined the children from *The Brady Bunch* in an escapade.

But cartoons were not the first visual experience of Superman. Actor Ray Middleton made a live appearance as Superman at the 1940 New York World's Fair, and Kirk Alyn famously brought him to life in two serials in the 1940s and a movie in 1948 (which also featured Noel Neill, who would be television's Lois Lane in the iconic 1950s series). Finally, Superman would not be Superman without the 1942 novel *The Adventures of Superman* by radio scriptwriter George Lowther. It was Lowther's book that changed Jor-L and Lora to Jor-El and Lara, offered more details about Krypton and Clark's early life (three full chapters' worth), and temporarily renamed the Kents Eben and Sarah.

The first years of Superman's evolution overlapped America's entry into the Second World War, which had a lasting but ambiguous effect on the Man of Steel, especially his divergent characteristics in various media. As early as February 1940, *Look* magazine asked Siegel and Shuster to contribute a brief story on the topic "How Superman Would

End the War," but as many observers have commented, Superman was so mighty that he could have made short—and unrealistic—work of the conflict, single-handedly winning a war that would take millions of men many years to prosecute. So, ironically, it was necessary for him to be largely absent from the war effort. Comic books featured him prominently on the covers tackling war subjects, but the actual comic book stories were surprisingly unrelated to the conflict. In fact, in 1941 Clark Kent was rejected by the military for poor eyesight, and a 1942 newspaper strip quoted him as saying, "The United States Army, Navy, and Marines are capable of smashing their foes without the aid of Superman!"[21] (Why the country could not handle its lesser problems without Kryptonian assistance was not addressed.) In print, Superman did play a domestic role in the war, and at one point in the radio program he worked undercover for the government, exposing saboteurs. Clark and Lois toured a Japanese internment camp (of which they essentially approved), but Superman's principal contribution to the war was encouraging citizens to buy war bonds to finance the effort: in *Action Comics* #58 (March 1943), his super speed allowed him to crank out flyers with the message, "Superman says, YOU can slap a Jap with WAR BONDS and STAMPS." Curiously, in cartoons and live-action films, he was much more directly involved in actual fighting against the Germans and Japanese.

How Superman affected the war is less important than how the war affected him. "By mid-1942, when the war effort demanded unquestioning loyalty to the state and increased collaboration between government and industry, Superman no longer operates outside the law but is made an honorary policeman."[22] This was the beginning of the domestication of Superman, of his association with—his virtual personification of— patriotism and "the American way." It was the beginning of what many fans and critics alike call "the big blue Boy Scout" phase of Superman. Interestingly, he also finally received a recurring enemy worthy of his power in Luthor—who is not only a mad scientist like the villain in Siegel's original Super-Man story but even looks like that character, bald and maniacal.

With the war won, the Superman legend could evolve yet again, and one strange and problematic direction was the 1945 introduction of Superboy, an idea proposed by Siegel and envisioned as a prankster without a costume. But with Siegel inducted into the army in 1943, the character was launched without him, as Superman's costumed younger self in 1945's *More Fun Comics* #101 (later moving to *Adventure Comics* before getting his own title in 1949). Running until 1979, the Superboy plotline presented a logical difficulty, since never before had Clark used or even recognized his powers and assumed his alter ego prior to adulthood; in fact, recall that in the radio show he did not have a childhood on Earth. The year 1949 also named his secret hideaway or base as the Fortress of Solitude, and in 1950, contrary to everything that had ever been said about Krypton, Superman met other survivors of the dead planet.

By 1948 Siegel was permanently off the Superman project, his very name expunged from the credits of comics, and Superman was free to develop in ways that Siegel neither controlled nor intended. The 1950s was a decade of notorious conformity and conservatism, which had an impact on Superman in two contradictory ways. He completed his metamorphosis from a social avenger and liberal vigilante into a superhero in a red-and-blue flannel suit, an organization man and supporter of the establishment. He also settled into his classic, and most formative, image—which many people regard as the "real" or "authentic" Superman—in the 1951 movie *Superman and the Mole-Men* and then the 1952 television series *The Adventures of Superman*, in both of which George Reeves played our hero. (By the way, in the first episode of the television show, the Kents were named Eben and Sarah.) Finally, Superman became the protector of "truth, justice, and the American way." Ironically, his conversion into a super-patriot was not enough to protect him from the McCarthyite campaign against subversives and youth culture in general. In what some dubbed the Great Comic Book Scare, Superman comics were censored and burned along with other unhealthy influences on America.

Superman survived the cultural onslaught and continued to grow in unexpected and downright odd ways. In 1955 (*Adventure Comics* #210) Superboy got a super dog, Krypto. Supergirl was introduced in 1958, becoming Superman's cousin Kara Zor-El in 1959. To make matters worse, 1958 also saw Superboy's weird double or opposite, Bizarro (brought back into popular culture by a *Seinfeld* episode about "Bizarro-Jerry"). Finally, in violation of everything that fans knew, in

1959 Superman returned to Krypton and met his birth parents; arch-villain Luthor also got a first name—Lex.

Obviously, Superman's storylines had become so tangled and inconsistent that, in effect, there were multiple simultaneous Supermen. In the 1960s, DC Comics made it official, by establishing that there were several parallel universes with different Earths, the original 1938 Superman occupying Earth 2, while the contemporary 1960s Superman inhabited Earth 1. Understandably, this situation became untenable by the 1980s, placing the entire Superman narrative in crisis and calling for an update and clarification. Although the various universes had come in contact before (in previous stories such as "Crisis on Earth—Two" and "Crisis on Earth—Three"), it was decided to return to a single, unified universe and storyline in the 1985–6 twelve-issue adventure "Crisis on Infinite Earths." Three incarnations of Superman literally fought each other, and in an almost biblical climax, Earth 2 (the original) Superman and his Lois Lane along with Superboy were sent to an off-Earth paradise, leaving the Earth 1 (modern) Superman as the only Superman.

As Jack Teiwes opines, "In essence, all Superman's previously-published adventures were rendered null and void as his origin story

Vincent Zurzolo of Metropolis Collectibles, holding a copy of *Action Comics* #1, purchased for $3.2 million.

could be reinvented with a blank slate that would allow for a new, updated version."[23] Not only had the competing biographies and storylines become discontinuous, but it was felt that Superman was too powerful and too non-human. So one of the key goals of the reinvention of Superman was to humanize him. In a series of comics after the unification of the universes, called "The Man of Steel" (July–September 1986), it was posited that Clark Kent was the real person while Superman was the disguise. Understandably, many fans and critics felt that Superman was ruined by this shift in direction, transformed into a "sensitive man," a yuppie, and a wimp.

Meanwhile, of course, Superman had other lives in other media, such as 1978's *Superman: The Movie* starring Christopher Reeve. Andrae considered the film to be a bellwether of changes to come in the comics, in which "Superman is presented as a thoroughly human, vulnerable, and even sexual character," eventually giving in to his passion for Lois Lane and surrendering his superpowers for his humanity.[24] Call it "Superman: The Love Story." The more human side of Superman was also highlighted in three television series, *Superboy* (premiering in 1988), *Lois & Clark: The New Adventures of Superman* (1993) concentrating on the romance between Clark and Lois, and *Smallville* (2001), set before Clark donned his Superman identity.

Even these reboots and reinventions were not enough. In 1987 a new comic book title, *Superman*, debuted, while the previous *Superman* was rebranded as *Adventures of Superman*. In 1992 (*Superman* #75), the unthinkable happened: Superman died. Happily, he was resurrected in 1993 (*Action Comics* #689). Since that harrowing experience, Superman's persona has varied wildly. At one point, he let his hair grow long; at another, he abandoned the Clark Kent charade to live as Superman; at yet another, he constructed an army of robots to rule the world—finally realizing the menace of previous supermen. In 2002, in a Tony Soprano moment, he started seeing the psychiatrist Dr Claire Foster. The "Superman: Birthright" storyline of 2005 represented a kind of fundamentalism, returning to the beginning of the whole story and retelling it. In 2005–6 Superman faced an "Infinite Crisis"—tossing out many of the "Birthright" elements—only followed by 2008's "Final Crisis." In the interim (2006–7), Superman, along with Batman and Wonder

Woman, withdrew from the world for a year. Finally, in 2010–11, Superman returned from New Krypton in a storyline called "Grounded" (*Superman* #700), in which he went on a walking tour of the United States to get back in touch with his country.

What Makes Superman So Darned American?

In probably the most often-cited essay in the Superman literature, Gary Engle asked precisely why the Man of Steel is "so darned American." His answer was Superman's dual status as an immigrant and an orphan. Orphan stories certainly appeal to us, but Engle stressed the former, insisting that the superhero is "the consummate and totally uncompromising alien, an immigrant whose visible difference from the norm is underscored by his decision to wear a costume of bold colors so tight as to be his very skin."[25] Think of his costume as "ethnic" garb. Superman then is a reminder that America is an immigrant society, always divided between being "from here" and being "from there." And Superman is the ultimate American success story, an immigrant who made it in the modern big city although he hails from foreign lands.

There is no doubt something to be said for this evaluation, although it cannot be the whole story. For one thing, Superman was a big hit long before his entire biography was revealed. Also, there have been other travelers and strangers in the hero genre, before and since. In fact, all heroes are travelers and strangers in a sense; they are the "other," the outsider, the cavalry riding over the hill to save the day. But we should not overlook other factors, not the least being the pragmatic marketing that kept him in the public imagination; by 1973, Weldon contends, "money from licensing Superman's likeness eclipsed the income from comic sales, as the launch of the action figure touched off a boomlet in licensed games, jigsaw puzzles, coloring books, play sets, stickers, and related merchandise."[26] And what could be more American than that?

Perhaps because he was the first American superhero, living several if not dozens of lives across multiple media and multiple universes for almost a century, Superman has a history not only with but like America. His story parallels our story: a forceful liberal in the 1930s, he became a confident, if naive, superpower, and then a law-and-order conservative, finding himself old-fashioned in the 1960s before turning sensitive, self-questioning, even cynical and a bit lost. Part of his appeal is pure nostalgia, for the country America used to be.

As we have amply demonstrated, there is not a single all-American Superman, any more than there is a single America. Most of all, he has not been unambivalently associated with America throughout his history. Blacklisted as un-American in the 1950s, few Americans remember that in 2006's *Superman Returns* movie, his famous nationalistic catchphrase was replaced with the sarcastic "truth, justice, and all that stuff" and that in 2011 (*Action Comics* #900) he expressed an intention to renounce his American citizenship in favor of a global identity. "Truth, justice, and the American way . . . it's not enough anymore," he said, "The world's too small. Too connected."[27]

FOURTEEN

Who's the Leader of the Club?
Mickey Mouse

★ ★ ★

Who is at the same time the icon of a corporation, a country, and a culture? The answer is M–I–C–K–E–Y–M–O–U–S–E, as they used to chant in the theme song of *The Mickey Mouse Club* in the 1950s, more than two decades after the creation of The Mouse and long past his heyday as a character in cartoons and animated films. In fact, it is rather odd that Mickey Mouse is such a recognizable figure when he has not appeared significantly in original features for a couple of generations. Unlike Superman and other fictional characters, Mickey Mouse truly has shifted from active star to retired tradition and ambassador of an empire that was born in the United States but straddles the globe.

Mickey Mouse's history is as interesting and invented as any American traditions—more so, because Walt Disney, his creator, was so overt about inventing not only the history of The Mouse but American history in general. In his critical analysis of Disney theme parks, which is where Mickey lives on today, Mike Wallace coined the term "Mickey Mouse History" to name Disney's entire "approach to the past," which was "not to reproduce it, but to *improve* it," as is clear in his romanticized and sanitized historical park attractions.[1] Worse is the fact that Wallace condemned Disney's corporate account of history, which "carefully program[s] out all the negative, unwanted elements," as "bad history" in which "the silences are profoundly distorting."[2] The same could be said about Disney Studios in general, which has made a career out of recycling already existing traditions (for example, folk tales such as Snow

White, Cinderella, and Mulan), along with historical characters such as Pocahontas, to forge a particularly Disneyfied version of traditions and history that is the only version many Americans know.

In a word, and more so than most or any of the Americans previously discussed, Mickey Mouse is part of a much larger private corporate project intentionally to create tradition and history and to influence the imagination of America and the world (after all, Disney Studios' creative minds are explicitly called "imagineers"—that is, people who engineer the imagination). This is why Mickey's history is not just the story of a man and his mouse.

Pre-Mickey Mouse

If the late nineteenth century was the era of patriotic traditions and new holidays, the early twentieth century was a time of creation of fictional characters, such as Superman in the previous chapter and Popeye and the Lone Ranger in the next chapter. I am not sure that anyone has ever pondered why the first three decades of the 1900s were so productive of fictional Americans and specifically of "heroes"; one hopes that it was not a symptom of a kind of pessimism about real Americans.

In the case of Mickey Mouse and his generation of characters, a prime mover was the new technology of motion pictures and animation. The first motion picture camera, the Kinetograph (literally "movement-write"), was demonstrated in 1890, designed by an associate of Thomas Edison named William Dickson, which was followed in 1892 by a system to project filmed images on a screen and, in 1894, by so-called Kinetograph parlors in which Edison played films for the public. Hence the twentieth century opened with the possibility of new ways of seeing, making, and distributing images and imagined characters.

Among the earliest inhabitants of the virtual world of film were cartoon characters, some of whom started out in newspaper comic strips and many of whom were animals. Before Mickey Mouse, for example, there was Krazy Kat and his mouse buddy Ignatz, dreamed up by George Herriman in 1913, and Felix the Cat, the brainchild of Otto Messmer in 1919; both felines starred in a series of animated cartoons over the years.

Cartooning and cartoon animation were thus real career paths in the first decades of the century, and a young Walter Elias Disney (1901–1966) joined the community, originally drawing "Newman Laugh-O-Grams" in Kansas City around 1919. Soon he formed his own studio and hired artists including Ubbe Eert Iwerks (1901–1971), better known as Ub Iwerks and a teen friend of Disney's who would become central to the success of the studio and The Mouse. After dabbling in nursery-rhyme-themed stories, Disney had the inspiration for a series of "Alice Comedies" pairing animation and live action. Disney and a team consisting of Iwerks, inker Lillian Bounds (eventually Disney's wife), and some other artists produced a series of "Alice Comedies" until 1927, by which time the Walt Disney Studio had been established. In that year, he was encouraged by his distributor to undertake an all-animation project based on a character named Oswald the Lucky Rabbit. Oswald, who appeared in a few animated shorts such as "Poor Papa," "Trolley Troubles," and "Oh, Teacher," looked remarkably like the yet-unborn Mickey Mouse, only with long ears.[3] Oswald, a mischievous bunny who got into a variety of sight gags and had a girlfriend named Fanny and an enemy named Pete (just as Mickey's arch-enemy was named Peg Leg Pete), was unfortunately lost to Disney in a contract dispute, which sent him on a search for a new character—a search that put him on a train to Los Angeles in March 1928 and led to Mickey Mouse.

Mickey Mouse Becomes a Sensation

"The exact details about the creation of Mickey Mouse have always been unclear because Walt Disney told different versions of how it happened," writes Jim Korkis, an authority on Mickey and all things Disney.[4] Later, for instance, Disney claimed that he came up with the idea during that fateful cross-country train trip, adding the appealing detail that an actual mouse had shared his drawing room back in Kansas City, which he had trained and/or saved and nicknamed Mortimer.[5] Most sources suggest that this story was pure fiction, but then perhaps it was the first instance of Disney imagineering. More likely, according to Korkis, is that Walt and his wife brainstormed on the train but conceived the character with her, his brother Roy, and Ub Iwerks in Los Angeles.

Two interesting but underappreciated facts about Mickey Mouse, then, are that he was not Disney's first character but was closely based on an earlier character and that Disney himself was not the principal illustrator of the Mickey Mouse cartoons. First, as Korkis explains, "Mickey Mouse was a 'mouse-ified' version of Oswald the Rabbit (designed by Iwerks), with mouse ears replacing rabbit ears and with a mouse tail replacing Oswald's small rabbit tail. Even the shorts remained the same"; Korkis quotes Iwerks himself as explaining, "Pear shaped body, ball on top, couple of thin legs. You gave it long ears and it was a rabbit. Short ears, it was a cat. Ears hanging down, a dog . . . With an elongated nose, it became a mouse."[6] It is also quite clear that, while Disney was the brains, and frequently the voice, behind The Mouse, he was not the main artist, initially or subsequently. Iwerks reportedly did all the drawing on the first three breakthrough Mickey Mouse cartoons (see below) and most of the work on the next few. Iwerks was also reputedly a prolific drawer,

Walt Disney with a drawing of Mickey Mouse, 1931.

completing hundreds of cells per day, which was much aided by the extremely simple look of Mickey Mouse at this point.

The first Mickey Mouse animation to be completed was "Plane Crazy," a six-minute cartoon inspired by Charles Lindbergh's recent flying accomplishments. As with its follow-up, "The Gallopin' Gaucho,"[7] a tribute to or parody of swashbuckling actors of the age like Douglas Fairbanks, the cartoon was done in 1928, was silent, and "was met with a wave of indifference" by potential distributors, as animated animals were no longer novel.[8] The key to Disney's and Mickey Mouse's success was the third incarnation, in a cartoon called "Steamboat Willie." Shortly before, the first sound motion picture, Al Jolson's *The Jazz Singer*, had been released, and Disney and his team set about devising a method to add sound to animations. The result debuted on November 18, 1928— eventually recognized as Mickey Mouse's official birthday—at a theater in New York City.

"Steamboat Willie," with Mickey as a ship's captain, was a smash hit, and Disney rushed to add sound to his previous Mickey Mouse cartoons, re-releasing them after "Steamboat Willie," which is remembered as the first Mickey animation although it was really the third. (Nor is it widely recalled that there was at least one earlier sound animation, a short titled "Dinner Time" produced by Paul Terry two months before Disney's cartoon.)[9] Within a year, fifteen Mickey Mouse cartoons had been shown in theaters, and January 1930 saw the introduction of a Mickey Mouse daily comic strip. Korkis notes that the strip commonly featured the title "Mickey Mouse by Iwerks," giving the official credit for the work to Ub Iwerks and not Walt Disney.[10]

When Iwerks left the studio in 1930, Floyd Gottfredson took over artistic duties, sketching Mickey Mouse comics for more than forty years. The Depression-era Mickey, however, bore little resemblance to the cute juvenile character that most Americans know today, either in appearance or personality. He was much more primitive-looking, a simple black-ink rendering with a more rat-like face; he also originally lacked his trademark gloves and shoes. (Korkis contends that the white gloves were implemented because Mickey's black hand disappeared when it moved across his black body.[11]) Mickey and his world were also quite different then: he was a bit of a tough guy, who talked and behaved like a ruffian—occasionally even using a gun—and was involved in a lot of visual gags, and he "lived in a rural area with farms, wide-open spaces, rustic devices, and barnyards filled with a variety of animals" such as Clarabelle Cow and Horace Horsecollar. That is, Mickey Mouse was born as a representative of pre-urban and rough-and-tumble America.

From the beginning, Mickey Mouse was a merchandising bonanza. According to Robert Heide and John Gilman, as early as September 1929 the idea of theater-based Mickey Mouse clubs was conceived—and not by Walt Disney. Rather, a theater manager named Harry W. Woodin, looking for ways to increase business, suggested the notion to Disney, and on Saturday, January 11, 1930, "at noon, the first official theater-based Mickey Mouse Club opened its doors to kids at the Fox Dome Theater in Ocean Park, California":

> Woodin invited local merchants and businesses to participate in the program, much to their benefit. Neighborhood bakeries offered up cakes to celebrate the birthdays of Club members each week. Delighted kids would walk away from Club meetings with MM masks, pins, and banners, all sponsored by local or national organizations or theater managers themselves. Dairies sponsored ice-cream prizes; banks offered piggy banks; and drugstores provided candy and trinkets. And the free goodies won more than the children's heart—the merchants gained a loyal customer base.[12]

Certainly, Mickey Mouse clubs were intended to drum up business and create loyal customers, but they also had the goal, as other potent American traditions of the era such as flag salutes and allegiance pledges had, "to aid children in learning good citizenship" by means of "inspirational, patriotic, and character building activities related to the Club."[13] Indeed, each meeting was scripted something like a political rally or patriotic celebration, with elected officers, a creed, and a pledge. The creed read,

> I will be a squareshooter in my home, in school, on the playgrounds, wherever I may be.

I will be truthful and honorable and strive always to make myself a better and more useful little citizen.

I will respect my elders and help the aged, the helpless and children smaller than myself.

In short, I will be a good American!

Members then pledged, "Mickey Mice do not swear, smoke, cheat, or lie" and sang a verse of "America" to the flag. At its height, the national Mickey Mouse movement claimed over one million young Americans— although, surprisingly, Disney soon turned against the idea of clubs, and no more were added after 1935. "Disney hoped the clubs would just fade away."[14]

With or without clubs, Mickey Mouse proved to be a juggernaut, enlisting many enthusiasts not directly associated with Walt Disney Studio. For instance, 1929 witnessed paper tablets for school children emblazoned with Mickey's image. In 1930, a seamstress named Carolyn Clark began making her own stuffed Mickey Mouse dolls, and by the end of the year she was supplying hundreds of dolls per week for two department stores in Los Angeles.[15] By 1934 the Knickerbocker Toy Company was mass-producing dolls based on Clark's design. Meanwhile, a company named Borgfeldt introduced a wooden Mickey Mouse figure with movable joints, adding other toys to its Mickey Mouse line such as drums, wagons, and balls. The year 1934 also gave us the first appearance of Mickey Mouse on a cereal box, and in 1935 the Mickey Mouse lunch box hit the market. As a sign of his fame, a Mickey Mouse balloon entered the Macy's Thanksgiving Day Parade in 1934. Partly out of concern for product quality, and partly so as not to miss out on the money-making opportunity, Walt Disney hired his own promotions expert in Herman "Kay" Kamen in 1932, who pioneered the classic Mickey Mouse watch in 1933 and a wind-up toy handcar with Mickey and Minnie Mouse in 1934—while refusing to permit Mickey's use on cigars, cigarettes, and alcohol. By the end of the decade, Disney Studio enjoyed more profit from Mickey Mouse's merchandise than from his cartoons.[16]

The Many Lives—and Afterlife—of a Mouse

Within two years of his premiere, Mickey Mouse had a biography independent of Walt Disney. Bobette Bibo, of the publishing house Bibo
and Lang, produced *Mickey Mouse Book* in 1930, which included an
origin story for The Mouse. Residing before he ever met Disney in a
realm called Mouse Fairyland and known only as Mouse #13, he was
exiled by the king for being too rambunctious and playful; kicked out of
the kingdom, he landed on a roof in Hollywood and, sliding down the
chimney like a rodent Santa, found himself in the presence of Walt
Disney. Disney named him Mickey (allegedly because the green cheese
Walt fed to him reminded Walt of Ireland), and after Mickey accompanied Disney to the studio and charmed the artists, they agreed to make
him a movie and cartoon star.[17] By the way, a copy of that 1930 book
fetches between $4,500 and $9,000 today.

And for a couple of decades, he was a major film star, appearing in
many guises mined from the catalogue of literature, folklore, and popular
culture; a prime example is 1934's "Gulliver Mickey," obviously appropriating Jonathan Swift's own classic *Gulliver's Travels*. Along the way,
many of Mickey's pals were introduced, including Donald Duck and
Goofy (who, Korkis tells us, was originally named Dippy Dawg); Minnie
Mouse was present from the start, in "Plane Crazy."

Surprisingly perhaps to many fans of Mickey, he did not command
Disney's attention for long. By the late 1930s Disney had bigger goals for
his studio and for animation, and he made plans for a feature-length
animated film bringing to life yet another folktale, *Snow White*, which
was released to great acclaim in 1937. Mickey Mouse short cartoons continued to flow from the studio, mixed among cartoon adventures of
Donald Duck, Pluto, and later other characters such as chipmunks Chip
and Dale. Mickey himself morphed from the hooligan of his original
incarnation into an increasingly innocent and juvenile ten-year-old
mouse-boy. (One problem for an eternally pre-pubescent Mickey is his
relationship with Minnie Mouse: officially, "Mickey and Minnie are not
married. Being married is an adult thing to do, and Mickey and Minnie
are not officially adults. Yet, Mickey and Minnie are capable of driving
cars, owning homes, having jobs, and pursuing other activities only

adults would do."[18] No one ever said that traditions had to be consistent.) Around the same time, similar to the history of Superman, Mickey Mouse moved into new media, such as radio: a *Mickey Mouse Theater of the Air* was inaugurated on October 5, 1937, running only for twenty episodes. A noteworthy fact about the short-lived radio program is that Mel Blanc, who later famously worked on Warner Brothers cartoon characters such as Bugs Bunny, did some of the voices on the show.

There is little doubt that Mickey's high point was his 1940 appearance in the sumptuous Disney movie *Fantasia*. The sequence "The Sorcerer's Apprentice" provided arguably the most lasting image of The Mouse, in wide-sleeved sorcerer's robe, but Korkis reveals two startling things about the sequence. First, Disney did not come up with the idea of a sorcerer's apprentice; rather, he borrowed it from a scherzo composed in 1897 by Paul Dukas, about "a lazy magician's apprentice who foolishly experiments with his mentor's magic to bring to life a broom that would do the apprentice's chores. The situation for the apprentice quickly gets out of control, leading to an exciting climax."[19] That is, of course, precisely the premise of the Mickey scene. Second, Disney did not even intend initially to use Mickey Mouse in the scene but rather envisioned Dopey, the dwarf from *Snow White and the Seven Dwarves*. Why make the unlikely switch from a dwarf to a mouse? "What Walt wanted," Korkis surmises, "was a good story to showcase Mickey Mouse, whose theatrical appearances had diminished because of the restrictions on the character now that he had become a role model."[20]

The truth is that, despite his popularity, Mickey Mouse's iconic status and his infantilization limited what could be done with the character. To be sure, he did not utterly fade from view, then or ever: instead, he was so important in the 1940s that a company manufactured a child's Mickey Mouse gas mask during the Second World War, and apparently the claim that "Mickey Mouse" was a password to the planning meeting for the D-Day invasion is true.[21] Nevertheless, even Disney himself lost enthusiasm for The Mouse by the 1950s, stating in 1951, "I'm tired of Mickey now. For him, it's definitely trap time. The Mouse and I have been together for about twenty-two years. That's long enough for any association."[22] The last Mickey Mouse cartoon was released in 1953,

yielding to other Disney characters that, quite honestly, had more narrative potential than he did, such as Donald and Goofy. In the words
of David Bain and Bruce Harris, "The benignly cute Mickey Mouse,
being poor competition to the wilder mania of his colleagues Donald
and Goofy (not to mention other studios' Tom and Jerry, Bugs Bunny,
and Road Runner), was the first to go."[23]

But Mickey got a second lease on life in 1955, with the debut of *The
Mickey Mouse Club* on television. It was the TV club, running through
1959, that helped solidify Mickey Mouse in the memories of Americans, especially Baby Boomers, and defined the image that survives
to this day. As told in many chronicles of the show, such as Jennifer
Armstrong's *Why? Because We Still Like You* and Jerry Bowles's
Forever Hold Your Banner High!,[24] as well as many biographies of cast
members, Walt Disney assembled a cast of young performers, called
Mouseketeers, the most memorable of whom were Cubby O'Brien
and Annette Funicello, the latter of whom would go on to a career in
1960s surf movies. Mickey himself featured in the show's musical
introduction, as an animated master of ceremonies, and in showings
of vintage cartoons that were made before the new audience was
born. Armstrong stresses that part of the appeal was the show's early
interactive quality:

> With *The Mickey Mouse Club*, kids could be part of the action.
> Fans could sign up to be official members of the Club, call
> themselves Mouseketeers in good standing—and even show
> proof if they sent in for a membership card. Belonging felt as
> essential as joining the Boy or Girl Scouts, complete with hats
> and theme songs. Viewers might even get a shot at appearing on
> Talent Round-Up Day—which featured "real" kids playing the
> trumpet, twirling the baton, performing magic, or any number
> of special skills—at mass auditions held in department stores
> throughout the country. They could play Club records, carry a
> Club lunchbox, strum a toy Club guitar. In short, *The Mickey
> Mouse Club* would extend into kids' everyday lives far beyond
> its five p.m. time slot.[25]

The irony of the televised Mickey Mouse club is, naturally, that Disney had come to oppose those theater-based clubs way back in the 1930s.

Mickey Mouse also had other ways of staying alive after his theatrical demise, as Disney made a number of wholesome television programs including *Walt Disney Presents* and *The Wonderful World of Color*. "Mickey appeared sporadically in these shows; his recycled cartoons were featured regularly. On the Disney variety show he could often be found perched on Disney's desk, talking with Walt."[26] These venues not only kept The Mouse, in a much diminished capacity, in the public eye but presaged his transition to his post-retirement career as an elder statesman for the Disney empire.

For its first nearly three decades, this empire had been a virtual or conceptual one only, but in 1955 it conquered an actual territory. On August 31, 1948, Walt Disney first announced his thoughts on a "Mickey Mouse Park," a theme park where fans could spend time in the physical presence of the virtual mouse. Consequently, the next year the skating show Ice Capades added Disney characters to its performances, giving audiences an experience of three-dimensional versions of Mickey, Donald, and the rest portrayed by skaters in costumes—costumes that would soon be used at the Disney park.

According to Sam Gennawey's history of Disneyland, by the middle of his life, Disney aspired to something more permanent, more tangible, than cartoons and movies. He also wanted to be about more than Mickey Mouse or animated films in general; Gennawey quotes Disney as saying that the park "would be a world of Americans, past and present, seen through the eyes of my imagination—a place of warmth and nostalgia, of illusion and color and delight."[27] To bring his vision to fruition, Disney proposed a project in Burbank, California— by then reconceived as Disneylandia—which was rejected by the city council on the argument that it would inject an unwanted "carny atmosphere" to their town. Undeterred, he scouted another location for the park, finding a site in Anaheim, not far from Los Angeles. Construction commenced on July 16, 1954, and the renamed Disneyland was opened on July 17, 1955.

Fascinatingly, Mickey Mouse was noticeably absent from his own park. Korkis explains that "when concerns arose even at the studio that

Entrance to Disneyland, 1957.

Disneyland might not be a successful venture, Mickey's role in the park was kept to a minimum. In particular, Walt's brother Roy expressed that he would like Mickey's involvement minimized so the brand would not be damaged if the park failed."[28] Instead, the source of all of Walt Disney's original success, and the ostensible reason for the amusement park in the first place, "would not appear in a Disney theme park until 1971 and the opening of the Magic Kingdom in Florida."[29]

Rather than visions of Mickey, visitors were treated to Walt Disney's personal imagining of American culture and history. Disneyland was designed as a composite of five themed "lands,"

- Frontierland, which "celebrated the Western frontier and its many legends";

- Adventureland, offering "jungle exploration";
- Fantasyland, which naturally "brought his animated films to life";
- Tomorrowland, a site dedicated to "innovation and future possibility"; and
- perhaps most memorably and significantly, Main Street USA, "hearken[ing] back to the small town U.S.A. Walt grew up in."[30]

But like all traditions, Disney did not consider his park settled once and for all. Disneyland, he intoned, "will never be completed. It will continue to grow as long as there is imagination left in the world."

What Have You Done for Me Lately, Mickey?

As mentioned previously, Mickey Mouse was conspicuously absent from The House that Mickey Built until Disney World, or Walt Disney World, was opened near Orlando, Florida, in 1971, five years after Walt Disney's death. (Presumably, a land was no longer sufficient to hold his vision; now a whole world was required.) The first phase of this new project was the Magic Kingdom, featuring replicas of the five lands of Disneyland. However, guests did not just want Disneyland East; they wanted The Mouse: "One of the biggest complaints by guests at the Magic Kingdom was that they weren't guaranteed an opportunity to meet Mickey Mouse in person or snap a souvenir photo or get an autograph. So for Walt Disney World's eighteen-month promotional event celebrating Mickey Mouse's sixtieth birthday, a temporary area was quickly built in Fantasyland called Mickey's Birthdayland."[31] Although intended to be temporary, it was preserved until 1990. In the meantime, both Mickey Mouse and the Disney empire enjoyed something of a renaissance. A second coming of *The Mickey Mouse Club* appeared on television in 1977. EPCOT Center was opened in 1982 as the second of four theme park projects in Florida and twice the size of its predecessor, the Magic Kingdom. The next year Mickey starred in his first new short film in thirty years, 1983's *Mickey's Christmas Carol*, yet another retelling of a popular culture standard. The Disney Channel was launched on cable the same year, followed in 1984 by a computer game, *Mickey's Space Adventure*.

Mickey's fate was also influenced by another cartoon character, Roger Rabbit, in the 1988 mixed animation and live-action movie *Who Framed Roger Rabbit*. This film introduced a new domain for animated characters, called Toontown. On May 26, 1990, the long-lived Mickey's Birthdayland was converted to Mickey's Starland, which was elaborated further in the original Disneyland as Mickey's Toontown:

> The Imagineering storyline was that Mickey and his friends had lived in Anaheim, even before Disneyland was built, and that their presence was one of the reasons Walt had chosen Anaheim as the location for his theme park. However, by 1993, it was time to tear down the wall that separated the town from the park and welcome guests to come and visit, so on January 24, 1993, Mickey's Toontown opened at Disneyland.[32]

So as not to lose continuity with the Florida park complex, it was told that California's Toontown was Mickey's full-time home, while Florida's kingdom was his vacation estate.

Contemporaneous with these developments was a third iteration of *The Mickey Mouse Club*, appropriately named *The All New Mickey Mouse Club*, running from 1989 to 1994 and promoting the talents of future stars Britney Spears, Justin Timberlake, Keri Russell, and Christina Aguilera.[33] In the twenty-first century, Mickey was revived for 52 episodes of *Disney's House of Mouse*, a half-hour television show that aired from 2001 to 2003. He rose yet again for the *Mickey Mouse Clubhouse* (2006–14) on the Disney Channel, a show "specifically aimed at pre-schoolers"[34] and securing his place in the hearts and minds of another generation of Americans, almost a century after his creation.

So despite the fact that most Mickey Mouse fans of the last two or three generations probably cannot name or describe a Mickey Mouse cartoon, he lives on as a favorite of Americans and, in many ways, an embodiment of America. He is, of course, not restricted to America, as evidenced by Tokyo Disneyland (opened 1983) and Disneyland Paris (1992). Mickey Mouse may have been conceived and owned by Walt Disney, but he was drawn, voiced, and loved by many others. He is the perfect mix of culture and corporation, which is as American as it gets, and he belongs to America as much as to Walt Disney or the Disney corporation—literally, since Lauren Vanpelt made the clever legal argument that the two short animations that introduced Mickey Mouse to the world in 1928 were never copyrighted and therefore that "Disney forfeited its copyright claims to Mickey Mouse. Mickey has fallen into the public domain where all are free to copy and enjoy him."[35] If she was correct—and I would not want to face the Disney empire in court—Mickey Mouse really is the property of America.

FIFTEEN

You'll Go Down in History:
Some American Characters

★ ★ ★

As every culture is, the culture of the United States is rich with folklore. The website American Folklore (www.americanfolk-lore.net) identifies multiple categories such as animal stories, children's stories, humorous stories, nursery rhymes, and ghost stories. Some of these tales feature (presumably fictitious) monsters and marvels such as Bigfoot, the jackalope, the skunk ape, and the Hodag (a part-reptile, part-bull forest creature in the northern Great Lakes region). Most tales focus on human characters, typically personifying key American values, places, or historical moments and often actually credited with shaping the American countryside and society. Many of these characters emerged from regional lore (for example, the South or the northern forests), such as Uncle Remus and his band of animal characters including Br'er (Brother) Rabbit, Br'er Fox, and Br'er Bear, collected and published by Joel Chandler Harris in 1881. A few characters originated outside the United States but have become stock figures in American popular culture, such as Sherlock Holmes, introduced by British novelist Sir Arthur Conan Doyle in a series of books and short stories beginning in 1887.

One of the most important and common genres of folklore in nineteenth- and early twentieth-century America was the "tall tale," an exaggerated and generally humorous account of great (verging on superhuman) deeds, frequently on the edges or frontier of expanding American society. In a 1921 article about tall tales, Esther Shephard related them to the tradition of humorous writing stretching back to

Mark Twain and long before; further, she described two lines of what she called "frontier humor"—the "down East" and the "wild West" traditions, with the latter characterized by "exaggerated adventure" and remarkable happenings.[1] That much of this action transpired on the frontier helps explain the existence and quality of tall tales, since not only did these events occur beyond the view of city-dwellers, who cannot question their truthfulness, but since, as Walter Blair contended in his 1944 study of American tall tales,

> When it comes to raising up heroes, there's nothing under the sun that's as helpful as hardships. This is because the way a man gets to be a hero is by overcoming hardships.

> Well, from the beginning, we Americans have had a better stock of snarling, snorting, rock-ribbed hardship than any other country in the world. And that's one good reason why we've had so many star-spangled heroes like Old Stormalong and Davy Crockett and Paul Bunyan and others that made our high, wide and handsome history.[2]

Added to Blair's list of folk heroes were Daniel Boone, Mike Fink "King of the Mississippi Keelboatmen," Johnny Appleseed, Pecos Bill, and John Henry, as well as lesser-known adventurers such as Windwagon Smith, Feboldson and Bridger, and Joe Magarac "Pittsburgh Steel Man."

Some of these characters were actual historical figures, such as Daniel Boone or Davy Crockett, although their exploits have frequently been embellished and reworked in multiple retellings. Others are loosely based on real people, such as Johnny Appleseed or John Henry; Appleseed, fancifully credited with planting apple trees across the country, was allegedly a man named John Chapman who lived in the late eighteenth century. John Henry "the steel-driving man" is widely believed to have been a large African American man, probably digging tunnels in the West Virginia hills in the late 1800s, although historian Scott Reynolds Nelson claimed that John William Henry of New Jersey, a convict laborer, was the hero of the ballad.[3] Another possibility is a John Henry who lived and worked in Alabama. Still other folk characters were pure fiction, and/or their original folk versions were distorted and augmented, making them fine examples of what folklorists have called "fakelore."

First coined in his 1950 essay "Folklore and Fakelore,"[4] Richard Dorson defined fakelore as contrived literature passed off as if it is authentic folklore, which "falsifies the raw data of folklore by invention, selection, fabrication, and similar refining processes, but for capitalistic gain rather than for totalitarian conquest. The end result is a conception of the folk as quaint, eccentric, whimsical, droll, primeval" and especially often more coherent and cleaner (much folklore being "coarse and obscene") than its sources—if it has any sources at all other than a writer's or advertiser's imagination.[5] But Dorson's outrage was slightly misplaced: it is difficult if not impossible to separate "authentic" folklore from later additions and interpretations; furthermore, all folklore, as with all of culture, is ultimately invented and necessarily selected, and it is one of the most venerable American traditions, as we have seen repeatedly, to mix what he called "romantic nationalism" with business interests.

This chapter presents a few of the more enduring American folklore or fictional characters, in regard to whom folklorist Marshall Fishwick commented in 1959 that the "most remarkable thing about American 'folk' heroes is not their differences but their similarity. Though their names and occupations vary (Paul Bunyan, lumberman; Pecos Bill, cowpoke; Kent Morgan, oil driller; Joe Magarac, steel worker; or John Henry, tunnel digger) they are cut out of the same bolt of cloth."[6] Some of them represented the people who literally helped build America during its prime building phase, the late 1800s, personifying the skill and strength that carved the country out of the North American landscape. Others are unabashed fictional creations but ones that have penetrated and replicated through American culture (as Superman and Mickey Mouse did in previous chapters) and express something fundamental about American personality and values.

American Hercules: Paul Bunyan

"A whole new pantheon of humorous heroes made their debut before the American public in the present century," Dorson wrote in 1959, and "at their head strode Paul Bunyan."[7] According to Dorson, Fishwick, and many others, Paul Bunyan is the archetype of these formative American characters, called "comic demigods" by Dorson. As John Henry, Joe Magarac, Mike Fink, and such characters did, Bunyan personified an occupation that made America great—and substantially made America—and a traditional way of life that was already fading at the time of the popularization of his lore.

Dorson disparaged Paul Bunyan as the very epitome of fakelore, arguing that the giant lumberjack made his first public appearance in a 1924 book,[8] but that is fairly clearly untrue. Apparently tales of Paul Bunyan (sometimes Bunyon, sometimes Bunion from the French) were told in the forests of the northern U.S. and Canada at least by the 1860s and were well established by the last decades of the 1800s. There may even have been an actual Paul Bunyan in Canada in the 1830s, associated with the Papineau Rebellion against Britain—making him originally French Canadian, not American. Esther Shephard opined that Paul Bunyan stories were told in lumber camps

> to string the tenderfoot or to put a smart-Alec in his proper place. If someone comes to camp who brags of the big logs they took out in the camp where he last worked it is not long before he is "taken down a peg" by a Paul Bunyan yarn, and the green-horn has always to be put through a number of practical jokes.[9]

Shephard's assessment was verified by the first documented mention of Paul Bunyan outside the world of lumberjacks, in an anonymous 1904 column in the *Duluth News Tribune*. That article claimed that the "pet joke" of the lumberjack, "and one with which the green horn at the camp is sure to be tried, consists of a series of imaginative tales about the year Paul Bunyan lumbered in North Dakota. The great Paul is represented as getting out countless millions of timber in the year of the 'blue snow'." So enormous were Bunyan and his team that, in order to feed them their morning pancakes, "they strapped two large hams to [the cook's] feet and started him running up and down a half mile of black glistening stove top."[10]

The legend of Paul Bunyan gathered momentum when another tale was printed in *The Press* of Oscoda, Michigan, in August 1906. In a story called "Round River," James MacGillivray recounted an adventure of Paul and his compatriots Canada Bill and Dutch Jake.[11] This was followed by a tale in verse in 1914 titled "The Round River Drive," published in the trade journal *American Lumberman*; referring to a drive occurring in 1864 or 1865, the poem features the lines,

> Paul Bunyan, (you have heard of Paul?
> He was the king pin of 'em all,
> The greatest logger in the land;
> He had a punch in either hand
> And licked more men and drove more miles
> And got more drunk in more new styles
> Than any other peavey prince
> Before, or then, or ever since.)[12]

There was also a passing reference to "the biggest steer that ever was."

It is worth recalling that the late 1800s and early 1900s were the great era of folklore collection, much of it for the same purpose as the invention of political traditions such as flags, anthems, and pledges—namely, to achieve and "prove" national identity and cohesion. Thus, between MacGillivray's two versions of the Paul Bunyan legend—which already evinced expansion of and addition to the basic outline—J. E. Rockwell published "Some Lumberjack Myths" in 1910, lamenting that "with the passing of the old time 'lumberjack' and the coming of the modern woodsman, the myths are rapidly being lost."[13] Among these vanishing legends were "innumerable" stories of Paul Bunyan, the "famous hero of lumberjack mythology [who] was the center of almost every tale told in the camps in the old days . . . Each camp has its own set of stories, and the men, in traveling from camp to camp—for the old time lumberjack was a rover—swapped these yarns in the long winter evenings." In one account, Paul was "eight feet tall and weighed three hundred pounds," and he oversaw a vast camp of three thousand men and a "huge blue ox" that hauled supplies for the men.

Paul Bunyan tales began to be reproduced in more and more essays and books, including Charles Albright's 1916 "Chronicle of Life and Works of Mr Paul Bunyan" (also published in *American Lumberman*) and Bernice Stewart and Homer Watt's "Legends of Paul Bunyan, Lumberjack," likewise from 1916.[14] But the work that really launched the popular legend, and undoubtedly the target of much of Dorson's ire against Paul Bunyan fakelore, was William Laughead's 1914 *Introducing Mr Paul Bunyan of Westwood, California.*[15] Laughead was not a lumberjack or a folklorist but instead an ad man, who wrote marketing materials for the Red River Lumber Company. In a series of pamphlets, he told and enlarged stories about Bunyan, not only allegedly giving the blue ox a name (Babe) but adding more characters such as Johnny Inkslinger, the head clerk of Bunyan's camp. Even Laughead confessed in the first advertising piece that Bunyan originally lived in North Dakota, but how he got to California is anybody's guess.

Laughead upped the ante in his 1922 *The Marvelous Exploits of Paul Bunyan* (full title, *The Marvelous Exploits of Paul Bunyan as Told in the Camps of the White Pine Lumbermen for Generations During Which Time the Loggers Have Pioneered the Way Through the North Woods From Maine to California Collected from Various Sources and Embellished for Publication*).[16] Not only did Laughead shamelessly associate the big man with the Red River Lumber Company—claiming for instance that "Red River 'Paul Bunyan's' California Pine and Sugar Pine meet the strict requirements of trade that have made white pine their standard" and "Everyone expects great things of Paul Bunyan and with the Red River outfit back of him he has the chance of his life to make good"—but he introduced many new exploits and characters and acknowledged the artificial nature of such collections of folklore:

> Paul Bunyan is the hero of lumbercamp whoppers that have been handed down for generations. These stories, never heard outside the haunts of the lumberjack until recent years, are now being collected by learned educators and literary authorities who declare that Paul Bunyan is "the only American myth." The best authorities never recounted Paul Bunyan's exploits in narrative form. They made their statements more impressive by dropping them casually, in an off hand way, as if in reference to actual events of common knowledge.

William Laughead's
"Paul Bunyan, with
Babe the Blue Ox."

Esther Shephard, a somewhat more serious scholar of Paul Bunyan lore, made much the same point a few years later. In her 1924 *Paul Bunyan: Twenty-one Tales of the Legendary Logger*, she allowed that the "super-lumberjack" may have had Canadian (Quebec or northern Ontario) or American roots and that his stories migrated westward with the itinerant lumbermen, picking up Scandinavian and Native American elements along the way. She added that the tales gathered in her volume

> have been selected from a great number and do not include stories which are too technical or too closely tied up with some small geographic detail to be of general interest, and stories which in my opinion seemed to be too new or too far outside the pale really to belong to the Paul Bunyan cycle. Where there have been several versions of the same story the one which seemed the most interesting has been chosen or the one which best fitted into the plan of the book.[17]

But such is the way with all folklore: multiple versions coexist, oral performance is transformed—and frozen—into written literature, and choices and selections are made that become the "official" version.

Along the way, Paul Bunyan's legend grew, until he was a towering giant who required five storks to deliver him as a baby, so big was he at birth. With his colossal companion, Babe the Blue Ox, he literally created the American landscape through superhuman feats such as dragging his humongous axe across the land to sculpt the Grand Canyon. In some accounts, he was even involved in other industries besides logging, for instance working as an oil driller. No wonder that Paul Bunyan still stands for some people as a "symbol of American size and ingenuity."[18] He was an earthly superman before Superman—a character who showed that all Americans, or at least all American workingmen, were supermen who forged a land and a country out of the wild and stubborn terrain of North America.

That self-congratulatory message sustained Paul Bunyan through multiple retellings, from Robert Frost's poem "Paul's Wife" to an opera libretto composed by W. H. Auden to, indeed, a 1958 Disney animated cartoon and a *Simpsons* episode featuring Homer as Paul.

The Lone Ranger

One of the most recurring tropes in American adventure literature is the cavalry charging over the hill to save the day. Another is vigilante justice—the civilian individual or group that takes matters into his or their own hands and punishes wrongdoers while protecting the weak and vulnerable. Superman was and is precisely such a vigilante, like other classic superheroes from Batman to Captain America, commonly breaking the law to defend a nobler law.

When the whole cavalry was not available, as in the wildest parts of the West, there was the army-of-one known as the Lone Ranger. The Lone Ranger of movie, radio, and eventually television fame can be traced back to a 1915 novel by prolific Western author Zane Grey. Titled *The Lone Star Ranger*, it featured an outlaw named Buck Duane who joined the storied Texas Rangers (whose glory was revived by the major league baseball team the Texas Rangers) for personal redemption. The book was made into a movie in 1919, 1923, and 1930. However, it was the 1933 radio program that secured the anonymous mask-wearing Lone Ranger as the great hero of the old West.[19] The radio show, debuting on January 30 on a Detroit station and running for nearly three thousand episodes, featured the equally iconic "William Tell Overture" theme music and catchphrases such as "Hi-yo, Silver, away!"—Silver, of course, being the name of his horse—and dramatic introductions such as "A fiery horse with a speed of light, a cloud of dust, and a hearty 'Hi-yo, Silver'—the Lone Ranger." In a 1938 episode of the show, it was stated that the Lone Ranger rode a horse called Dusty before the arrival of Silver.

The Lone Ranger never took off his mask or revealed his true identity; the most we know is that his surname was Reid (in some sources his first name is given as John), although in a 1938 installment of the movie serial his name was said to be Allen King, and in a later episode he called himself Bill Andrews—all false names, perhaps. (The 1981 movie *The Legend of the Lone Ranger* revived the John Reid moniker.) Further, as Superman and Mickey Mouse (or at least human members of the Mickey Mouse theater club) were, the Lone Ranger was a highly moral figure, living by a strict code of good. He even had his own Lone Ranger creed, to the effect of

I believe that to have a friend,
a man must be one.
   That all men are created equal
and that everyone has within himself
the power to make this a better world.
   That God put the firewood there
but that every man
must gather and light it himself.
   In being prepared
physically, mentally, and morally
to fight when necessary
for that which is right.
   That a man should make the most
of what equipment he has.
   That "This government,
of the people, by the people
and for the people"
shall live always.
   That men should live by
the rule of what is best

for the greatest number.

    That sooner or later . . .

somewhere . . . somehow . . .

we must settle with the world

and make payment for what we have taken.

    That all things change but truth,

and that truth alone, lives on forever.

In my Creator, my country, my fellow man.[20]

At least as interesting is his companion, the Native American Tonto (*tonto*, coincidentally or not, means "foolish" or "silly" in Spanish). Tonto was not added to the story until the eleventh episode of the radio show and was initially identified as a member of the Potawatomi tribe—a people originally inhabiting the upper Mississippi valley, not the southwest, until they were dislocated and resettled in Nebraska, Kansas, and Oklahoma in the 1800s. Tonto's horse was named Scout, and Tonto's affectionate term for his white friend was *kemosabe*. Much speculation has

Clayton Moore as television's "Lone Ranger," with Jay Silverheels as Tonto, 1956.

gone into the origin and significance of that word. In the old television series (1949–57), Tonto asserted that *kemosabe* meant "faithful friend" or "trusty scout." Some scholars have looked for and claimed to find words in Native American languages that resemble it: one explanation is that *sabe* is a Tewa name for the Apaches and *kema* means "friend," while renowned Native American author Sherman Alexie ventured that *kemosabe* is the Apache word for "idiot"; another possibility is that it is a corruption of the Yavapai term *kinmasaba* or *kinmasabeh* for "white man."[21] Finally, a more pedestrian answer is that it means nothing: it has been speculated that the director of the radio series, James Jewell, made up the word by appropriating the name of a camp in Mullet Lake, Michigan, called Ke Mo Sah Bee.

The Lone Ranger has proven to be as durable a fixture in popular culture as some of his contemporaries like Superman. In addition to the radio show, early movies, and television series, he starred in a number of feature films such as *The Lone Ranger* (1956), *The Lone Ranger and the Lost City of Gold* (1958), and *The Legend of the Lone Ranger* (1981). There has been a stream of novels, comic books and strips, cartoons and at least one video game, and the rather ill-conceived 2013 Disney film *The Lone Ranger*, starring Johnny Depp as Tonto with some outrageous bird headdress.

Finally and most fascinatingly, some students of the Lone Ranger have claimed that there was an actual historical figure behind the fictional character. Identified as Bass Reeves, he was a former slave in Arkansas and a deputy U.S. marshal in the 1800s. There is even a book on Reeves, Art Burton's 2006 *Black Gun, Silver Star: The Life and Legend of Frontier Marshal Bass Reeves*, which notes the similarities between the (black) man and the (white) myth.[22] Bass was apparently a John Henry of a man, over 6 ft (1.8 m) tall and muscular; he reportedly lived among the Native peoples of Indian Territory (Oklahoma) after the Civil War, learning western skills, and was deputized in 1875. His celebrity during his lifetime has since been forgotten, eclipsed by the Caucasian masked hero, although a 23-ft (7-m) bronze statue commemorates him at Fort Smith, Arkansas.[23] We do not know if Reeves was the real Lone Ranger, an indirect inspiration for the character, or merely an incidental match, but it would be disappointing to discover that another African American source of tradition, as in the case of Memorial Day, had been denied his place in history.

Popeye the Sailor Man

If the American frontier—whether the virgin forests or the Wild West—has been the most fertile site for American folk characters, then the other great frontier has always been the sea. Sailing has long been associated with adventure, romance, and danger, and it has produced an array of heroes and anti-heroes, from Davy Jones to Johnny Depp's Captain Jack Sparrow. The most enduring cartoon sailor in American culture is without doubt Popeye the Sailor Man.

In fact, Fred Grandinetti, a leading chronicler of Popeye, maintains that Popeye fans rather resent all the attention paid to Mickey Mouse, as if the rodent is America's greatest cartoon character. As recounted in the previous chapter, Mickey's acting career effectively ended in the 1950s, but "for the sheer volume of animated cartoons produced starting in the 1930s to the 1980s, Popeye still holds the record as the most successful animated cartoon character for both film and television."[24]

Unlike Mickey Mouse (who was born on the screen) and Superman (who debuted in comic books), Popeye originally appeared in newspaper comic strips. Surprisingly, though, he was not the first character created by his maker, E. C. (Elzie Crisler) Segar (1894–1938). As a young illustrator, he published his first comic strip in 1916, based on the real-life actor Charlie Chaplin. Three years later, he was hired by the *New York Journal* to design a strip called "Thimble Theater," for which he invented his first great character—not Popeye but Olive Oyl. Olive and her kin (Castor Oyl, Cole Oyl, and her boyfriend Ham Gravy) graced the pages of the newspaper for a decade before Popeye came along. It was only in a June 17, 1929, strip that Ham and Castor, planning a sailing trip, met a salty seaman; in one frame, Castor pointed a finger at someone out of view and asked, "Hey there! Are you a sailor?" to which the first-ever image of Popeye responds, "Ja think I'm a cowboy?"

"Segar never intended for the sailor to become a permanent addition to the strip"; when that particular storyline ended within a few months, "he retired the character from Thimble Theater."[25] However, popular demand drove him to revive the sailor, and by 1931 Popeye had top billing in the renamed Thimble Theater . . . Starring Popeye. As any good American hero would,

> Popeye would often perform feats of strength to assist people but never wanted any reward in return . . . Over the next few years Segar introduced several memorable characters to the strip, including J. Wellington Wimpy, the hamburger moocher whose phrase, "I will gladly pay you Tuesday for a hamburger today," is known worldwide; Swee'Pea, Popeye's adopted son; Oscar, Popeye's big-nosed, buck-toothed buddy; the Sea Hag, Popeye's first real enemy and the last true witch on earth; Poopdeck Pappy, Popeye's tough-as-nails father; Bluto, whom Popeye first battled in 1932; Alice the Goon, hulking monster who later became the family babysitter; Toar, a monstrous brute; and Rough House, the belligerent café owner.[26]

Many of those characters are fixtures of Popeye lore, while others have been forgotten.

Interestingly, Grandinetti insisted that the key characters in the Popeye universe had real human inspirations. Olive Oyl, for instance, was modeled after one Dora Paskel of Chester, Illinois, Segar's hometown; Ms Paskel was described as "tall, lanky, and wore her hair tightly in a bun" and is reputed even to have "dressed like Miss Oyl."[27] Wimpy emulated William Schuchert, manager of the Chester Opera House where Segar once worked and an actual fan of hamburgers. Popeye himself was purportedly inspired by a local Polish tough guy named Frank "Rocky" Fiegel with a reputation as a brawler.

In 1933 Max Fleischer (who also produced some Superman cartoons in the 1940s) began producing "Popeye the Sailor Man" animations, first cautiously acquainting audiences with him in a Betty Boop cartoon before giving him his own vehicle. Based on that success, by 1957 Fleischer starred Popeye in 233 shorts and one longer feature, 1936's "Popeye the Sailor Meets Sindbad the Sailor" starring a Sindbad who strongly resembled Popeye's nemesis, Bluto.[28] "From the very beginning," Grandinetti stated, "the Popeye series was a success, and in many key markets the Popeye cartoons were more popular than Disney's short subjects," owing partially to the sumptuous three-dimensional back-grounds in the animations.[29] Popeye's classic theme song, "I'm Popeye the Sailor Man," was composed by Sammy Lerner in 1934.

Several other additions to the Popeye universe were made in the animations, a number of them after Segar's untimely death in 1938. The most important was the role of spinach. Every late twentieth-century fan knows that Popeye derived his prodigious strength from spinach—yet in the original Thimble Theater strip, his superhuman power came not from spinach but from rubbing the head of the magical Whiffle Hen.[30] In fact, Grandinetti asserted that Segar seldom used the spinach trope in the comic strip; it was in the animated cartoons that the tradition of consuming a can of spinach was elaborated. (Amusingly, Sarah Griffith reports that Popeye's affair with spinach was based on his animators' acceptance of the erroneous data that spinach is unusually nutritious, and despite the miscalculation, "the cartoon character is responsible for boosting consumption of spinach in the U.S. by a third."[31] Nor has that discovery prevented the Allen Canning Company from putting Popeye on its label.) Popeye's nephews—Pipeye, Peepeye, Pupeye, and Poopeye—premiered as his children by Olive in 1940, although there was never any mention that he and his lady love were married. Finally, the coarse, pugilistic Popeye mellowed after the 1940s, as he became more popular with children.

Before that, however, Popeye fought in the Second World War, in such cartoons as 1942's "Scrap the Japs" and 1943's "Spinach fer Britain." Also in 1942, a new owner, Famous Studios, acquired the Popeye franchise and, despite keeping on some of Fleischer's talent, "played fast and loose with traditional Popeye elements. Though nec-essarily triumphant in his war adventures, Famous's Popeye in other cartoons was often portrayed as a buffoon rather than a hero, letting his nephews and his little sailor pal, Shorty, get the better of him."[32] Furthermore, long-established characters such as Wimpy and Swee'pea either underwent changes or faded from view. Worse was the fact that

By the mid-1950s, the basic plot line of the series was Bluto stealing Olive from Popeye, who would then eat his spinach

Popeye the Sailor Meets Sindbad the Sailor (1936).

and save Olive. While the standards on the animation remained high throughout the production of the series, the repeated plot lines began to wear thin . . . With the 1957 film "Spooky Swabs," Popeye's movie career as a cartoon character came to a close. Most of the Fleischer and Famous cartoons were sold to Associated Artists Productions for television syndication the year before.[33]

Popeye would live on, though, in that afterlife called television syndication. Like Mickey Mouse, who was retired around the same time, Popeye was resuscitated in the 1950s in various local children's television programs. (There was a brief two-year radio series of Popeye in the mid-1930s.) New Popeye cartoons continued to be drawn for television, often with noticeable alterations or inconsistencies, such as in Popeye's uniform, Olive's clothes and hair, and Bluto's name (for some reason, he began to be referred to as Brutus). Being so strong (at least when he ate his spinach), Popeye figured in a 1962 Physical Fitness Campaign and in a 1971 educational video on street safety. He joined forces with other cartoon characters on the 1972 *The ABC Saturday Superstar Movie* along with Beetle Bailey, Hi and Lois, Snuffy Smith, and such newspaper comic strip staples. He moved to CBS in the late 1970s, where *The All New Popeye Hour* boasted a more liberated Olive, and a whole new batch of 192 cartoons was produced.[34] He even starred in a Dr Pepper commercial in the 1970s, adding his voice to the "I'm a Pepper" marketing scheme by singing "I'm Popeye the Pepper Man."

Although Popeye is probably not held in the same wide esteem today as his rival Mickey Mouse, he remains a part of popular culture. In the late 1980s, CBS ran a *Popeye and Son* cartoon series—with a married Popeye and Olive but no Swee'pea. Moreover, in 1980 a live-action feature film cast Robin Williams as the sailor man and Shelley Duvall as Olive; among the innovations in the movie was Popeye's hometown of Sweethaven.

> The film attempts to explain the origins of the characters: why Popeye sailed to Sweethaven, why Pappy remained hidden all these years, the discovery of Swee'pea left in a basket by his mother and the growing attraction between Popeye and Olive Oyl . . . Whatever the flaws of the script, the major reason for the film's commercial failure is probably its attempt to recreate Segar's Popeye. Audiences came expecting to see the Popeye they knew best: the animated film star. No matter how wonderful Segar's strip was (and still is), Segar's Popeye is not the version that the mass audience knows.[35]

Without a promoter like Walt Disney or today's Disney corporation, Popeye has not enjoyed the cultural saturation of Mickey Mouse, but this hardly means that he is forgotten. As The Mouse did, he found a home in the theme park world (the MGM Grand in Las Vegas and Universal Studios in Florida), and a CGI-animated movie was in the works in 2016 but was apparently canceled.[36] Hilariously, a 2012 comic book even depicted Popeye in the classic Superman pose from the Kryptonian's debut publication, lifting a car over his head as Wimpy and the gang run for cover.

Rudolph the Red-nosed Reindeer

Do you recall the most famous reindeer of all? In a textbook case of implanted memory, this brilliant question proclaims Rudolph not as an innovation but as knowledge that we had or should have had, despite the fact that he was not counted among the team in Clement Clark Moore's eternal poem "'Twas the Night Before Christmas," which was actually published only in 1823 and under the original name "A Visit from St Nicholas." That rhyme helped institute many of the conventions of Santa Claus and Christmas Eve, which were further solidified by Coca-Cola. But nowhere was Rudolph to be found. He is pure fakelore.

From tribal mythology to Aesop's fables, animals have always been a central part of folklore. Although animal characters were conspicuously absent in nineteenth-century American popular culture, they multiplied like rabbits in the early twentieth century—many actually being rabbits, such as Disney's pre-Mickey Oswald, Bugs Bunny, and Roger Rabbit. Many more were cats (Felix, Krazy, Tom) and mice (Mickey, Jerry, Herman, and Mighty). Rudolph is the only reindeer, conceived in the mind of Robert May, an ad man like Paul Bunyan's William Laughead, the latter of whom at least had some lumberjack lore to draw on. May was drafting marketing copy for the Montgomery Ward department store, which, as other businesses did, aspired to associate itself with a cute mascot or appealing character. During the store's 1939 Christmas season, according to Sara and Tom Pendergast, he adapted his own childhood experience of bullying into a sympathetic reindeer-boy named Rudolph.[37]

After rejecting the names Rollo and Reginald, May penned a poem about Rudolph in close imitation of Moore's Christmas Eve tale. Published in 1939, it began,

'Twas the day before Christmas, and all through the hills
The reindeer were playing, enjoying their spills.
While every so often they'd stop to call names
At one little deer not allowed in their games.

"Ha ha! Look at Rudolph! His nose is a sight!
It's red as a beet! Twice as big! Twice as bright!"
While Rudolph just cried. What else could he do?
He knew that the things they were saying were true!

Making very little of Rudolph's tribulations other than that he was lonely, most of the verse deals with the fog that made his bright nose useful to the sleigh team and with the delivery of presents. The fairly long poem ends with these lines:

And that's why—whenever it's foggy and gray,
It's Rudolph the Red-nosed who guides Santa's sleigh.
Be listening, this Christmas, but don't make a peep,
'Cause that late at night children should be asleep!
The very first sound that you'll hear on the roof
That is, if there's fog, will be Rudolph's small hoof.
And soon after that, if you're still as a mouse,
You may hear a "swish" as he flies 'round the house,
And shines enough light to give Santa a view
Of you and your room. And when they're all through . . .
You may hear them call, as they drive out of sight,
"Merry Christmas to all, and to all a good night!"[38]

More than two million copies of this fakelore-built-on-fakelore were distributed by Montgomery Ward that year.

More than likely, most Americans have never heard, or even heard of, May's advertising poem about Rudolph. Their familiarity with the red-nosed reindeer comes from two later sources. The first is Johnny Marks's popular song, "Rudolph, the Red-nosed Reindeer," recorded by singing cowboy Gene Autry in 1949. That song asked the musical question, "But do you recall the most famous reindeer of all?" and proceeded to elaborate on Rudolph's backstory, about reindeer games and calling names. In true American fashion, the plucky reindeer overcame disability and public scorn to be the hero and savior of Christmas, securing his spot in history.

Second and equally unforgettable is the stop-motion animated television special, initially aired in 1964. Interestingly, it was not the first visual portrayal of Rudolph: he appeared in an animated cartoon in 1947 produced by none other than Max Fleischer, and he also featured in a series of DC Comics through the 1950s and a 1958 illustrated children's book from Golden Books. However, all of us who grew up in the 1960s and after know Rudolph and his family (his parents Donner and Mrs Donner are named in the television program), as well as the adventures that were only revealed in that show—*Rudolph the Red-nosed Reindeer*, hosted and narrated by an animated Burl Ives in the form of a snowman—with his girlfriend Clarice, Hermey the dentist, Yukon Cornelius, the Abominable Snowman, and the Island of Misfit Toys. Two less memorable sequels were made, 1976's *Rudolph's Shiny New Year* and 1979's *Rudolph and Frosty's Christmas in July*, pairing him with another seasonal character from song and story.

Do you recall the 1998 animated film *Rudolph the Red-nosed Reindeer: The Movie*? Probably not, as it quickly went straight to home video, along with its new villain Stormella, Rudolph's new girlfriend Zoey, his friend Slyly, and his protector Leonard. There was also a 2001 version, *Rudolph the Red-nosed Reindeer and the Island of Misfit Toys*, seeking to bring back the glory of the 1964 production. In other songs and films, Rudolph was given a brother (Rusty), a cousin (Leroy), and a different father (Blitzen).

Some Forgotten American Characters

As with Rusty, Leroy, Stormella, and many augmentations of the Rudolph universe (does anyone recall his pal Fireball from the 1964 program?), American folklore has produced a plethora of characters that never caught on or that have since receded from consciousness. Not every invention or addition lodges firmly and permanently in the national psyche.

Long forgotten, for instance, is Uncle Mistletoe, the answer of department store Marshall Field's to Montgomery Ward's Rudolph. Launched in 1946 and worked into a Little Golden Book in 1953—and even starring in his own *The Adventures of Uncle Mistletoe* television series from 1948 to 1952—he was a sort of Victorian figure in a red coat and black top hat who supposedly assisted Santa with his gift delivery (and presumably moms and dads with their gift purchasing, at Marshall Field's, ideally).[39]

Paddy O'Cinnamon, the Cinnamon Bear, was a local character, limited mostly to the Portland, Oregon, vicinity. He was introduced in 1937, at the height of the Depression, as a television character in a show sponsored by Lipman-Wolfe and Company, a Portland-area department store. According to one source dedicated to his history, the Cinnamon Bear lives on in Portland and in Chicago, for some reason, where he is sponsored by a local toy store.

Even some of Paul Bunyan's venerable peers have waned into relative obscurity, such as Pecos Bill. Emerging at almost the same moment as Paul (1917), Pecos Bill, the American cowboy, was recorded in stories by Edward O'Reilly for *The Century Magazine* and collected in the 1923 book *Saga of Pecos Bill*. Richard Dorson also rejected Pecos Bill, despite O'Reilly's claims, as a fabrication and not genuine Texas folklore. Nevertheless, Bill was turned into a comic strip in the 1930s and made into a Disney animation in 1948. Joe Magarac, Pittsburgh's greatest steel man, suffered a similar fate. His adventures debuted in a 1931 article by Owen Francis in *Scribner's* magazine, claiming to be authentic folklore among the city's steelworkers. His exploits were recounted in a 1964 song by The New Christy Minstrels, describing how it was Magarac who made the steel for the railroad west to San Francisco and south to Mexico.

Why some characters stick in American popular culture, and even attract new tellings and continual embellishments, is a mystery. But for more than a century, American writers, artists, singers, and filmmakers have been breeding and promoting new characters, some as alleged folklore and some as novel creations that may become or already have become part of American folklore: Charlie Brown, Yogi Bear, Spiderman, Homer Simpson, and SpongeBob SquarePants are just a few examples. In fact, there are few things that Americans produce more of than folk and fictional characters—all images of some part of themselves.

Conclusion: The Future of American Tradition

Consider these:

- *Star Trek: The Next Generation*,
- Bruce Springsteen's "Born in the USA,"
- the "Gatorade shower" for winning football coaches,
- the mobile phone,
- Homer Simpson, and
- *Abraham Lincoln: Vampire Hunter* (movie based on the novel).

These and many more (such as the annual MTV Video Music Awards) are American traditions that have been introduced, extended, or modified—sometimes wildly modified, such as reconceptualizing Abraham Lincoln as a vampire hunter—since the 1980s.

Admittedly, these new or revamped (pardon the pun) traditions do not have the *gravitas* of the national anthem or Thanksgiving, but then neither do National Cousins Day or Rudolph the Red-nosed Reindeer. Granted, most of America's weightiest traditions have been around for a while now (although, as we have learned, not as long as most people think), and the society has turned, for the better part of the last century, to fluffier fare. But American tradition is not finished and never can be. Americans, as members of all societies have, have continuously invented and altered traditions throughout their history and continue to do so. The late nineteenth century was only an especially fertile era for traditioning, as we have seen and will discuss in this chapter. But this hardly means that traditions are all in the past. Some things that started yesterday and have not yet risen to national consciousness may become traditions tomorrow or ten years from now. Events that have not occurred yet and individuals who have not performed their acts yet—or have not even been born yet—will provide new raw material for traditioning: there will be more wars and war dead to commemorate, more foods and clothes to design, more characters to invent. And future generations will continue to reconceive and reimagine past traditions—and the very past itself. It is fair to say that the past is not over, that as the future unfolds, the past is retold.

Before America was a Traditional Society

The conventional view is that older societies are or were traditional and that as they modernize, societies become less traditional. But that is not how the United States has worked, for comprehensible and significant reasons. The previous chapters have shown, for instance, that in 1776, in 1812, and even in 1865 (and certainly in 1620, when the Pilgrims founded Plymouth Colony), most of America's traditions were far in the future. In some cases the rudiments or precursors of a tradition, such as a flag or an anthem, were in place but had not been transformed into an official and enduring tradition; in other cases, no inkling of the tradition had been dreamed yet, as with the Pledge or Veterans Day.

The United States was not born as a "traditional" society because it lacked in its early days most, if not all, of the traditions that would distinguish it. But more profoundly, the early U.S. was overtly disinterested in, almost hostile to, traditions and to the past in general. As Mike Wallace asserted paradoxically in his study of "Mickey Mouse history," "the ahistorical strain that runs through our culture is deeply rooted in our history and economy":

> Revolutionary forebears believed they had broken free both of
> England and the past's dead hand. Shattering tradition's chains
> became the young nation's go-ahead mantra. In succeeding cen-
> turies, millions of immigrants shed their pasts and moved to
> America, land of the future . . . Few Americans, even the elite,
> had a stake in the past.[1]

The lack of sentimentality toward even the proudest past was evident in the attempt in the second decade of the 1800s (in the heat of the War of 1812, no less) by the state of Pennsylvania "to tear down Independence Hall and sell the land to commercial developers. Protests saved the building, but not before two wings had been demolished and the woodwork stripped from the room in which the Declaration of Independence had been signed."[2]

The dean of early American amnesia or indifference to the past is Michael Kammen, whose *Mystic Chords of Memory: The Transformation of Tradition in American Culture* told the tale of how the United States became "a land of the past, a culture with a discernible memory,"[3] literally "its own historian,"[4] although this history was not always accurate or innocent. As he demonstrated forcefully, Americans of the seventeenth, eighteenth, and the first half of the nineteenth century were not enamored with and were sometimes actively averse to history and tradition. The very notion of a "New World" and a "new order" (recall that American money bears the saying *novus ordo seclorum* or "new order of the ages") communicates the American orientation to the new and away from the old. Many Americans felt that they were escaping the burdensome history of Europe if not slipping off the yoke of history altogether.

> In many societies the force of tradition has served as a source of authority. But for much of American history the inhabitants of the continent clearly indicated that they did not want power to reside in pastness. They preferred, instead, the sovereignty of morality or perhaps natural law in tandem with their colonial charters . . . "We have outgrown tradition," boasted Orestes A. Brownson in 1836. "Probably no other civilized nation has at any period," proclaimed the *Democratic Review* in 1842, "so completely thrown off its allegiance to the past as the American."[5]

Great American thinkers from Thomas Paine to Ralph Waldo Emerson were conspicuously anti-tradition, Emerson asking in his 1840 essay "Self-Reliance," "What have I to do with the sacredness of traditions, if I live wholly from within?"

Such neglect of the past was not limited to scholars and poets, though; the average American citizen had not yet acquired the habit of tradition. "In 1837, for example, which was the fiftieth anniversary of the Constitutional Convention that had met in Philadelphia, the press remarked upon the absence of public celebrations in Baltimore and Alexandria, Virginia, on the Fourth of July. Apart from a military parade and an oration, the holiday even passed rather quietly in Washington, DC."[6] Likewise, Kammen noted "the widespread indifference to historic sites, which often resulted in neglect or actual damage," including the destruction of Benjamin Franklin's home and George Washington's presidential residence.[7] Slavish worship of great men actually felt undemocratic to Americans of that era: "memorials that elevated heroes above the folk seemed antithetical to popular sovereignty."[8] And neither schools nor government accepted a responsibility to instill a sense of tradition: "For most of the nineteenth century formal education gave short shrift to the past. American history remained very much a minor subject in the schools—rarely a required part of the curriculum."[9]

We must acknowledge that the United States, born in strife after 1776 and keen to distinguish itself from its European ancestry, literally had little history and tradition in the mid-1800s. To be sure, the absence of basic national traditions like a flag or anthem was soon felt, although, as their respective chapters have shown, the vacuum was only gradually filled. But Americans discounted or ignored the need for traditions as collective memory for binding the nation until it became abundantly clear just how close to unbinding the nation came. That is, America began to become self-consciously "traditional" when America itself became *a problem*, a country that seemed on the verge of unraveling.

If the previous chapters have illustrated anything, it is how traumatic the Civil War was to the American identity and psyche. Indeed, for four years, America did unbind, and suddenly it was palpable that the country lacked and desperately needed traditions. Additionally, those who sacrificed so much for their restored Union, especially the veterans of the Civil War as well as the kin of the casualties, were determined to keep the memory of their achievement alive. These figures, as in the highly influential Grand Army of the Republic encountered throughout this book, engaged intentionally and aggressively in what scholars have come

G. A. R. 25TH REUNION, KEENE, NH C.1890

The 25th reunion of the Grand Army of the Republic (GAR), *c.* 1890.

to call "memory work," actively forming and fomenting memory in the guise of symbols, parades, speeches, museums, and holidays. Kammen referred to all of this activity and the resources committed to it as "the nation's arsenal of memory devices," with "the astonishing diversity of its stockpile."[10]

The Civil War was only one of two threats to American unity and identity that inclined the society to become more "traditional." The second, as we have also discovered in the preceding cases of invented traditions, was immigration and the danger of non-assimilation and dis-integration of the nation. New immigrants obviously lacked a memory of America, since it was foreign to them, and such memory had to be constructed and inculcated. School was one site for the production of "Americans" and of "American memory," as were all manner of patriotic displays and performances. The imperative for new arrivals, Kammen argued, was loyalty, which goes a long way toward explaining practices like the Pledge of Allegiance. Meanwhile, for those who already called themselves Americans (the "nativists") and particularly the elites who enjoyed power and prestige, the imperative was to protect that privilege and to preserve the America that they knew. "When we look more closely at the passion for tradition on the part of most nativists during the later nineteenth century," Kammen wrote, "we discover a deep-seated resistance to (often resulting from a genuine fear of) change."[11] Wallace concurred that in the final two decades of the nineteenth century,

> the dominant classes' attitude toward history began to change. By the 1890s it had undergone a remarkable transformation. Upper and middle-class men and women established great numbers of ancestral societies and historical associations. They also set about rescuing old buildings and displaying them to the public, preserving battlefield sites, and erecting shrines and monuments.[12]

Among the organizations formed to wage what Wallace called "the patricians' cultural offensive" were the Association for the Preservation of Virginia Antiquities (founded in 1888), Native Sons of the Golden West (1888), Sons of the American Revolution (1889), Daughters of the American Revolution (1890), and Mayflower Descendants (1897),[13] not to mention the omnipresent Grand Army of the Republic.

Remembering America

In short, the concentrated traditioning of the late 1800s and early 1900s amounted, in Wallace's words, to a coordinated set of "Americanization campaigns,"[14] motivated by the trauma of the Civil War and the anxiety of the ongoing peril of immigration and the dissolution of American identity, if not of American society itself. Tradition was medicine for a grave and potentially fatal disease, "the antidote to the bane" (in the words of John Fiske, a member of the ominously named Immigration Restriction League)[15] of political and/or cultural schism that loomed in the person of rebels and foreigners (not to mention socialists, communists, unionists, and others guilty of "un-American activities"). Subsequently, Americans evolved from a people suspicious of the past and tradition into, according to historian Diane Britton, a people "in love with their pasts,"[16] who endowed themselves with a rich complement of traditions. This hardly means that Americans are clear-headed historians—indeed, quite the opposite in Britton's estimation: "Generally speaking, our culture promotes a sense of the past that clashes with what historians have documented to be true."[17] But then, as Wallace, among others, reminded us, "There is, after all, no such thing as 'the past.' All history is a production—a deliberate selection, ordering, and evaluation of past events, experiences, and processes."[18] This is why we can and must say, and only partly facetiously, that the past is constantly changing—or more extremely, that the past has not happened yet and only achieves reality when and as it is known in the present and the future.

This awareness raises the question of memory. Numerous scholars observed that the United States, and the world as a whole, went through something of a "memory boom" in the twentieth century. Jay Winter, one of the key thinkers on the memory boom, captured its essence in his polysemous phrase "the generation of memory":[19] generations living through and since the two world wars and especially the Holocaust have been inundated with memory, such that (excess) memory has been the curse of twentieth-century generations, while people in our time have actively cultivated memory as they have struggled with how to remember and commemorate (and sometimes simply how to bear) the historical burdens of the century. Calling it a memory boom suggests, as Gavriel Rosenfeld articulates, that

> memory has developed into what Andreas Huyssen has called "a cultural obsession of [such] monumental proportions" that it has become, in the words of Jay Winter, "the historical signature of our own generation." So frequently have public controversies erupted over contested historical legacies worldwide that a shorthand designation for them—"the politics of memory"—has entered popular parlance to describe the phenomenon. In short, few would disagree with Susan Suleiman's contention that "the era we are living in is . . . the era of memory."[20]

War has predictably figured prominently in contemporary memory, but war has not been alone. Sharing the space of modern memory are the ordeals of colonialism, nationalism, ethnic conflict, and modernization and globalization.

All of these stressful experiences have one element in common—loss. Hence Joel Candau coined the French term *mnémotropisme* to refer to the "problem in identity caused by our incapacity to master the anxiety of loss"; stricken by "a profuse production of information, images and traces,"[21] twentieth- and twenty-first-century citizens are fixated on memory and activate it to stake their identity while also carrying it like a weight or even a disease. After all, Freud long ago diagnosed that hysterical patients suffered mainly from reminiscences.

Accordingly, Rosenfeld made the meaningful comment that one "of the most important preconditions for the recent memory boom has been the presence of numerous 'unmastered' pasts throughout the West and other parts of the world. The concept of an 'unmastered' past . . . refers to a historical legacy that has acquired an exceptional, abnormal, or otherwise unsettled status in the collective memory of a given society."[22] Such memories are unmastered and perhaps unmasterable because they often contain a heritage of injustice and cruelty that "has been remembered differently by, and has caused discord between, the original perpetrators, victims, and their respective descendants . . . The result," Rosenfeld asserted, ironically for an alleged boom in memory, "is the emergence of what some scholars have referred to as a 'great silence' toward—or what others have imperfectly called the general 'repression' of—the past."[23]

This perspective casts tradition and memory work in general in a different light, less as celebration and more as a curious and problematic combination of therapy and politics. The past is something simultaneously to recover and to recover from. One classic process of recovery of or from the past is irredentism, reclaiming a lost homeland, often by armed struggle. More widely and usually less violently, recent decades have witnessed a boom in a specific kind of memory—namely, nostalgia. In an edited volume pointedly subtitled "Yearning for the Past, Present, and Future," Katharina Niemeyer says that nostalgia is "the name we commonly give to a bittersweet longing for former times and spaces,"[24] usually recalled as the good old days. Niemeyer further explains that nostalgia is not only an old term for homesickness but was actually used as a medical term, derived from *nostos* for "return home" and *algia* for "pain/longing" (and related to "neuralgia" or nerve pain). Nostalgia was a medical diagnosis applied, for instance, to soldiers fighting far from home and suffering from real clinical symptoms: "The sufferer did not eat or drink, and had fever or gastric illness. Hallucinations and schizophrenia were also described as symptoms of homesickness. All in all, nostalgia mostly led to death."[25]

Today we are less likely to regard nostalgia as a medical pathology than as a memory that is at once gladdening and saddening: we are glad to have had it but sad to have lost it. Michael Pickering and Emily Keightley characterized it as a "longing for what is lacking in a changed present . . . a yearning for what is now unattainable, simply because of the irreversibility of time."[26] Oddly, in parts of Europe, nostalgia is sometimes expressed today for regimes that were loathed in their day, such as the Soviet Union or even Nazi Germany; symptoms include constructing historical museums and exhibitions, collecting memorabilia, and occasionally dreaming of the return of the defunct party or leader. In Iraq and Syria, one could say with more than a little justification that ISIS/Islamic State is a clinical case of what Olivia Angé and David Berliner call the "current overdose of nostalgia,"[27] not only yearning for the early, pure days of Islam but striving to recreate the seventh century in the twenty-first.

Two final points about memory are worth mentioning, one well known and the other somewhat less so. First, as psychologists have understood since Frederic Bartlett's book on remembering in 1932, memory is notoriously imperfect and porous. Bartlett emphasized that, in thinking about what we claim to remember, the "first notion to get rid of is that memory is primarily or literally reduplicative, or reproductive"; he went so far as to opine that "literal recall is extraordinarily unimportant."[28] More than eighty years ago, Bartlett realized that memory is "an imaginative reconstruction or construction, built out of the reaction of our attitude towards a whole active mass of organized past reactions or experience . . . It is thus hardly ever really exact, even in the most rudimentary cases of rote recapitulation, and it is not at all important that it should be so."[29] Surely ample evidence has accumulated since then that memory is subject to all sorts of biases, especially suggestibility, which can cause (false) memories to be implanted and accepted as true.

The second and closely related point is that memory is intrinsically retrospective: it is not "what happened" but how we look back upon what happened. We are limited by what we know about the past, and then we select from those facts to, as Bartlett taught, reconstruct or reassemble memory. Biases again intervene, such as "rosy retrospection," which encourages us to judge the past more positively than people did as they lived through it, or "hindsight bias," with its tendency to filter the past through present experience and knowledge and to presume that the past was more similar to the present than it truly was. Consequently, what Nicholas Dames says of nostalgia is equally applicable to all memory and all tradition: it is not only or mostly an idea or fact that refers to something but "a force that *does* something," and what it does is "to transform the past by imagination."[30] In the final analysis, tradition, as is all memory and history,

> is not something waiting out there, always over one's shoulder.
> It is rather plucked, created, and shaped to present needs and
> aspirations in a given historical situation. Men refer to aspects
> of the past as traditional in grounding their present actions in
> some legitimating principle. In this fashion, tradition becomes
> an ideology, a program of action in which it functions as a goal
> or as a justificatory base.[31]

That is, tradition is and always has been more about the present and the future than the past.

Inventing Tomorrow's American Traditions

America's traditions, like those of all societies, invoke the past and purport to be concerned about yesterday, but the crucial concerns, as we have now established beyond doubt, are today and tomorrow. What happened back then is, quite frankly, only tangentially relevant to our memories of it and our traditions surrounding it. Diane Britton gave us a dramatic example, in regard to the fabled ride of Paul Revere as immortalized in the poem by Longfellow:

In 1923, as Warren G. Harding toured the country, a critic pointed out to him that [Paul] Revere had been captured by the British and never made the ride that Longfellow immortalized in verse. Unfazed, Harding told a crowd, "Suppose he did not; somebody made the ride and stirred the minutemen of the colonies to fight the battle of Lexington, which was the beginning of independence in the new Republic of America. I love the story of Paul Revere whether he rode or not."[32]

Verily, we love our traditions whether they happened or not.

Traditions are a story that we tell ourselves about ourselves. And like every story, there is no single right way to tell it and an infinite variety of ways to tell it—including ways we have not thought of yet. We have proven that American traditions have a history, each tradition singly and tradition or traditioning as a whole. In its founding days, America did little traditioning and was little interested in traditions. In the second half of the nineteenth century, for reasons thoroughly illustrated, America embarked on a campaign of muscular if not manic traditioning; the result was many new national and patriotic traditions—some completions of projects already under way (the flag, the anthem, the motto), and some new projects not previously envisioned (the pledge, various holidays, clothing, food, etc.).

By the turn of the twentieth century, America was well on its way to becoming a "traditional" society. To a considerable extent, the fundamental "tradition work" was more or less complete; a few new holidays were yet to come, and many traditions were not fully encoded and institutionalized, but the big traditions were in place. Potentially, the tradition-invention process could have stopped, or at least slowed, except for events that waited in the future such as the First World War, the Second World War, the Depression, the Cold War, the Korean War, the Vietnam War, September 11, and more. But in those critical first decades, Kammen spied a new trend in or ethos of tradition, a "democratizing" of tradition that allowed more individuals to participate in the traditioning process. The result was what he called multiple "creative modes of traditionalism"[33] (and this was long before the Internet and social media!).

Perhaps because the big, obligatory, national traditions were ready or nearing readiness, and because of new technologies such as the automobile and the motion picture, and because of a significant shift in American society and psyche, by the 1920s and 1930s there was a sea change in America's restless energy of self-invention and self-recognition. American traditioning started following a different path, by any standard a lighter or even more frivolous path, as in the invention of fictional characters like Superman, the Lone Ranger, and Popeye. In this era, we see a third phase of American traditioning arise, from original non- or anti-traditionalism to conventional modern traditionalism to nostalgia. For some Americans no doubt, the good old days of WASP America were either fading or faded; for others, the heroic days of the frontier were gone once and for all; for still others, the drudgery and smallness of urban and office life seemed to drain all of the adventure out of the country (producing, for instance, a "crisis of manhood" in the new century and the establishment of organizations such as the Boy Scouts in 1910 to teach manly virtues and skills); and for the entire population, the First World War and the Depression were jarring experiences, causing people to dream of the past and despair of the future.

Combined with a new (and, by some measures, juvenile) focus on humor after the turn of the century, American nostalgia and self-doubt, verging on hopelessness, spawned an invention of a constellation of traditions featuring fictional characters who would right the world and fight our battles for us. We might consider the likes of Superman, the Lone Ranger (an outstanding instance of frontier nostalgia), Paul Bunyan, or even Popeye as the *last American individual*, one who is self-sufficient and at least a little outside the confines of society. What much of the traditioning of the first half of the twentieth century appears to have in common is a compulsive (some would say pathetic) grasping for a hero, suggesting disconcertingly the absence of heroes or of opportunities for heroism in contemporary life. This attitude transcends nostalgia, Americans seeming to have lost faith in their own abilities and looking instead for an outsider—even a being from another planet—to save them.

We might say that by the mid-1900s the United States had become a land of plentiful, almost crushing memory but of declining prospects; to invoke Angé and Berliner, Americans suffered from an overdose of the past but no real prognosis. But Kammen's "creative modes of tradition-alism" or merely the society's creative energies had to go somewhere. In the final quarter of the twentieth century, America's nostalgia and back-ward/other-looking orientation morphed into cynicism, symbolized most clearly by the new tradition since 1972 of adding "-gate" to the name of every scandal after Nixon's "Watergate," giving us "Monica-gate" (for Bill Clinton's dalliance with Monica Lewinsky), Nipple-gate (for Janet Jackson's 2004 "wardrobe malfunction" during the Super Bowl), and Deflate-gate (for the charges of tampering with footballs against the New England Patriots in 2014), among many others.[34]

As the whimsical case of "-gate" reveals, the creative and traditioning juices of Americans have not stopped flowing, nor can or will they. People cannot live by the traditions of yesterday alone, and tomorrow's traditions will come from two main sources. One, naturally, is events that have not transpired yet, that are still in our future but that will eventually be in someone else's past. Contrary to the assertions of Francis Fukuyama and his ilk, history has not ended, and many memory-worthy happenings— entirely unforeseen and unforeseeable—await Americans, including wars, natural disasters, and national achievements. Great men and women will emerge in the future, and new fictional characters will be created while new stories shall be told. And new knowledge of the past may be discov-ered, giving Americans currently unknown things to either celebrate or mourn.

The other source of tomorrow's traditions is the ongoing rework-ing of today and yesterday. As mentioned at the outset of this chapter, there is always the possibility of adding another generation to the *Star Trek* universe or of syncretizing two different sources such as Abraham Lincoln and vampires. There is absolutely no limit to the potential of reimagining already-existing knowledge or traditions, and two of the most familiar vehicles for doing so are the *sequel* and the *prequel*. Either way, people can add, subtract, or modify elements of traditions currently in hand. The ultimate act of reappropriating traditions and giving them a new spin is the *reboot*, as was done several times with the Superman character (and with Captain America, among others), with Batman, and most conspicuously with *Star Trek* in J. J. Abrams's 2013 *Star Trek: Into*

Darkness (which was personally an offense to my hallowed memories of the original—invented—television series). What all of this proves is that traditions will likely, if not necessarily, change through the sheer passing of the generations, as those traditions are transferred from one hand to another (a chain of ownership and authorship, if you will) and those same traditions are then continuously reimagined in the eyes and experiences of another age.

Sequels, prequels, and reboots can reconfigure our very memory of the originals, especially for the young who never knew the originals. Indeed, studies have shown how the present and future can forge the past (in both senses of the term—make it and falsify it). A series of experiments by Elizabeth Loftus and colleagues documented the phenomenon that became known as "destructive updating," by which people over-write their old knowledge and memory with new. In the experiments, misinformation was presented to people after they were exposed to the facts of an event; when tested subsequently on their recall of the event, the subjects quickly and confidently remembered the false details as much as the true ones. The inescapable conclusion is that "people can come to accept misinformation and adopt it faithfully as their own."[35] Destructively updating, and along the way erasing, memory is facilitated by imagery, instruction, and storytelling, which are all inherent in trad-itioning and celebrating traditions. The nineteenth-century philosopher Friedrich Nietzsche used a still-more-forceful term for the same process, *Beschlag genommen* or "confiscation," the retroactive seizure (in the lit-eral military sense) of an idea, event, or narrative and then reinterpretation, rearrangement, and transformation of that information. Thus it is always possible for the present or future to seize or confiscate a memory and reshape it anew.

Gregory Stewart offers a model for envisioning this never-ending traditioning process. He describes four steps in the circulation of trad-itions and cultural materials, expressed by the acronym DVND.[36] These four phases are displacement, validation, narration, and deployment. The model applies particularly well to popular culture, which is the site of much of contemporary tradition-(re)making, and can be elucidated by a specific example like the televised retelling of the classic American tale "The Legend of Sleepy Hollow." Published by Washington Irving

John Quidor, *The Headless Horseman Pursuing Ichabod Crane*, 1858, oil on canvas.

in 1819, the story is extensively reimagined in the television series *Sleepy Hollow*, debuting on FOX in 2013. In Stewart's first stage of displacement, the action is most obviously lifted from its early nineteenth-century context to the early twenty-first century, and aspects of another Irving story, "Rip Van Winkle" (specifically, a soldier from the Revolutionary War era waking up in the present day), are borrowed from that source and stirred into the show. Over the seasons of the television program, other displacements occurred, from conceiving the Revolutionary War as some sort of supernatural struggle (and George Washington as a possessor of arcane knowledge) to introducing a madly displaced Greek mythology of Pandora into modern-day America. The final episode of 2015 was actually titled "*Novus Ordo Seclorum*."

Validation happens in a number of ways. Destructive updating or the authority of confiscation (that is, when the one doing the confiscation has social or political authority) is, of course, its own validation. In the case of *Sleepy Hollow*, the creators of the show took various intentional measures to ensure the "truth effect" of the show. First, the series was set in a real place, a town in New York, and everything else about the setting was normal and familiar. The show linked (loosely and fancifully) to actual historical eighteenth-century persons (Washington, Revere, Franklin, and Betsy Ross) and events, and it was made more believable by recognizing twenty-first-century realities such as racial diversity (Ichabod Crane's modern partner is an African American woman) and institutions such as the FBI. Furthermore, various aspects of Revolutionary War-era and present-day America were given explanations in terms of the doings of Crane and his eighteenth-century companions, and the whole narrative was integrated by a vaguely Christian/biblical sense of Revelation and doomsday.

Speaking of narration, everyone recognizes the power of a good story. In *Sleepy Hollow*, all of these past and present, true and false, elements were bundled into an entertaining and appealing narrative rather than a didactic lesson. Furthermore, they were just believable enough because many of those elements were already familiar to and accepted by the audience, not least the aforementioned Christian and biblical themes. The same recycling and re-presentation of culturally available themes is met in many offerings of popular culture, such as the "chosen one" or savior motif in movies from *The Matrix* to *Star Wars*. Finally, then, the displaced, validated, and narrated product is deployed, rolled out, and added to the society's cache of both updated and confiscated memories, to become a major or minor, enduring or fleeting, bit of tradition.

Stewart's DVND is a never-ending cycle, today's deployment being a candidate for tomorrow's displacement, mixing with the details of its historical moment and any of the other ideas, beliefs, images, and traditions that came before it. Thus every tradition is grist for future traditioning, in a process that does not and cannot end. In ten years, twenty years, fifty years someone else may resurrect the legend of Sleepy Hollow and re-narrate it for another generation.

And these two points—that traditioning never stops and that traditions may be enduring or fleeting—are the final message for us. In this book, we have been concerned primarily with the traditions that succeeded and endured, but naturally there have been many other attempts at traditioning that failed or faded. We cannot know today what traditions will catch on tomorrow, and we cannot assume that the traditioning process of tomorrow will resemble that of yesterday. One huge difference between the past and the present or future is the omnipresence of communication technologies. Potential traditions—which we might better call in the contemporary moment "memes" or "viruses"—are easily created and easily transmitted, but they also find themselves in fierce competition. Indeed, a synonym for the success of a new tradition today might be "going viral." We could fairly say that the spread of the national anthem or the Pledge of Allegiance, of Coca-Cola or blue jeans, was the nineteenth-century equivalent of going viral.

There have always been local and short-lived traditions or potential traditions, and in today's saturated and distracted information-world, a new and future tradition may be a "niche tradition" that some community follows or observes while another ignores or even resists it. At the extreme, we may see (and most likely have already seen) "flash traditions" that pop up suddenly, exist temporarily, and disappear again—but then more than a few older traditions had similarly short lives. And there is a definite trend toward the commodification of tradition, but this too is nothing new: people made money or exercised power in nineteenth- and twentieth-century traditioning, and as we saw, not only burgers and comic books but flags and other venerable traditions were opportunities to make a buck.

If we think of American traditions as a set of shared habits—which truly they are—then perhaps it is fitting to end with Friedrich Nietzsche's thoughts on habits. In a section of *The Gay Science* titled "Brief Habits," he wrote, in part,

> I love brief habits and consider them an inestimable means for getting to know *many* things and states, down to the bottom of their sweetness and bitterness . . .
>
> Enduring habits I hate. I feel as if a tyrant had come near me and as if the air I breathe had thickened when events take such a turn that it appears that they will inevitably give rise to enduring habits; for example, owing to an official position, constant association with the same people, a permanent domicile, or unique good health . . .

Most intolerable, to be sure, and the terrible par excellence would be for me a life entirely devoid of habits, a life that would demand perpetual improvisation.[37]

Let us then celebrate American traditions past and future and the constant invention, updating, and confiscation of traditions—but not too many and not too enduring.

References

PREFACE

1 Meyer Fortes and E. E. Evans-Pritchard, *African Political Systems* (London, 1940), p. 9.
2 Jacqueline Knörr, *Creole Identity in Postcolonial Indonesia* (New York and Oxford, 2014), p. 53.
3 Melissa Schrift, *Becoming Melungeon: Making an Ethnic Identity in the Appalachian South* (Lincoln, NE, and London, 2013), p. 91.
4 Of course, other countries such as Canada celebrate their own Thanksgiving holiday, while others have invented their own patriotic remembrances of great battles or other events.
5 Richard Howard, "Introduction," in Marcel Proust, *In Search of Lost Time*, vol. I: *Swann's Way*, trans. C. K. Scott Moncrieff and Terence Kilmartin (New York, 2003), p. xiii.

INTRODUCTION:
TRADITION IS NOT WHAT IT USED TO BE

1 Nandini Sikand, *Languid Bodies, Grounded Stances: The Curving Pathway of Neoclassical Odissi Dance* (New York and Oxford, 2017), p. 41.
2 Ibid., p. 110.
3 Quoted in Kristina M. Jacobsen, *The Sound of Navajo Country: Music, Language, and Diné Belonging* (Chapel Hill, NC, 2017), p. 31.
4 Newell S. Booth, Jr, "Tradition and Community in African Religion," *Journal of Religion in Africa*, XIX/2 (1978), pp. 81–2.
5 Dan Ben-Amos, "The Seven Strands of Tradition: Varieties in its Meaning in American Folklore Studies," *Journal of Folklore Research*, XXI/2 (1984), pp. 102–24.
6 Ibid., p. 106.
7 Richard Bauman, "Differential Identity and the Social Base of Folklore," *Journal of American Folklore*, LXXIV/331 (1972), p. 33.
8 Ruth Finnegan, "Tradition, But What Tradition and For Whom?," *Oral Tradition*, VI/1 (1991), p. 112.
9 Richard P. Heitzenrater, "Tradition and History," *Church History*, LXXI/3 (2002), pp. 622–4.
10 Anthony F. C. Wallace, "Revitalization Movements," *American Anthropologist*, LVIII/2 (1956), p. 264.
11 Ibid., p. 265.

12 Ibid.
13 Although diverse, cargo cults tended to be movements that anticipated the arrival of Western goods (as "cargo") if locals adopted certain aspects of Western culture, combining them with aspects of indigenous culture or abandoning and destroying indigenous culture altogether.
14 Wallace, "Revitalization Movements," p. 269.
15 Ibid., p. 275.
16 Eric Hobsbawm, "Introduction: Inventing Traditions," in *The Invention of Tradition*, ed. Eric Hobsbawm and Terence Ranger (Cambridge, 1983), p. 1.
17 W.G.V. Balchin, "The Swastika," *Folklore*, LV/4 (1944), p. 168.
18 Hobsbawm, "Introduction," p. 2.
19 Ibid.
20 Ibid.
21 Dell Hymes, "Folklore's Nature and the Sun's Myth," *Journal of American Folklore*, LXXXVIII/350 (1975), p. 353.
22 Ibid., p. 354.
23 Ibid.
24 Ibid., p. 355.
25 Edward Shils, "Tradition," *Comparative Studies in Society and History*, XIII/2 (1971), p. 135.
26 Ibid., p. 122.
27 Ibid., p. 151.
28 Ibid., p. 130.
29 Alan Gailey, "The Nature of Tradition," *Folklore*, C/2 (1989), p. 155.
30 Shils, "Tradition," p. 140.
31 Ibid., pp. 132–3.
32 Henry Glassie, "Tradition," *Journal of American Folklore*, CVIII/430 (1995), p. 395.
33 Ibid.
34 Tom Mould, "The Paradox of Traditionalization: Negotiating the Past in Choctaw Prophetic Discourse," *Journal of Folklore Research*, XLII/3 (2005), p. 257.
35 Ibid., p. 263.
36 Ibid., p. 261.
37 Dorothy Noyes and Roger D. Abrahams, "From Calendar Customs to National Memory: European Commonplaces," in *Cultural Memory and the Construction of Identity*, ed. Dan Ben-Amos and Liliane Weissberg (Detroit, MI, 1999), p. 79.
38 Ibid., p. 90.
39 Bernhard W. Anderson, "Tradition and Scripture in the Community of Faith," *Journal of Biblical Literature*, C/1 (1981), p. 8.
40 Ibid.
41 Ibid., p. 9.
42 Ibid., p. 13.
43 Walter Brueggemann, *An Introduction to the Old Testament: The Canon and Christian Imagination* (Louisville, KY, 2003), pp. 11–12.
44 Ibid., p. 9.
45 Ibid., p. 7.

46 Orlando O. Espin, "Traditioning: Culture, Daily Life and Popular Religion, and Their Impact on Christian Tradition," in *Futuring Our Past: Explorations in the Theology of Tradition*, ed. Orlando O. Espin and Gary Macy (Maryknoll, NY, 2006), p. 2.

47 Ibid., p. 4.

48 Ibid., p. 5; italics in original.

49 Ibid., p. 15; italics in original.

50 H. Neill McFarland, *The Rush Hour of the Gods: A Study of New Religious Movements in Japan* (New York, 1967).

51 John Clammer, "Colonialism and the Perception of Tradition in Fiji," in *Anthropology and the Colonial Encounter*, ed. Talal Asad (New York, 1973), p. 202.

52 Deborah Bird Rose, *Dingo Makes Us Human: Life and Land in an Australian Aboriginal Culture* (Cambridge, 1992), p. 2.

53 Jianhua Zhao, *The Chinese Fashion Industry: An Ethnographic Approach* (London and New York, 2013), pp. 69–73.

54 Shils, "Tradition," p. 154.

55 Monica M. Ringer, *Pious Citizens: Reforming Zoroastrianism in India and Iran* (Syracuse, NY, 2011), p. 145.

56 Ibid., p. 151.

57 Benedict Anderson, *Imagined Communities: Reflections on the Origin and Spread of Nationalism* (London, 1983).

58 Maurice Halbwachs, *On Collective Memory*, ed. and trans. Lewis A. Coser (Chicago, IL, and London, 1992 [1925]), p. 47.

59 Richard Bauman, *A World of Others' Words: Cross-cultural Perspectives on Intertextuality* (Oxford, 2004), p. 27.

60 Mircea Eliade, *Myth and Reality*, trans. Willard R. Trask (Prospect Heights, IL, 1998 [1963]), p. 141.

61 Heitzenrater, "Tradition and History," p. 637.

62 Ibid.

63 Ibid., p. 633.

64 Ka-Ming Wu, *Reinventing Chinese Tradition: The Cultural Politics of Late Socialism* (Urbana and Chicago, IL, 2015), p. 36.

65 Ibid., p. 49.

66 Nicholas Thomas, "The Inversion of Tradition," *American Ethnologist*, XIX/2 (1992), p. 216.

67 Richard Handler and Jocelyn Linnekin, "Tradition, Genuine or Spurious," *Journal of American Folklore*, XCVII/385 (1984), p. 279.

68 Réka Szilárdi, "Neopaganism in Hungary: Under the Spell of Roots," in *Modern Pagan and Native Faith Movements in Central and Eastern Europe*, ed. Kaarina Aitamurto and Scott Simpson (Durham, and Bristol, CT, 2013), p. 230.

69 Ibid., p. 232.

70 Ibid., p. 236.

71 Ibid., p. 233.

72 Thomas Sowell, *Race and Culture: A World View* (New York, 1994), pp. 28–9.

73 Remo Guidieri and Francesco Pellizi, "Introduction: 'Smoking Mirrors'— Modern Polity and Ethnicity," in *Ethnicities and Nations: Processes of*

Interethnic Relations in Latin America, Southeast Asia, and the Pacific, ed. Remo Guidieri, Francesco Pellizi, and Stanley Tambiah (Austin, TX, 1988), p. 155.
74 Liisa Malkki, *Purity and Exile: Violence, Memory, and National Cosmology among Hutu Refugees in Tanzania* (Chicago, IL, and London, 1995), p. 3.

I OF THEE I SING:
NATIONAL ANTHEM

1 Marc Ferris, *Star-Spangled Banner: The Unlikely Story of America's National Anthem* (Baltimore, MD, 2014), p. 4.
2 Ibid., p. 8.
3 Stephen Salisbury, *An Essay on the Star Spangled Banner and National Songs* (Worcester, MA, 1873), pp. 11–12.
4 For complete lyrics, visit the National Anthems website at www.nationalanthems.info. To hear this virtually forgotten song being sung, see "Hail Columbia! With Lyrics; First American National Anthem—United States of America," at www.youtube.com.
5 Ferris, *Star-Spangled Banner*, pp. 13–14.
6 George J. Svejda, *History of the Star Spangled Banner from 1814 to the Present* (Washington, DC, 1969), p. 56.
7 Lonn Taylor, Kathleen Kendrick, and Jeffrey L. Brodie, *The Star-Spangled Banner: The Making of an American Icon* (New York, 2008), pp. 40–41.
8 Svejda, *History of the Star Spangled Banner*, p. 76.
9 Ibid., p. 69.
10 Oscar George Theodore Sonneck, *Report on "The Star Spangled Banner," "Hail Columbia," "America," "Yankee Doodle"* (Washington, DC, 1909), p. 7.
11 Ferris, *Star-Spangled Banner*, p. 21.
12 Sonneck, *Report on "The Star Spangled Banner,"* p. 20.
13 Svejda, *History of the Star Spangled Banner*, p. 109.
14 Sonneck, *Report on "The Star Spangled Banner,"* p. 27.
15 Svejda, *History of the Star Spangled Banner*, p. 103.
16 Ibid., pp. 124–7.
17 Taylor, Kendrick, and Brodie, *The Star-Spangled Banner*, p. 51.
18 Svejda, *History of the Star Spangled Banner*, p. 130.
19 Ferris, *Star-Spangled Banner*, p. 49.
20 Quoted in Svejda, *History of the Star Spangled Banner*, p. 261.
21 Salisbury, *An Essay on the Star Spangled Banner*, p. 11.
22 Svejda, *History of the Star Spangled Banner*, p. 219.
23 Ibid., p. 221.
24 Ferris, *Star-Spangled Banner*, p. 125.
25 Quoted in Svejda, *History of the Star Spangled Banner*, p. 340.
26 Ferris, *Star-Spangled Banner*, p. 129.
27 Irvin Molotsky, *The Flag, the Poet, and the Song: The Story of the Star-Spangled Banner* (New York, 2001), p. 3.
28 Taylor, Kendrick, and Brodie, *The Star-Spangled Banner*, p. 48.
29 Ferris, *Star-Spangled Banner*, p. 188.

2 YOU'RE A GRAND OLD RAG: AMERICAN FLAG

1 Marc Leepson, *Flag: An American Biography* (New York, 2006), p. 1.
2 Arnaldo Testi, *Capture the Flag: The Stars and Stripes in American History*, trans. Noor Giovanni Mazhar (New York and London, 2010), p. 1.
3 Ibid., p. 79.
4 Leepson, *Flag*, p. 3.
5 Ibid., p. 26.
6 Ibid., p. 17.
7 Kevin Keim and Peter Keim, *A Grand Old Flag: A History of the United States through its Flags* (London and New York, 2007), p. 92.
8 Leepson, *Flag*, pp. 35–6.
9 Lonn Taylor, Kathleen Kendrick, and Jeffrey L. Brodie, *The Star-Spangled Banner: The Making of an American Icon* (New York, 2008), p. 72.
10 Keim and Keim, *A Grand Old Flag*, p. 33.
11 Ibid.
12 Leepson, *Flag*, p. 39.
13 William Canby, "The History of the Flag of the United States," www.ushistory.org, 1870.
14 Leepson, *Flag*, p. 43.
15 Ibid., p. 44.
16 Thomas Ayres, *That's Not in My American History Book* (Lanham, MD, 2000), p. 212.
17 Leepson, *Flag*, p. 58.
18 Keim and Keim, *A Grand Old Flag*, p. 34.
19 Testi, *Capture the Flag*, p. 80.
20 Kit Hinrichs and Delphine Hirasuna, *Long May She Wave: A Graphic History of the American Flag* (Berkeley, CA, and Toronto, 2001), p. 13.
21 Quoted in Leepson, *Flag*, pp. 91–2.
22 Leepson, *Flag*, p. 155.
23 Testi, *Capture the Flag*, p. 38.
24 Ibid.

3 THE NEW AMERICAN MAN: UNCLE SAM

1 Hector St John de Crèvecoeur, "Letters from an American Farmer," xroads. virginia.edu, 1782, "Letter III."
2 Phillis Wheatley, "His Excellency General Washington," www.poets.org, 1775.
3 Stephen Hess and Sandy Northrop cited in Ruth Miller, "Stuck or Star-struck with Uncle Sam? Reevaluating Relations between the U.S. and its National Personification," *Americana: Journal of the American Studies Student Association*, VIII (2010), p. 23.
4 Winifred Morgan, *An American Icon: Brother Jonathan and American Identity* (Newark, DE, 1988), p. 21.

5 James Kirke Paulding, *The Diverting History of John Bull and Brother Jonathan*, 3rd edn (Philadelphia, PA, 1827 [1812]).
6 Albert Matthews, *Uncle Sam*, repr. from the Proceedings of the American Antiquarian Society, V/19 (Worcester, MA, 1908), p. 21.
7 Ibid., p. 63.
8 Ibid., pp. 64–5.
9 Alton Ketchum, *Uncle Sam: The Man and the Legend* (New York, 1959), p. 41.
10 Ibid., p. 40.
11 Alton Ketchum, "The Search for Uncle Sam," *History Today*, XL/4 (1990), p. 23.
12 Ibid.
13 Ibid.
14 Ketchum, *Uncle Sam*, p. 41.
15 Ibid., p. 42.
16 Matthews, *Uncle Sam*, p. 23.
17 Ketchum, "The Search for Uncle Sam," p. 23.
18 Matthews, *Uncle Sam*, p. 42.
19 Ibid., p. 43.
20 Ketchum, *Uncle Sam*, p. 60.
21 Ibid., p. 66.
22 Ibid., p. 80.
23 Ibid., p. 96.
24 Quoted in ibid., p. 118.
25 Quoted in Miller, "Stuck or Star-struck with Uncle Sam," pp. 29–30.
26 Miller, p. 29.
27 Ketchum, *Uncle Sam*, p. 122.
28 Miller, "Stuck or Star-struck with Uncle Sam," p. 22.

4 THE REPUBLIC FOR WHICH IT STANDS: PLEDGE OF ALLEGIANCE AND MOTTO

1 Richard J. Ellis, *To the Flag: The Unlikely History of the Pledge of Allegiance* (Lawrence, KS, 2005), p. 210.
2 "Oath of Allegiance," www.alexlibraryva.org, 1862.
3 Marc Leepson, *Flag: An American Biography* (New York, 2006), p. 164.
4 Ellis, *To the Flag*, p. 6.
5 Ibid., pp. 27–8.
6 Ibid., p. 50.
7 Ibid., p. 37.
8 Ibid., p. 30.
9 Ibid., p. 52.
10 Ibid., p. 54.
11 Ibid., p. 125.
12 Ibid., p. 132.
13 Ibid., p. 133.
14 Quoted in Leepson, *Flag*, p. 174.
15 Ibid., p. 176.

16 Jim Walker, "History to Consider," www.nobeliefs.com, July 28, 2015.
17 U.S. Treasury, "History of 'In God We Trust'," www.treasury.gov, 2011.
18 Religioustolerance.org, "The U.S. National Mottos: Their History and Constitutionality," www.religioustolerance.org, 2012.
19 U.S. House of Representatives, "The Legislation Placing 'In God We Trust' on National Currency," history.house.gov, July 29, 2015.
20 Ellis, *To the Flag*, p. 85.
21 Ibid., p. 86.
22 Ibid., p. 138.
23 U.S. Ninth Circuit Court of Appeals, *Michael A. Newdow v. U.S. Congress et al.* (2002), p. 9123.
24 George W. Bush, "50th Anniversary of Our National Motto, 'In God We Trust,' 2006," georgewbush-whitehouse.archives.gov, 2006.

5 WE GATHER TOGETHER: THANKSGIVING

1 Diana Karter Appelbaum, *Thanksgiving: An American Holiday, an American History* (New York, 1984), p. 26.
2 Ibid., p. 7.
3 James W. Baker, *Thanksgiving: The Biography of an American Holiday* (Durham, NH, 2009), p. ix.
4 Godfrey Hodgson, *A Great and Godly Adventure: The Pilgrims and the Myth of the First Thanksgiving* (New York, 2006), p. 61.
5 Edward Winslow, *Mourt's Relation*, www.pilgrimhall.org, 1622.
6 Appelbaum, *Thanksgiving*, pp. 9–10.
7 Ibid., p. 10.
8 Andrew Smith, "The First Thanksgiving," *Gastronomica*, III (2003), p. 81.
9 Appelbaum, *Thanksgiving*, p. 35.
10 William DeLoss Love, *Fast and Thanksgiving Days in New England* (Boston, MA, 1895), p. 69.
11 Appelbaum, *Thanksgiving*, p. 36.
12 Quoted in Baker, *Thanksgiving*, p. 42.
13 Appelbaum, *Thanksgiving*, p. 40.
14 Ibid., p. 53.
15 George Washington, "Thanksgiving Proclamation, 3 October 1789," founders.archives.gov, 1789.
16 Applebaum, *Thanksgiving*, p. 133.
17 Ibid., p. 163.
18 Baker, *Thanksgiving*, p. 63.
19 Abraham Lincoln, "Proclamation of Thanksgiving," www.abrahamlincolnonline.org, 1863.
20 Baker, *Thanksgiving*, p. 75.
21 Appelbaum, *Thanksgiving*, p. 113.
22 Sarah Josepha Hale, *Northwood Life North and South*, www.pilgrimhall.org, 1827.
23 Pilgrim Hall Museum, "The Godmother of Thanksgiving: The Story of Sarah Josepha Hale Continued," www.pilgrimhall.org, 2005.

24 Appelbaum, *Thanksgiving*, p. 113.
25 Abraham Lincoln Papers, Library of Congress, womenshistory.about.com, July 9, 2012.
26 Baker, *Thanksgiving*, p. 115.
27 Ibid., p. 143.
28 Ibid., p. 16.
29 Ibid., p. 112.
30 Appelbaum, *Thanksgiving*, pp. 186–8.
31 Baker, *Thanksgiving*, p. 148.
32 Ibid., p. 168.
33 United American Indians of New England, "39th National Day of Mourning," iacenter.org, 2008.
34 Appelbaum, *Thanksgiving*, p. 126.
35 Smith, "The First Thanksgiving," p. 85.

6 HONOR THY MOTHER AND FATHER, ETC.: MOTHER'S DAY AND FATHER'S DAY

1 Cai Hua, *A Society without Fathers or Husbands: The Na of China*, trans. Asti Hustvedt (Brooklyn, NY, 2001).
2 Stephanie Coontz, *The Way We Never Were: American Families and the Nostalgia Trap* (New York, 1992), pp. 25–6.
3 W.H.R. Rivers, *Social Organization: A History of Civilization* (London and New York, 1996 [1924]), p. 52.
4 Dorothy A. Mays, *Women in Early America: Struggle, Survival, and Freedom in a New World* (Santa Barbara, CA, 2004), pp. 246–8.
5 Barbara Welter, "The Cult of True Womanhood: 1820–1860," *American Quarterly* XVIII/2 (1966), p. 152.
6 Ibid., p. 153.
7 Ibid., p. 158.
8 Ibid., p. 162.
9 Ibid., p. 171.
10 Ibid., p. 172.
11 Brian Handwerk, "Mother's Day Turns 100: Its Surprisingly Dark History," news.nationalgeographic. com, 2014.
12 Julia Ward Howe, "Mother's Day Proclamation," www.peace.ca, 1870.
13 Research History, "Mother's Day History," www.researchhistory.org, 2011.
14 The History Channel, "Mother's Day," www.history.com, accessed August 24, 2017.
15 Katherine Lane Antolini, "The Tenacious Woman Who Helped Keep Mother's Day Alive," www.smithsonianmag.com, 2015.
16 Ibid.
17 The History Channel, "Mother's Day."
18 Antolini, "The Tenacious Woman."
19 Research History, "Mother"s Day History."
20 Joey Butler, "Father's Day Has Methodist Ties," www.umc.org, 2010.
21 Vicky Smith, "First Father's Day Service," *Martinsburg Journal*, www.wvculture.org, 2003.

22 "History of Father's Day," www.fathersdaycelebration.com, accessed August 24, 2017.
23 Ibid.
24 Timothy Marr, "Father's Day," in *American Masculinities: A Historical Encyclopedia*, ed. Bret Carroll (New York, 2003), p. 166.
25 Ibid.
26 Ralph LaRossa and Jaimie Ann Carboy, " 'A Kiss for Mother, A Hug for Dad: The Early 20th Century Parents' Day Campaign," *Fathering* VI/3 (2008), p. 249.
27 Ibid., p. 252.
28 Ibid., p. 256.
29 Ibid., p. 259.
30 Ibid., p. 261.
31 Ibid., p. 255.
32 Ibid., p, 251.
33 Legacy Project, "The History of Grandparents Day," www.legacyproject.org, accessed August 24, 2017.
34 Melanie Notkin, "25 Reasons Why Aunts Deserve a Day," melanienotkin.com, 2014.
35 Colleen Paige, "National Pet Day," www.petdayusa.com, 2017.

7 LEST WE FORGET:
PATRIOTIC HOLIDAYS

1 Jacob R. Straus, "Federal Holidays: Evolution and Current Practices," www.crs.gov, 2014, p. i.
2 Quoted in Michael Kammen, *Mystic Chords of Memory: The Transformation of Tradition in American Culture* (New York, 1993 [1991]), p. 71.
3 The History Channel, "Presidents' Day," www.history.com, accessed August 25, 2017.
4 Yoni Appelbaum, "When Presidents Day was Bicycle Day," www.theatlantic.com, 2015.
5 Chris Hedges, *War is a Force that Gives Us Meaning* (New York, 2002).
6 U.S. Department of Veterans Affairs, "Memorial Day History," www.va.gov, 2015.
7 Daniel Bellware and Richard Gardiner, *The Genesis of the Memorial Day Holiday* (Columbus, GA, 2014), pp. 1–2.
8 Quoted in ibid., p. 3.
9 Ibid., p. 5, emphasis in original.
10 The History Channel, "Memorial Day," www.history.com, 2015.
11 *Calhoun County Courier*, Calhoun County GA Newspaper Microfilm, files.usgwarchives.net, 1866.
12 Bellware and Gardiner, *The Genesis of the Memorial Day Holiday*, p. 56.
13 Ibid., p. 53.
14 Quoted in ibid., p. 35.
15 Grand Army of the Republic, "General Order Number 11," memorialdayorigin.info, 1868.
16 Marc Leepson, *Flag: An American Biography* (New York, 2006), p. 134.

17 David W. Blight, "Decoration Days: The Origins of Memorial Day in North and South," in *The Memory of the Civil War in American Culture*, ed. Alice Fahs (Chapel Hill, NC, 2004), pp. 94–129. Also *Race and Reunion: The Civil War in American Memory* (Cambridge, MA, 2001).
18 David W. Blight, "The First Decoration Day," zinnedproject.org, 2011.
19 U.S. Department of Veterans Affairs, "Memorial Day History."
20 U.S. Department of Veterans Affairs, "Celebrating America's Freedoms: The Origins of Flag Day," www.va.gov, August 12, 2015.
21 Leepson, *Flag*, p. 145.
22 National Flag Day Foundation, "Bernard J. CiGrand," www.nationalflagday. com, August 12, 2015.
23 Baptist Heritage Journal, "The History of Flag Day," baptistheritagejournal. blogspot.com, 2014.
24 Leepson, *Flag*, p. 151.
25 U.S. Army, "The History of Veterans Day," www.history.army.mil, 2015.
26 U.S. Department of Veterans Affairs, "Veterans Day," www.va.gov, 2015.
27 Quoted in the History Channel, "Veterans Day," www.history.com, 2015.

8 WE ARE THE WORLD:
ETHNIC AMERICAN HOLIDAYS

1 Yuson Jung, "Experiencing the 'West' Through the 'East' in the Margins of Europe: Chinese Food Consumption Practices in Postsocialist Bulgaria," in *Re-Orienting Cuisine: East Asian Foodways in the Twenty-first Century*, ed. Kwang Ok Kim (New York and London, 2015), pp. 150–69.
2 Mike Cronin and Daryl Adair, *The Wearing of the Green: A History of St Patrick's Day* (London and New York, 2002), p. xxi.
3 James Mooney, "The Holiday Customs of Ireland," *Proceedings of the American Philosophical Society*, XXVI/ 130 (1889), pp. 377–427.
4 Philip Freeman, *St Patrick of Ireland: A Biography* (New York, 2004).
5 Josiah Cox Russell, "The Problem of St Patrick the Missionary," *Traditio*, XII (1956), pp. 393–8.
6 Cronin and Adair, *The Wearing of the Green*, p. xxvii.
7 Ibid., p. 25.
8 John Daniel Crimmins, *St Patrick's Day: Its Celebration in New York and Other American Places, 1737–1845; How the Anniversary was Observed by Representative Irish Organizations, and the Toasts Proposed* (New York, 1902), p. 9.
9 See www.friendlysons.com for The Society of the Friendly Sons of Saint Patrick for the Relief of Emigrants from Ireland, founded in Philadelphia in 1771.
10 Kenneth Moss, "St Patrick's Day Celebrations and the Formation of Irish-American Identity, 1845–1875," *Journal of Social History*, XXIX/ 1 (1995), p. 126.
11 Ibid., p. 125.
12 Sallie A. Marston, "Public Rituals and Community Power: St Patrick's Day Parades in Lowell, Massachusetts, 1841–1874," *Political Geography Quarterly*, VIII/3 (1989), p. 259.
13 Ibid., p. 263.

14 Moss, "St Patrick's Day Celebrations," p. 126.

15 Ibid., p. 130.

16 Susan G. Davis, *Parades and Power: Street Theatre in Nineteenth Century Philadelphia* (Philadelphia, PA, 1986).

17 Moss, "St Patrick's Day Celebrations," pp. 136–7.

18 Marston, "Public Rituals and Community Power," p. 264.

19 Ibid., pp. 261–6.

20 Moss, "St Patrick's Day Celebrations," p. 139.

21 Cronin and Adair, *The Wearing of the Green*, p. 52.

22 Ibid.

23 Ibid., p. 74.

24 Ibid., p. 166.

25 David Boyle, *Toward the Setting Sun: Columbus, Cabot, Vespucci, and the Race for America* (New York, 2008), p. 4.

26 Lakshmi Gandhi, "How Columbus Sailed into U.S. History, Thanks to Italians," www.npr.org, 2013.

27 Ibid.

28 Ibid.

29 William J. Connell, "What Columbus Day Really Means," theamericanscholar.org, 2012.

30 Quoted in Gandhi, "How Columbus Sailed into U.S. History."

31 Ibid.

32 American Indian Movement, "Goodbye Columbus!," www.indians.org, 1994.

33 David E. Hayes-Bautista, *El Cinco de Mayo: An American Tradition* (Berkeley, CA, 2012), p. 11.

34 Joanna Kaftan, "National Identity during Periods of Controversy: Celebrating Cinco de Mayo in Phoenix, Arizona," *Nations and Nationalism*, XIX/1 (2013), p. 168.

35 Ibid.

36 Hayes-Bautista, *El Cinco de Mayo*, p. 183.

37 Ibid., pp. 185–6.

38 Ibid., p. 186.

39 Alvar W. Carlson, "America's Growing Observance of Cinco de Mayo," *Journal of American Culture*, XXI/2 (1998), p. 8.

40 Ibid., pp. 12–13.

41 Todd Leopold, "Why Do We Celebrate Cinco de Mayo?," www.cnn.com, 2015.

42 Carlson, "America's Growing Observance of Cinco de Mayo," p. 12.

43 Hayes-Bautista, *El Cinco de Mayo*, pp. 190–91.

44 Keith A. Mayes, *Kwanzaa: Black Power and the Making of the African American Holiday Tradition* (New York and London, 2009).

45 Frederick Douglass, "What to the Slave is the Fourth of July?," teachingamericanhistory.org, 1852.

46 Mayes, *Kwanzaa*, p. 4.

47 Ibid., p. 2.

48 Association for the Study of African American Life and History, "The Origins of Black History Month," asalh.net, 2011.

49 Mayes, *Kwanzaa*, p. 65.

50 Maulana Karenga, *Kwanzaa: A Celebration of Family, Community and Culture* (Los Angeles, CA, 2008).
51 Official Kwanzaa website, www.officialkwanzaawebsite.org, August 17, 2015.
52 Mayes, *Kwanzaa*, p. 94.
53 Ibid., p. 97.
54 Ann Coulter, "Kwanzaa: The Holiday Brought to You by the FBI," www.anncoulter.com, 2013.
55 William J. Bennett, "The Kwanzaa Hoax," www.textbookleague.org, 2000.
56 Mayes, *Kwanzaa*, p. 84.

9 AMERICA IN A WORD: "OK"

1 Woodford A. Heflin, "'O.K.,' But What Do We Know About It?," *American Speech*, XVI/2 (1941), p. 89.
2 Ibid.
3 H. L. Mencken, *The American Language: An Inquiry into the Development of English in the United States*, 2nd edn (New York, 1921 [1919]), p. 31.
4 Ibid., p. 188.
5 Allen Walker Read, "Later Stages in the History of 'O.K.'" *American Speech*, XXXIX/2 (1964), p. 95.
6 Allen Walker Read, "The First Stage in the History of 'O.K.'" *American Speech*, XXXVIII/1 (1963), p. 5.
7 Ibid., p. 12.
8 Ibid.
9 Ibid., pp. 26–7.
10 Allen Walker Read, "The Second Stage in the History of 'O.K.'" *American Speech*, XXXVIII/2 (1963), p. 86.
11 Ibid., p. 88.
12 Ibid., p. 94.
13 Ibid., p. 97.
14 For scans of the original sheet music pages, see the John H. Hewitt, "OK Gallopade" (1840), Johns Hopkins University Sheridan Libraries and University Museums Lester S. Levy Sheet Music Collection, Box 015, Item 031, http://levysheetmusic.mse.jhu.edu.
15 See "O.K. Quick Step," www.loc.gov.
16 Allan Metcalf, *OK: The Improbable Story of America's Greatest Word* (Oxford and New York, 2011), p. 50.
17 Quoted in Read, "Later Stages," p. 85.
18 Ibid., p. 94.
19 Ibid., p. 95.
20 Ibid., p. 96.
21 Paul R. Beath, "'O.K.' in Radio Sign Language," *American Speech*, XXI/3 (1946), p. 235.
22 Read, "Later Stages," p. 100.
23 Ibid.
24 Allen Walker Read, "The Folklore of 'O.K.'" *American Speech*, XXXIX/1 (1964), p. 9.

25 Ibid., p. 25.
26 Metcalf, *OK*, p. 2.
27 Ibid., p. 14.
28 Ibid., p. 15.
29 Ibid.
30 Ibid., p. 113.
31 Ibid., pp. 19–20.
32 Ibid., p. 196.
33 Ibid., p. 197.

10 I'D LIKE TO TEACH THE WORLD: COCA–COLA

1 The Coca-Cola Company, "Coke Lore: A Story of Special Moments," www.thecoca-colacompany.com, August 9, 2012.
2 Mark Pendergrast, *For God, Country, and Coca-Cola: The Definitive History of the Great American Soft Drink and the Company that Makes It*, 2nd edn (New York, 2000), p. 442.
3 Ibid.
4 Ibid., p. 356.
5 Gyvel Young-Witzel and Michael Karl Witzel, *The Sparkling Story of Coca-Cola: An Entertaining History Including Collectibles, Coke Lore, and Calendar Girls* (Stillwater, MN, 2002), p. 90.
6 See Robert N. Bellah, "Civil Religion in America," *Daedalus*, XCVI/1 (1967), pp. 1–21. Bellah posited that America's civil religion gave supernatural authority to its institutions and policies and also provided the country with a transcendent mission, like spreading democracy.
7 Pendergrast, *For God, Country, and Coca-Cola*, pp. 442–3.
8 Ibid., p. 9.
9 Ibid., p. 11.
10 Pat Watters, *Coca-Cola: An Illustrated History* (Garden City, NY, 1978), p. 5.
11 Pendergrast, *For God, Country, and Coca-Cola*, p. 22.
12 Watters, *Coca-Cola*, p. 18.
13 Pendergrast, *For God, Country, and Coca-Cola*, p. 51.
14 Young-Witzel and Witzel, *The Sparkling Story of Coca-Cola*, p. 39.
15 Ibid., p. 42.
16 Watters, *Coca-Cola*, p. 50.
17 Pendergrast, *For God, Country, and Coca-Cola*, p. 79.
18 Ibid., pp. 103–4.
19 Young-Witzel and Witzel, *The Sparkling Story of Coca-Cola*, p. 44.
20 Ibid., p. 92.
21 Ibid.
22 Michael Blanding, *The Coke Machine: The Dirty Truth Behind the World's Favorite Soft Drink* (New York, 2010), p. 42.
23 Young-Witzel and Witzel, *The Sparkling Story of Coca-Cola*, p. 107.
24 Watters, *Coca-Cola*, p. 151.
25 Blanding, *The Coke Machine*, p. 49.
26 Ibid., p. 50.

27 Young-Witzel and Witzel, *The Sparkling Story of Coca-Cola*, p. 64.
28 Pendergrast, *For God, Country, and Coca-Cola*, p. 87.
29 Young-Witzel and Witzel, *The Sparkling Story of Coca-Cola*, pp. 69–70.
30 Ibid., p. 22.
31 Watters, *Coca-Cola*, p. 102.
32 Pendergrast, *For God, Country, and Coca-Cola*, p. 192.
33 Ibid., p. 274.
34 Thomas Oliver, *The Real Coke, The Real Story* (New York, 1986), p. 51.
35 Ibid., pp. 155–6.
36 Watters, *Coca-Cola*, p. 235.
37 Blanding, *The Coke Machine*, p. 3.
38 Ibid., p. 4.
39 Constance L. Hay, *The Real Thing: Truth and Power at the Coca Cola Company* (New York, 2004), p. 86.
40 Blanding, *The Coke Machine*, p. 94.
41 Watters, *Coca-Cola*, p. 234.

11 MEALS ON WHEELS: HAMBURGER

1 Josh Ozersky, *The Hamburger: A History* (New Haven, CT, and London, 2008), p. 1.
2 John T. Edge, *Hamburgers and Fries: An American Story* (New York, 2005), p. 13.
3 Ronald T. McDonald, *The Complete Hamburger: The History of America's Favorite Sandwich* (Secaucus, NJ, 1997), p. 5.
4 Edge, *Hamburgers and Fries*, p. 13.
5 Andrew F. Smith, *Hamburger: A Global History* (London, 2008), p. 10.
6 Ozersky, *The Hamburger*, p. 6.
7 Edge, *Hamburgers and Fries*, p. 14.
8 Jeffrey Tennyson, *Hamburger Heaven: The Illustrated History of the Hamburger* (New York, 1993), p. 13.
9 Ozersky, *The Hamburger*, p. 9.
10 Smith, *Hamburger*, p. 10.
11 Tennyson, *Hamburger Heaven*, p. 15.
12 Smith, *Hamburger*, p. 14.
13 Ozersky, *The Hamburger*, p. 7.
14 Smith, *Hamburger*, p. 15.
15 Bee Wilson, *Sandwich: A Global History* (London, 2010), p. 15.
16 Ibid., p. 16.
17 Ibid., p. 23.
18 Ozersky, *The Hamburger*, p. 15.
19 Ibid., p. 16.
20 Edge, *Hamburgers and Fries*, p. 22.
21 Smith, *Hamburger*, p. 18.
22 Ozersky, *The Hamburger*, p. 10.
23 Ibid., p. 13.

24 Ibid., pp. 12–13.
25 Ibid., p. 15.
26 McDonald, *The Complete Hamburger*, p. 14.
27 Ibid., p. 15.
28 Ozersky, *The Hamburger*, p. 36.
29 Quoted in Tennyson, *Hamburger Heaven*, p. 24.
30 Smith, *Hamburger*, p. 44.
31 See George Ritzer, *The McDonaldization of Society* (Newbury Park, CA, 1993). Among the highly generalizable characteristics of McDonaldization, he identified efficiency, calculability, predictability and standardization, and control.
32 Tennyson, *Hamburger Heaven*, p. 62.
33 Andrew F. Smith, *Potato: A Global History* (London, 2011), p. 31.
34 Ibid., p. 76.
35 Tennyson, *Hamburger Heaven*, p. 74.
36 Smith, *Hamburger*, p. 90.
37 Ibid.
38 Ozersky, *The Hamburger*, p. 133.

12 AMERICA'S INDIVIDUALISTIC UNIFORM: BLUE JEANS

1 For a version of the television commercial from 1977, see WalperMarketingGroup, "Dr. Pepper—'I'm a Pepper' TV Commercial 70's," March 2, 2008, www.youtube.com.
2 David Little, *Denim: An American Story* (Atglen, PA, 2007), p. 5.
3 John Fiske, *Understanding Popular Culture* (London and New York, 1989), p. 3.
4 Graham Marsh and Paul Trynka, *Denim: From Cowboys to Catwalks—A Visual History of the World's Most Legendary Fabric* (London, 2002), p. 4.
5 Lynn Downey, "A Short History of Denim," www.levistrauss.com, 2014, p. 1.
6 James Sullivan, *Jeans: A Cultural History of an American* Icon (New York, 2006), p. 13.
7 Ibid., p. 14.
8 Downey, "A Short History of Denim," p. 3.
9 Sullivan, *Jeans*, p. 15.
10 Ibid., p. 38.
11 Ibid., pp. 25–6.
12 Downey, "A Short History of Denim," p. 6.
13 Sullivan, *Jeans*, p. 27.
14 Downey, "A Short History of Denim," p. 7.
15 Sullivan, *Jeans*, p. 32.
16 Ibid., p. 33.
17 Little, *Denim*, p. 28.
18 See, for example, the men's Jacob Davis line for sale on www.buckle.com.
19 Marsh and Trynka, *Denim*, p. 44.
20 Downey, "A Short History of Denim," p. 9.
21 Marsh and Trynka, *Denim*, p. 56.
22 Little, *Denim*, p. 66.

23 A video of the performance can be seen at "Gene Vincent—Blue Jean Bop," July 26, 2014, www.youtube.com.
24 Downey, "A Short History of Denim," p. 12.
25 Sullivan, *Jeans*, p. 85.
26 Marsh and Trynka, *Denim*, p. 66.
27 Sullivan, *Jeans*, p. 112.
28 Todd Gitlin, *The Sixties: Years of Hope, Days of Rage* (New York, 1987), p. 162.
29 Little, *Denim*, p. 99.
30 Marsh and Trynka, *Denim*, p. 102.
31 Little, *Denim*, p. 104.
32 Sullivan, *Jeans*, p. 199.
33 To watch a video of the commercial, see Kid 80s, "Kid80s.com: Banned Calvin Klein Commercial from 1980 with Brooke Shields," April 15, 2014, www.youtube.com.
34 Sullivan, *Jeans*, p. 264.
35 Ibid., pp. 264–5.
36 Karl Smallwood, "The Surprisingly Recent Invention of the T-Shirt," www.todayifoundout.com, 2014.
37 Ibid.
38 Zani, "The Social History of the T-Shirt," www.zani.co.uk, 2015.
39 Eric Silverman, *A Cultural History of Jewish Dress* (London and New York, 2013).
40 Lynne S. Neal, "The Ideal Democratic Apparel: T-Shirts, Religious Tolerance, and the Clothing of Democracy," *Material Religion*, XIX/2 (2014), p. 203, emphasis in original.

13 AND THE AMERICAN WAY: SUPERMAN

1 Ben Saunders, *Do the Gods Wear Capes? Spirituality, Fantasy, and Superheroes* (London and New York, 2011), pp. 3–5.
2 Glen Weldon, *Superman: The Unauthorized Biography* (Hoboken, NJ, 2013), p. 2.
3 Thomas Andrae, "From Menace to Messiah: The Prehistory of the Superman in Science Fiction Literature," *Discourse*, II (Summer 1980), p. 85.
4 Ibid., p. 88.
5 Ibid., p. 91.
6 Ibid.
7 Weldon, *Superman*, p. 16.
8 Jeffrey K. Johnson, *Super-History: Comic Book Superheroes and American Society, 1938 to the Present* (Jefferson, NC, 2012), p. 11.
9 To read the original story, see Jerry Siegel and Joe Schuster, "Reign of the Superman," in *Science Fiction: The Vanguard of Future Civilization*, no. 3 (January 1933) at https://archive.org.
10 Weldon, *Superman*, p. 13.
11 Johnson, *Super-History*, p. 15.
12 Ibid., p. 8.
13 Andrae, "From Menace to Messiah," p. 100.
14 Ibid., p. 98.

15 Ibid., p. 100.

16 Ibid., p. 102.

17 Larry Tye, *Superman: The High-flying History of America's Most Enduring Hero* (New York, 2012), p. 89.

18 Ibid.

19 Josh Wilson, "Superman on Radio and Audio: Clayton 'Bud' Collyer," at www.supermanhomepage.com.

20 Weldon, *Superman*, p. 41.

21 Quoted in Tye, *Superman*, p. 60.

22 Andrae, "From Menace to Messiah," p. 100.

23 Jack Teiwes, "The New 'Man of Steel' is a Quiche-Eating Wimp! Media Reactions to the Reimagining of Superman in the Reagan Era," in *The Ages of Superman: Essays on the Man of Steel in Changing Times*, ed. Joseph J. Darowski (Jefferson, NC, 2012), p. 126.

24 Andrae, "From Menace to Messiah," p. 106.

25 Gary Engle, "What Make Superman So Darned American?," in *Superman at Fifty: The Persistence of a Legend*, ed. Dennis Dooley and Gary Engle (New York, 1988), p. 80.

26 Weldon, *Superman*, p. 152.

27 Quoted in Randy Duncan, "Traveling Hopefully in Search of American National Identity: The 'Grounded' Superman as a 21st Century Picaro," in *The Ages of Superman*, ed. Darowski, p. 224.

14 WHO'S THE LEADER OF THE CLUB? MICKEY MOUSE

1 Mike Wallace, "Mickey Mouse History: Portraying the Past at Disney World," *Radical History Review*, 32 (1985), p. 35.

2 Ibid., p. 48.

3 To watch the 1927 short cartoon "Trolley Troubles," see laughland, "Trolley Troubles—Oswald the Lucky Rabbit—1927," June 28, 2006, www.youtube.com.

4 Jim Korkis, *The Book of Mouse: A Celebration of Walt Disney's Mickey Mouse* (Winter Garden, FL, 2015 [2013]), p. 3.

5 Robert Heide and John Gilman. *Mickey Mouse: The Evolution, the Legend, the Phenomenon* (New York, 2001), p. 9.

6 Korkis, *The Book of Mouse*, p. 6.

7 To watch "Crazy Plane," see Walt Disney Animation Studios, "Plane Crazy, Mickey Mouse Classic Walt Disney 1928 Sound Cartoon," August 27, 2009, www.youtube.com.

8 Korkis, *The Book of Mouse*, p. 15.

9 To watch "Dinner Time 1928," see www.youtube.com.

10 Korkis, *The Book of Mouse*, p. 36.

11 Ibid., p. 9.

12 Heide and Gilman, *Mickey Mouse*, p. 22.

13 Jim Korkis, "The First Mickey Mouse Convention," www.mouseplanet.com, 2012.

14 Korkis, *The Book of Mouse*, p. 104.

15 Ibid., p. 52.

16 Ibid., p. 55.
17 David Bain and Bruce Harris, eds, *Mickey Mouse: Fifty Happy Years* (New York, 1997), p. 20.
18 Ibid., p. 14.
19 Ibid., p. 114.
20 Ibid., p. 115.
21 Ibid., pp. 67 and 32.
22 Quoted in ibid., 113.
23 Bain and Harris, *Mickey Mouse*, pp. 25–7.
24 Jennifer Armstrong, *Why? Because We Still Like You: An Oral History of the Mickey Mouse Club* (New York, 2010). Jerry Bowles, *Forever Hold Your Banner High! The Story of the Mickey Mouse Club and What Happened to the Mouseketeers* (Garden City, NY, 1975).
25 Armstrong, *Why?*, p. 7.
26 Bain and Harris, *Mickey Mouse*, p. 28.
27 Sam Gennawey, *The Disneyland Story: The Unofficial Guide to the Evolution of Walt Disney's Dream* (Birmingham, AL, 2014), p. 2.
28 Korkis, *The Book of Mouse*, p. 200.
29 Ibid., p. 201.
30 "Disneyland," www.disneyparkhistory.com, September 9, 2015.
31 Korkis, *The Book of Mouse*, p. 203.
32 Ibid., p. 204.
33 For a montage of performances from the show by the three singers, see ThisIsTheMusicTV, "Britney Spears-Justin Timberlake-Christina Aguilera Best Moments @ The MMC," September 21, 2012, www.youtube.com.
34 Korkis, *The Book of Mouse*, p. 192.
35 Lauren Vanpelt, "Mickey Mouse: A Truly Public Character," www.public.asu.edu, 1999.

15 YOU'LL GO DOWN IN HISTORY: SOME AMERICAN CHARACTERS

1 Esther Shephard, "The Tall Tale in American Literature," *Pacific Review* (December 1921).
2 Walter Blair, *Tall Tale America: A Legendary History of our Humorous Heroes* (Chicago, IL, and London, 1987 [1944]), p. 1.
3 Scott Reynolds Nelson, *Steel Drivin' Man: John Henry, the Untold Story of an American Legend* (Oxford and New York, 2006).
4 Richard M. Dorson, "Folklore and Fake Lore," *The American Mercury* (March 1950).
5 Richard M. Dorson, *American Folklore* (Chicago and London, 1959), p. 4.
6 Marshall W. Fishwick, "Sons of Paul: Folklore or Fakelore?," *Western Folklore*, XVIII/4 (1959), p. 277.
7 Dorson, *American Folklore*, p. 214.
8 Ibid., p. 215.
9 Esther Shephard, *Paul Bunyan: Twenty-one Tales of the Legendary Logger* (Orlando, FL, 2000 [1924]), p. xii.
10 Anonymous, "Caught on the Run," *Duluth News Tribune* (August 4, 1904), p. 4.

11 James MacGillivray, "Round River," *The Press* (August 10, 1906).

12 Douglas Malloch and James MacGillivray, "The Round River Drive," *American Lumberman* (April 25, 1914), p. 33.

13 J. E. Rockwell, "Some Lumberjack Myths," *The Outer's Book* (February 1910), p. 157.

14 Charles Albert Albright, "Chronicle of Life and Works of Mr. Paul Bunyan," *American Lumberman* (June 17, 1916), pp. 40–41; K. Bernice Stewart and Homer A. Watt, "Legends of Paul Bunyan, Lumberjack," *Transactions of the Wisconsin Academy of Sciences, Arts, and Letters* (1916), pp. 639–51.

15 William B. Laughead, *Introducing Mr. Paul Bunyan of Westwood, California* (Minneapolis, MN, 1914).

16 William B. Laughead, *The Marvelous Exploits of Paul Bunyan as Told in the Camps of the White Pine Lumbermen for Generations During Which Time the Loggers Have Pioneered the Way Through the North Woods From Maine to California Collected from Various Sources and Embellished for Publication* (Minneapolis, MN, and Westwood, CA, 1922).

17 Shephard, *Paul Bunyan*, pp. xii–xiii.

18 Fishwick, "Sons of Paul," p. 278.

19 To hear some of the old radio shows, visit The Lone Ranger Official Fan Club at www.lonerangerfanclub.com.

20 Fran Striker, "The Lone Ranger Creed," www.npr.org, 2008.

21 Aisha Harris, "What Do You Mean 'Kemosabe,' Kemosabe?," www.slate.com, June 26, 2013.

22 Art T. Burton, *Black Gun, Silver Star: The Life and Legend of Frontier Marshal Bass Reeves* (Lincoln, NE, and London, 2006).

23 Sheena McKenzie, "Was an African American Cop the Real Lone Ranger?," www.cnn.com, 2013.

24 Fred M. Grandinetti, *Popeye: An Illustrated Cultural History* (Jefferson, NC, 2004), p. 105.

25 Miss Cellania, "I Yam What I Yam: The Story of Popeye," www.neatorama.com, 2012.

26 Grandinetti, *Popeye*, p. 5.

27 Ibid., p. 4.

28 Watch the entire original 1936 full-color sixteen-minute cartoon "Popeye the Sailor Meets Sindbad the Sailor" at captainbijou.com, "1936 *Popeye Meets Sinbad The Sailor* Cartoon," January 25, 2014, www.youtube.com.

29 Grandinetti, *Popeye*, p. 37.

30 Ibid., p. 179.

31 Sarah Griffiths, "Sorry Popeye, Spinach doesn't Make Your Muscles Big: Expert Reveals Sailor's Love of the Food Was Due to a Misplaced Decimal Point," www.dailymail.co.uk, 2013.

32 Grandinetti, *Popeye*, p. 52.

33 Ibid., p. 54.

34 Ibid., p. 100.

35 Ibid., p. 141.

36 To watch a trailer for the 2016 Popeye feature, see Movieclips Coming Soon, "Popeye SNEAK PEEK 1 (2016)—Animated Movie HD," September 18, 2014, www.youtube.com.

37 Sara Pendergast and Tom Pendergast, *Bowling, Beatniks, and Bell-bottoms: Pop Culture of 20th-Century America*, vol. 3: *1940s–1950s* (Detroit, MI, 2002), p. 58.
38 Robert L. May, *Rudolph the Red-nosed Reindeer* (New York, 2001 [1939]).
39 To watch a clip of Uncle Mistletoe's show, see "Adventures of Uncle Misteltoe," 1949, https://archive.org.

CONCLUSION:
THE FUTURE OF AMERICAN TRADITION

1 Mike Wallace, *Mickey Mouse History and Other Essays on American Memory* (Philadelphia, PA, 1996), p. ix.
2 Ibid., pp. 4–5.
3 Michael Kammen, *Mystic Chords of Memory: The Transformation of Tradition in American Culture* (New York, 1993 [1991]), p. 7.
4 Ibid., p. 17.
5 Ibid., p. 42.
6 Ibid., p. 49.
7 Ibid., p. 53.
8 Ibid., p. 19.
9 Ibid., p. 51.
10 Ibid., p. 94.
11 Ibid., p 248.
12 Wallace, *Mickey Mouse History*, p. 6.
13 Ibid., p. 7.
14 Ibid., p. 8.
15 Ibid.
16 Diane Britton, "Public History and Public Memory," *Public Historian*, XIX/3 (1997), p. 11.
17 Ibid., p. 14.
18 Wallace, *Mickey Mouse History*, p. 24.
19 Jay Winter, "The Generation of Memory: Reflections on the 'Memory Boom' in Contemporary Historical Studies," *Canadian Military History*, X/3 (2001). See also Jay Winter, *Sites of Memory, Sites of Mourning: The Great War in European Cultural History* (Cambridge, 1995).
20 Gavriel D. Rosenfeld, "A Looming Crash or a Soft Landing? Forecasting the Future of the Memory Industry," *Journal of Modern History*, LXXXI/1 (March 2009), p. 125.
21 Joel Candau, *Mémoire et identité* (Paris, 1998), pp. 104–5.
22 Rosenfeld, "A Looming Crash," pp. 126–7.
23 Ibid., p. 127.
24 Katharina Niemeyer, "Introduction: Media and Nostalgia," in *Media and Nostalgia: Yearning for the Past, Present, and Future*, ed. Katharina Niemeyer (New York, 2014), p. 1.
25 Ibid., p. 8.
26 Michael Pickering and Emily Keightley, "The Modalities of Nostalgia," *Current Sociology*, LIV/6 (2006), p. 920.
27 Olivia Angé and David Berliner, "Introduction: Anthropology of

Nostalgia—Anthropology as Nostalgia," in *Anthropology and Nostalgia*, ed. Olivia Angé and David Berliner (New York and Oxford, 2015), p. 3.

28 Frederic Charles Bartlett, *Remembering: A Study in Experimental and Social Psychology* (Cambridge, 1932), p. 204.

29 Ibid., p. 213.

30 Nicholas Dames, "Nostalgia and its Disciplines: A Response," *Memory Studies*, III/3 (2010), p. 271.

31 Joseph R. Gusfeld, "Tradition and Modernity: Misplaced Polarities in the Study of Social Change," *American Journal of Sociology*, LXXII/4 (1967), p. 358.

32 Britton, "Public History and Public Memory," p. 14.

33 Kammen, *Mystic Chords of Memory*, p. 299.

34 For a remarkably extensive list of recent "-gate" scandals, see "List of scandals with '-gate' suffix," November 10, 2017, https://en.wikipedia.org.

35 Elizabeth F. Loftus and Hunter G. Hoffman, "Misinformation and Memory: The Creation of New Memories," *Journal of Experimental Psychology*, CXVIII/1 (1989), p. 103. See also Elizabeth F. Loftus, Karen Donders, Hunter G. Hoffman, and Jonathan W. Schooler, "Creating New Memories that are Quickly Accessed and Confidently Held," *Memory and Cognition*, XVII/5 (1989), pp. 607–16.

36 Gregory Stewart, *Just Another Day in Paradise: In Science Fiction America— The Signs and Symbols of the American Life Mythology* (Denver, CO, 2006).

37 Friedrich W. Nietzsche, *The Gay Science, with a Prelude in Rhymes and an Appendix of Songs*, trans. Walter Kaufmann (New York, 1974 [1882]), pp. 236–7.

Further Reading

GENERAL WORKS

Anderson, Benedict, *Imagined Communities: Reflections on the Origin and Spread of Nationalism* (London, 1983)

Ben-Amos, Dan, "The Seven Strands of Tradition: Varieties in its Meaning in American Folklore Studies," *Journal of Folklore Research*, XXI/2 (1984), pp. 97–131

Brueggemann, Walter, *An Introduction to the Old Testament: The Canon and Christian Imagination* (Louisville, KY, 2003)

Coontz, Stephanie, *The Way We Never Were: American Families and the Nostalgia Trap* (New York, 1992)

Dorson, Richard M., *American Folklore* (Chicago, IL, and London, 1959)

Gailey, Alan, "The Nature of Tradition," *Folklore*, C/2 (1989), pp. 143–61

Glassie, Henry, "Tradition," *Journal of American Folklore*, CVIII/430 (1995), pp. 395–412

Heitzenrater, Richard P., "Tradition and History," *Church History*, LXXI/3 (2002), pp. 621–38

Hobsbawm, Eric, and Terence Ranger, eds, *The Invention of Tradition* (Cambridge, 1983)

Kammen, Michael, *Mystic Chords of Memory: The Transformation of Tradition in American Culture* (New York, 1993 [1991])

Shils, Edward, "Tradition," *Comparative Studies in Society and History*, XIII/2 (1971), pp. 122–59

Wallace, Anthony F. C., "Revitalization Movements," *American Anthropologist*, LVIII/2 (1956), pp. 264–81

TRADITION-SPECIFIC WORKS
National Symbols

Ellis, Richard J., *To the Flag: The Unlikely History of the Pledge of Allegiance* (Lawrence, KS, 2005)

Ferris, Marc, *Star-Spangled Banner: The Unlikely Story of America's National Anthem* (Baltimore, MD, 2014)

Hinrichs, Kit, and Delphine Hirasuna, *Long May She Wave: A Graphic History of the American Flag* (Berkeley, CA, and Toronto, 2001)

Keim, Kevin, and Peter Keim, *A Grand Old Flag: A History of the United States through its Flags* (London and New York, 2007)

Ketchum, Alton, *Uncle Sam: The Man and the Legend* (New York, 1959)

Leepson, Marc, *Flag: An American Biography* (New York, 2006)

Molotsky, Irvin, *The Flag, the Poet, and the Song: The Story of the Star-Spangled Banner* (New York, 2001)

Svejda, George J., *History of the Star Spangled Banner from 1814 to the Present* (Washington, DC, 1969)

Taylor, Lonn, Kathleen Kendrick, and Jeffrey L. Brodie, *The Star-Spangled Banner: The Making of an American Icon* (New York, 2008)

Testi, Arnaldo, *Capture the Flag: The Stars and Stripes in American History*, trans. Noor Giovanni Mazhar (New York and London, 2010)

Holidays

Antolini, Katharine Lane, *Memorializing Motherhood: Anna Jarvis and the Struggle for Control of Mother's Day* (Morgantown, WV, 2014)

Appelbaum, Diana Karter, *Thanksgiving: An American Holiday, an American History* (New York, 1984)

Baker, James W., *Thanksgiving: The Biography of an American Holiday* (Durham, NH, 2009)

Bellware, Daniel, and Richard Gardiner, *The Genesis of the Memorial Day Holiday* (Columbus, GA, 2014)

Blight, David W., "Decoration Days: The Origins of Memorial Day in North and South," in *The Memory of the Civil War in American Culture*, ed. Alice Fahs (Chapel Hill, NC, 2004), pp. 94–129

Crimmins, John Daniel, *St Patrick's Day: Its Celebration in New York and Other American Places, 1737–1845; How the Anniversary was Observed by Representative Irish Organizations, and the Toasts Proposed* (New York, 1902)

Cronin, Mike, and Daryl Adair, *The Wearing of the Green: A History of St Patrick's Day* (London and New York, 2002)

Freeman, Philip, *St Patrick of Ireland: A Biography* (New York, 2004)

Hayes-Bautista, David E., *El Cinco de Mayo: An American Tradition* (Berkeley, CA, 2012)

Hodgson, Godfrey, *A Great and Godly Adventure: The Pilgrims and the Myth of the First Thanksgiving* (New York, 2006)

Karenga, Maulana, *Kwanzaa: A Celebration of Family, Community and Culture* (Los Angeles, CA, and London, 2008)

Marr, Timothy, "Father's Day," in *American Masculinities: A Historical Encyclopedia*, ed. Bret Carroll (New York, 2003), pp. 165–6

Mayes, Keith A., *Kwanzaa: Black Power and the Making of the African American Holiday Tradition* (New York and London, 2009)

Moss, Kenneth, "St Patrick's Day Celebrations and the Formation of Irish-American Identity, 1845–1875," *Journal of Social History*, XXIX/1 (1995), pp. 125–48

Lifestyles

Blanding, Michael, *The Coke Machine: The Dirty Truth Behind the World's Favorite Soft Drink* (New York, 2010)

Edge, John T., *Hamburgers & Fries: An American Story* (New York, 2005)

Helfin, Woodford A., "'o.k.,' But What Do We Know About It?," *American Speech*, xvi/2 (1941), pp. 87–95

Little, David, *Denim: An American Story* (Atglen, PA, 2007)

McDonald, Ronald T., *The Complete Hamburger: The History of America's Favorite Sandwich* (Secaucus, NJ, 1997)

Marsh, Graham, and Paul Trynka, *Denim: From Cowboys to Catwalks—A Visual History of the World's Most Legendary Fabric* (London, 2002)

Metcalf, Allan, OK: *The Improbable Story of America's Greatest Word* (Oxford and New York, 2011)

Oliver, Thomas, *The Real Coke, The Real Story* (New York, 1986)

Ozersky, Josh, *The Hamburger: A History* (New Haven, CT, and London, 2008)

Pendergrast, Mark, *For God, Country, and Coca-Cola: The Definitive History of the Great American Soft Drink and the Company that Makes It*, 2nd edn (New York, 2000)

Read, Allen Walker, "The Folklore of 'o.k.'" *American Speech*, xxxix/1 (1964), pp. 5–25

Smith, Andrew, *Hamburger: A Global History* (London, 2008)

Sullivan, James, *Jeans: A Cultural History of an American Icon* (New York, 2006)

Tennyson, Jeffrey, *Hamburger Heaven: The Illustrated History of the Hamburger* (New York, 1993)

Watters, Pat, *Coca-Cola: An Illustrated History* (Garden City, NY, 1978)

Young-Witzel, Gyvel, and Michael Karl Witzel, *The Sparkling Story of Coca-Cola: An Entertaining History Including Collectibles, Coke Lore, and Calendar Girls* (Stillwater, MN, 2002)

Characters

Armstrong, Jennifer, *Why? Because We Still Like You: An Oral History of the Mickey Mouse Club* (New York, 2010)

Bain, David, and Bruce Harris, ed., *Mickey Mouse: Fifty Happy Years* (New York, 1997)

Blair, Walter, *Tall Tale America: A Legendary History of our Humorous Heroes* (Chicago, IL, and London, 1987 [1944])

Bowles, Jerry, *Forever Hold Your Banner High! The Story of the Mickey Mouse Club and What Happened to the Mouseketeers* (Garden City, NY, 1975)

Darowski, Joseph J., ed., *The Ages of Superman: Essays on the Man of Steel in Changing Times* (Jefferson, NC, 2012)

Gennawey, Sam, *The Disneyland Story: The Unofficial Guide to the Evolution of Walt Disney's Dream* (Birmingham, AL, 2014)

Grandinetti, Fred M., *Popeye: An Illustrated Cultural History* (Jefferson, NC, 2004)

Heide, Robert, and John Gilman, *Mickey Mouse: The Evolution, the Legend, the Phenomenon* (New York, 2001)

Korkis, Jim, *The Book of Mouse: A Celebration of Walt Disney's Mickey Mouse* (Winter Garden, FL, 2015 [2013])

May, Robert L., *Rudolph the Red-nosed Reindeer* [1939] (New York, 2001)

Nelson, Scott Reynolds, *Steel Drivin' Man: John Henry, the Untold Story of an American Legend* (Oxford and New York, 2006)

Shephard, Esther, *Paul Bunyan: Twenty-one Tales of the Legendary Logger* [1924]
   (Orlando, FL, 2000)
Tye, Larry, *Superman: The High-flying History of America's Most Enduring Hero*
   (New York, 2012)
Wallace, Mike, *Mickey Mouse History and Other Essays on American Memory*
   (Philadelphia, PA, 1996)
Weldon, Glen, *Superman: The Unauthorized Biography* (Hoboken, NJ, 2013)

WEBSITES AND ASSOCIATIONS

American Folklore
www.americanfolklore.net

The American Grandparents Association
https://aga.grandparents.com

Father's Day
www.fathersdaycelebration.com

Generations United
www.gu.org

History
www.history.com

National Day Calendar
www.nationaldaycalendar.com

National Parents' Day Coalition
www.parentsday.com

Plimoth Plantation, Inc.
www.plimoth.org

Superman Homepage
www.supermanhomepage.com

Photo Acknowledgements

The author and publishers wish to express their thanks to the below sources of illustrative material and/or permission to reproduce it. Some locations of artworks are also given below, in the interests of brevity:

Academy of Motion Picture Arts and Sciences, Margaret Herrick Library: p. 133; Adam Murphy/Alamy Stock Photo: p. 204; Apavlo (Wikimedia Commons): p. 176; Arkell Publishing Company, New York, 1898/Historical Society of Pennsylvania: p. 85; author's collection: p. 120; Benevolent and Protective Order of Elks 1919: p. 150; from Myer Solis-Cohen, *Women in Girlhood, Wifehood, Motherhood* (Philadelphia, 1906): p. 128; Daderot (Wikimedia Commons): p. 38; Hilltoppers (Wikimedia Commons): p. 96; Hoshie (Wikimedia Commons): p. 67; Keene Public Library and the Historical Society of Cheshire County: p. 293; from W. B. Laughead, *The Marvelous Exploits of Paul Bunyan*: p. 275; Library of Congress, Washington, DC: pp. 20, 57, 70, 79, 80, 86, 93, 184, 257; Maryland Historical Society: p. 56; Robert Satterfield 1919: p. 147; Seattle City Council: p. 166; from Jerry Siegel, *Science Fiction #3* (USA, 1933)/illustration Joe Shuster: p. 242; Smithsonian American Art Museum: p. 303; Stedelijk Museum De Lakenhal, Netherlands: p. 111; United States Department of Veterans Affairs: p. 142; United States Information Service/Bureau of Public Affairs: p. 265.

Joshua Rappeneker, the copyright holder of the image on p 219; Kawanet, the copyright holder of the image on p. 208; Michael Carian, the copyright holder of the image on p. 225; Michael Clarke Stuff, the copyright holder of the image on p. 32; S Pakhrin, the copyright holder of the image on p. 170 and Wilerson S Andrade, the copyright holder of the image on p. 196 have all published them online under conditions imposed by a Creative Commons Attribution-Share Alike 2.0 Generic License. Infrogmation of New Orleans, the copyright holder of the image on p. 216; Jon Harder, the copyright holder of the image on p. 124; mk2010, the copyright holder of the image on p. 231 and Usaf 1832, the copyright holder of the image on p. 160 have all published them online under conditions imposed by a Creative Commons Attribution-Share Alike 3.0 Generic License. Gary Dunaier, the copyright holder of the image on p. 250, has published it online under conditions imposed by a Creative Commons Attribution-Share Alike 4.0 Generic License.

Readers are free:
    to share – to copy, distribute and transmit the work
    to remix – to adapt this image alone

Under the following conditions:

attribution – You must attribute the work in the manner specified by the author or licensor (but not in any way that suggests that they endorse you or your use of the work).

share alike – If you alter, transform, or build upon this work, you may distribute the resulting work only under the same or similar license to this one.

Index

Page numbers for illustrations are in *italics*